# Teach Thinking by Discussion

*Edited by* DONALD BLIGH

The Society for Research into
Higher Education & NFER-NELSON

Published by SRHE & NFER-NELSON
At the University, Guildford, Surrey GU2 5XH

First published 1986
© The Contributors

**Library of Congress Cataloging-in-Publication Data**

Teach thinking by discussion.
   Sequel to: Varieties of group discussion in university teaching.
   Bibliography: p.221
   Includes index.
   1. Forums (Discussion and debate) 2. Group work in education. 3. Thought and thinking–Study and teaching.
I. Bligh, Donald A. II. Varieties of group discussion in university teaching.
LC6519.T4   1986      371.3'7      86-2506
ISBN 1-85059-004-4

Code 8939-02-1

Typeset by First Page Ltd., Watford.

Printed in Great Britain by A. Wheaton & Co., Ltd., Exeter

# Contents

# Preface and Acknowledgements

The importance of learning to think hardly needs justification. No one will doubt it, though people with different values will give different reasons for it. Those concerned about education for employment will emphasize thinking as part of any job; others, the way later learning builds upon previous thought; others, that the preservation of democracy requires citizens to exercise their own judgement and criticism, particularly when the power of the media, the military or big business is strong.

There is a great deal of evidence that discussion methods teach people to think better than methods, like lectures and television, that simply present information (cf Bligh 1978, pp. 12–17). If you present information, information is what the students acquire. But in discussion, at least something has to go on in students' minds before they speak.

Of course there are many different kinds of thought, so we should not be surprised that there are many different discussion methods and techniques to promote them. Yet most teachers use a remarkably limited range.

This book aims to help all teachers widen their range of discussion methods. It is the sequel to a book, long ago out of print, published in 1972 by the University of London's University Teaching Methods Unit entitled *Varieties of Group Discussion in University Teaching*. Chapter 2, taken from that book, lists sixteen discussion methods and the thinking they teach.

I have selected all the other readings in this book with several factors in mind. Firstly they should be introductory and self-contained in the sense of not assuming familiarity with the literature on discussion methods. They need to describe the methods, techniques or principles, and not to be commentaries assuming previous knowledge of them. And they need to be generally applicable, not over specialized in one subject or level of learning. While articles advocating particular viewpoints have been included, I have tried to exclude those biased in the sense of covertly promoting a narrow doctrine. Conciseness has been important too, and where a seminal work is long, I have attempted an abridgement. Finally, many of the best articles on discussion methods are out of print or not widely available and I hope this volume will serve to make them more accessible.

One consequence of these criteria is the selection of several articles from before 1970, but it would be a mistake to think they are out of date. They are about human nature; and human nature does not change that fast. Indeed, compared with many aspects of education, there has been remarkably little change in recent years in teaching and learning by discussion. I hope this collection of readings will be timely in bringing together the variety of ideas from which new discussion techniques can evolve when fertilized by current developments in cognitive and social psychology.

I am indebted to the authors and publishers whose kind permission to reproduce their work is acknowledged at the opening of each piece and in the bibliography. I hope that the few whom I have been unable to trace will see the book and allow me to acknowledge their permission in a subsequent edition.

# 1

# Introduction to the Varieties of Learning Group

There are many ways of teaching by discussion or learning in a group, yet words such as 'seminar', 'tutorial', 'brainstorming' or 'T-Group' which describe these methods are often carelessly used. The following two short chapters are an attempt to sharpen customary usage.

There is no pretence that the list of methods given in Chapter 1 is complete. Indeed, Huczynski (1983) has listed several hundred. Those described here are those most generally applicable.

Chapter 2 sets out the types of thinking best achieved by the different methods: methods which vary mostly according to a group's tasks, norms, size, structure and patterns of interaction; although composition, physical environment and history, and the motivation of group members also play a part. Indeed, the interaction of these nine factors can be used to explain most of the differences between one learning group and another, and will underlie many of the points made in the rest of the book.

# 2

# Glossary

The following meanings are given in order to avoid as far as possible in this book the ambiguity that arises in much other work in the use of some of the most common terms.

## Elements in Teaching

*Lesson* Teaching given at one time. The teaching may be by any method or combination of methods. (Although some teachers feel this term is childish, no such connotation is implied here. It is used as the only general term available.)

*Period* The whole or part of the time taken by a lesson. For example, 'a period of discussion' may be a whole lesson or ten minutes at the end of a lecture.

*Session* An academic year (normally consisting of three terms starting in September or October).

*Teacher* A general name for one who teaches (as distinct from 'lecturer', one who lectures).

*Group* A number of people, each of whom can interact with all the others face to face.

*Class* A set of students taught together. (This term has many other uses. It is given here in contrast to 'group'.)

## Categories of Teaching Methods

The vast majority of teaching methods can be categorized under four headings. This book is solely concerned with one of them, 'discussion methods'.

*Presentation or reception methods* Methods in which information is presented to the students (the students receive the information). These methods include lectures, demonstrations, audio-tapes, films, CCTV and reading. (Programmed learning is not normally included here since a student's active response is essential, but it does have a strong presentation, or reception, element.)

*Independent learning methods* Methods by which students learn on their own. They usually include presentations and an activity required of the student. Examples include programmed learning, Keller Plan, tape-slide programmes, private study and correspondence courses.

Adapted by permission from Bligh 1972c.

*Practical teaching* Creating the conditions (including setting tasks) so that students acquire skills by performance (ie practice) of those or similar skills. Practical teaching essentially involves getting students to do something rather than talking about it (discussion methods) or receiving information about it (presentation methods).

*Discussion methods* Methods of teaching using spontaneous conversation in which all students may take part. (NB 'discussion methods' and 'group teaching' are not the same, although many specific teaching methods are both.)

# Presentation Methods

*Lecture* A period of uninterrupted talk (not necessarily a complete lesson). This term is here restricted to a particular form of presentation and is defined in terms of the particular psychological conditions it imposes on the listener. It is distinguished here from a 'lesson'.

*Step-by-step lecture* A lecture organized around 3 or 4 topics, each of which is talked about for, say, ten minutes and followed by discussion or other activity.

*Demonstration* The teacher performs some operation exemplifying a phenomenon or skill while the students watch. (A presentation or reception method.)

# Discussion Methods

*Task-oriented groups or task-centred groups* Groups whose behaviour is directed towards the accomplishment of a task.

*Buzz groups* Groups of 2-6 members who discuss issues or problems for a short period within a lesson.

*Brainstorming* An intensive discussion in which spontaneous suggestions as solutions to a problem are received uncritically.

*Synectics* A development of brainstorming in which special techniques, such as choosing group members from diverse backgrounds, are used to produce a creative solution to the problem.

*Horseshoe groups* Groups (normally 4-12 members) sitting in a horseshoe arrangement in a class, each with a specific task.

*Syndicate method* Teaching where the class is divided into groups of about 6 members who work on the same or related problems with intermittent teacher contact and who write a joint report for the critical appraisal of the whole class.

*Subject-centred tutorial* In which the topic and general direction of discussion are given by the tutor. Includes some, but not all, case discussion and seminars.

*Group tutorial* General name for a learning group with a teacher and more than one student. It includes both subject-centred and student-centred (group) tutorials. It does not include individual tutorials and individual counselling.

*Individual tutorial* Teaching by discussion with a single student.

*Case discussion* Real or simulated complex problems analysed in detail with students suggesting their own solutions or decisions.

*Controlled discussion* Teaching in which students may raise questions or comment, but the general direction is under the strict control of the teacher. This is normally used after a presentation method with a class but not with a group.

*Step-by-step discussion* Teaching by a carefully prepared sequence of issues and questions to draw out the required information and thought from students.

*Seminars* Group discussion introduced by the presentation of an essay or other work.

*Student-centred discussion* Discussion in which the organization (or lack of it), content and direction respond to students' needs. Includes free group discussion, T-Groups and counselling.

*Free group discussion (FGD)* Group discussion in which the topic and direction are controlled by the student group; the teacher observes.

*T-group method* A method of teaching self-awareness and interpersonal relations based on therapeutic group techniques; individual group members discuss their relationships with each other. Also known as sensitivity groups or encounter groups.

*Simulation exercises* Teaching in which a real situation is duplicated in its essential features, perhaps in the form or a game or a problem; participants adopt an appropriate role or status, if possible.

*Role-play* In which students are given certain social roles and freely dramatize them in a group, ie act out their specified role.

*Counselling* Students voluntarily consult a trained tutor, doctor or welfare officer about their private or academic problems.

# 3

# A Classification of Discussion Methods

| TEACHING METHOD | OBJECTIVES | TEACHER'S ROLE | LEADER | TIME | SIZE OF GROUP | SIZE OF CLASS | COMMENT | REFERENCES |
|---|---|---|---|---|---|---|---|---|
| INDIVIDUAL TASKS | Involvement by all Problem-solving | Set task Pose problem | None | ½–4 mins | 1 | Any | Not strictly a 'group' method | |
| BUZZ GROUPS | Encouraging reticent students | Set task | None | 2–15 mins | 2–6 | 4 or more up to 500 | | Abercrombie 1979; Bligh 1978b (see extracts on pp. 63–66); Gorman 1969; Strauss and Strauss 1960 |
| | Group cohesion | Ensure formation of groups | A 'secretary' may record decisions or answers to problems | | No more than 3 in one row | | | |
| | Consolidating memory by 'rehearsal' of facts | Circulate to help groups, meet students, get feedback | | | | | | |
| | Learning terminology by use | | | | | | | |
| | Thought (at all levels) | Control reporting back, if any | | | | | | |

Adapted by permission from Bligh 1972b.

| Method | Objectives | Procedure | Leadership | Time | Optimum size | Maximum size | Comments | Reference |
|---|---|---|---|---|---|---|---|---|
| | Arousal | | | | | | | |
| | Feedback | | | | | | | |
| | Training in discussion techniques | | | | | | | |
| BRAINSTORMING | New ideas (creativity) | Establish the group(s) | None | 2 mins – 2 weeks | 5-14 | Up to 50 | | de Bono 1977 (see extracts on pp. 79–86) |
| | Problem-solving | Pose problem | | Varies with the problem | | | | |
| | Decision-making | Non-critical attitude | | Time pressure may be used to force suggestions | | | | |
| SYNECTICS | Creativity, including creative problem-solving and decision-making | Grouping | None, or administrator, or several ideas-leaders, or both | A series of meetings, say 5 hours to 5 years | 3-14, preferably 5 or 6; varied in background | Up to 50 | Useful in industry | Gordon 1961 (see extracts on pp. 87–99) |
| HORSESHOE GROUPS | Evaluation | Preparation | Designated by teacher, elected, self-appointed, or none | 5-20 mins | 4-12 | Up to 100 | | Bligh 1978c (see extracts on pp. 70–76) |
| | Decision-making | Pose problem | A 'secretary' may record decisions | | | | | |
| | Analytical thinking | Organization of groups | | | | | | |
| | Knowing how to apply principles | Circulate to help groups | | | | | | |
| | | Co-ordinate reporting back as necessary | | | | | | |

## 8  *Varieties of Learning Group*

| TEACHING METHOD | OBJECTIVES | TEACHER'S ROLE | LEADER | TIME | SIZE OF GROUP | SIZE OF CLASS | COMMENT | REFERENCES |
|---|---|---|---|---|---|---|---|---|
| CASE DISCUSSION | Understanding complex inter-relationships<br><br>Application of principles | Orientation, elicitation, clarification, pinpointing | Teacher, or none | 10 mins–2 hours (obviously, very variable with the case); one or many meetings | 4–30 | Normally same as group, but many could be organized as horseshoe groups | | Gorman 1969; Henderson 1969 |
| SYNDICATE METHOD | Skills in seeking and organizing information<br><br>Harnessing individual expertise<br><br>Teamwork | Design of tasks<br><br>Prescribe specific reading<br><br>Encourage individuals and groups | Elected, selected, emergent, or none | 1 hour – 1 term or longer; very variable | 5 or 6 | Up to 30 | | Collier 1966, 1969 (see extracts on pp. 105–118) |
| GROUP TUTORIAL | Understanding<br><br>Thinking at all levels | Organization of previous presentation methods<br><br>Initiate discussion<br><br>Praise, encourage, listen<br><br>Standard setting<br><br>Resource person<br><br>Unobtrusive group maintenance | Teacher | 10–90 mins | Up to 15 if skilled; normally 3–6 | | | Rudduck 1978 |

| | | | | | | | |
|---|---|---|---|---|---|---|---|
| CONTROLLED (CLASS) DISCUSSION | Knowledge of facts<br><br>Understanding, including revision<br><br>Feedback | Chairman<br><br>Answer questions<br><br>Clarification<br><br>Summary | Teacher | 5 mins-1 hour | Could be used, but normally inappropriate | Any | Not strictly a 'small group' teaching method: the class is not a 'group' |
| STEP-BY-STEP DISCUSSION | Knowledge of facts<br><br>Understanding, especially logical argument or developmental sequence | Chairman<br><br>Elicitation<br><br>Clarification<br><br>Group maintenance | Teacher | 10-90 mins | Any 'group' | Same as group | Instruction rather than teaching but thorough |
| SEMINAR | 'Critical' thinking<br><br>Ability to present an argument<br><br>Thought at all levels | Usually choose topic<br><br>Prepare arguments on key issues<br><br>Listen | Teacher | Over 45 mins | 3-14 only; more if teacher is skilled and/or students are mature | Same as group | Relies on a suitable introductory essay, a low level of student anxiety and sensitive handling |
| FREE GROUP DISCUSSION | Observation<br><br>Change in attitudes, feelings, human relations<br><br>Self-awareness<br><br>Willingness to receive and consider new ideas | Observation<br><br>Facilitate free expression of opinion<br><br>Tolerance<br><br>Human understanding<br><br>Listen | Perhaps, but not the teacher; but student leaders may emerge and subside | Over 45 mins for at least several weeks | 4-12; could be larger with a cohesive group used to the method | Same as group | Quite difficult to do well |

Abercrombie 1960; Abercrombie 1970; Barnett 1958 (see extracts on pp. 165-168)

10 *Varieties of Learning Group*

| TEACHING METHOD | OBJECTIVES | TEACHER'S ROLE | LEADER | TIME | SIZE OF GROUP | SIZE OF CLASS | COMMENT | REFERENCES |
|---|---|---|---|---|---|---|---|---|
| T-GROUP or SENSITIVITY GROUP or ENCOUNTER GROUP | Sensitivity in human relations<br><br>Self-awareness, especially of feelings, motives | Facilitate experimental and 'open' attitude | Teacher at first | Short intensive courses, eg several hours per day for several weeks | 4-25, preferably 8-14 | Same as group | Teaching by this method requires previous experience as a participant, and knowledge of group dynamics | P.B. Smith 1969 |
| ROLE PLAY or 'SOCIODRAMA' including SOCIAL SIMULATION | Empathy<br><br>Working off tensions | Very variable<br><br>Self-direction by students is preferable, but considerable encouragement may be necessary | Variable | Varies with roles to be played; open-ended lessons an advantage | 6-25 | Same as group | Previous group harmony an advantage | |
| INDIVIDUAL TUTORIAL | Individual development of student thought, especially at higher levels<br><br>Asking questions<br><br>Giving reasons<br><br>Feeling for others | Listen<br><br>Encourage student questions of himself<br><br>Sympathize, praise | Student, or none | Indefinite | 1 | Same as group | | |
| COUNSELLING | Very varied<br><br>Student welfare | Varied, but listening nearly always important | None | Indefinite | Usually 1, could be 2 | | Training preferable | Blaine and McArthur 1961; Payne 1969 |

# 4

# Introduction to Participation
# in Groups

Young people are usally quite talkative. So why is it that they often remain silent in discussion groups? Something prevents them talking. It is not that something is needed to make them participate.

This part of the book is about social and psychological factors influencing participation in discussion. It is also about practical teaching techniques to make participation easier. Thus it is about theory and practice.

Meyer Cahn reminds us in Chapter 5 that mutual trust affects confidence to participate. In Chapter 6 I suggest that trust can gradually be built up if the risks of participation are reduced by first giving students simple tasks, in small groups for short periods without the presence of the teacher, and by then gradually increasing the task difficulty, group size and length of time. Only later should the teacher become a group member.

A great deal of experimental work is cited in this volume. John Powell's article is included (Chapter 7) partly as an example of what experimental work in classrooms involves, and partly as a further illustration of the value of tutorless groups – a theme taken up in Part III.

Gordon Lawrence (Chapter 8) describes some of the social processes which larger groups experience as they develop, while Jane Abercrombie reviews in Chapter 9 some of the underlying psychological factors which can be applied to small group teaching.

Then, anticipating Part IV, Colin Flood Page gives practical advice in Chapter 10 to teachers who are to become group members.

# 5

# The Development of Trust in Learning Groups

*Meyer M. Cahn*

The trouble with many learning environments is that the social climate is not sufficiently developed for students to admit to what they understand or do not understand. Too often, the admission of what a student knows or does not know carries a price with it, a price of embarrassment or shame – of ugly anxiety than which anything else is better. And so the student's condition, particularly the condition which applies to the immediate learning situation, stays locked within him, unrevealed to the teacher, and even to peers. It seems a psychological fact that given a choice between sitting in abject boredom or revealing some measure of incompetence, in most groups, students will select the path of boredom. (This is not unrelated to the point which Maslow (1968) makes, that given the choice of psychological safety or self-actualization, safety will most often be the first choice.) Unrevealing students learn to tolerate endless ennui. (*This*, they learn.) They learn to retreat into their internal life without complaint, living in the private domain of the day-dream, the fantasy, the half-sleep of the student which gave rise to this poem.

### Professor's Lecture

Continues to say more
Say more, say more
Yet little I reap

I continue to pray for
Pray for, pray for
More eye-open sleep

Missing in such learning groups is the capacity of students to posit their position, to announce to the others, 'You owe me a part of your energy and attention!' Missing is the ground work that provides a group with the capacity to appreciate the wisdom of such a remark, and the capacity to respond to it.

Reproduced by permission from Cahn 1975.

Missing is the state of trust that will afford all members the right to speak their mind, that will assist them to do so, and that will help them to realize that trust is one of the main pillars upon which their mutual learning life depends.

The measurement of trust is to a group what the measurement of body temperature is to a state of health. Low trust is a symptom of group difficulty. Such difficulty can come from many sources including leadership, goal orientation and a host of interpersonal issues.

According to one source, trust is a 'state of mind of one who feels sure that a person or a thing will not fail him.' Human beings being what they are, that point of confidence is not likely to be reached until it is tested in graduated degrees. Because the course of increasing trust is rarely approached directly (Do you trust me?), it is necessary, most of the time, to deduce this trust from other things which are said and done. Put another way, people learn to trust in their own rather secretive ways. they test here and there, move forward, and then test again at a greater level of disclosure and risk. In initial stages of relationship, trust is a very unsure matter, perhaps because determinations of trust are usually made by intuition and through the senses. Because trust is such an internal process, it is, therefore, a difficult thing to be phony about. One may behave in a false manner, but one's sense of trust is generally treated as a real thing.

Without trust, a group must be on guard. Without it, members must spend energy preparing defences and strategies in order to cope with the trustless situation. Low trust groups are generally characterized by a minimum of participation, an awkward flow of conversation, a high degree of covert behaviour, a low amount of impulse sharing, and much negative feeling ranging from anger to depression. In low trust groups, there is usually much anger against the leader, even though he may seemingly not have earned this. When trust is low, someone will have to pay for this frustrating condition sooner or later. It will usually be the leader who will be sacrificed first. The form usually takes the shape of scapegoating. The place is usually in the safe caverns of the informal channels of comunications.

The development of trust in a group is not an abstract norm beyond reach. It is a condition resulting from the establishment of trust relationships between specific people in that group. These relationships can be observed and measured. A programme for trust development will therefore focus upon those relationships.

There are various ways, for instance, to measure trust between people. One simple way is to ask members to rate their trust in the group from 0 to 9, with 0 measuring minimum trust, and 9 measuring maximum trust. A mean score will provide one measure of group trust. If this is done at various times in the group's history, a measure of trust development can be made apparent. (These scores would best be presented to the group without names attached.) (See pp.17-18 for a more extended method of measuring group trust.)

A programme designed to increase trust must help members to meet each other, and to test each other's capacity for trusting one another. To be sure, this is not done directly by asking for trust. It is facilitated so that trust may grow in the special and unpredictable way trust has for determining its own development in relationships between people. In such a programme of trust development, some of the following facilitating steps might be taken.

*Create trust-producing structures.* These are small groups such as diads, trios, quartets or quintets which are geographically separated from the rest of the group, structures which afford private discussion, while at the same time members are placed in a no-exit relationship with each other. (The 'no-exit' is implied.) The inability to retreat forces disclosure. The privacy facilitates the consequent disclosure. Certain no-so-subtle means of escaping disclosure, such as retreating inwardly, engaging in reverie, leaving the scene physically, doodling, reading, and other such obvious methods of withdrawal which are used in larger groups, are not as likely in this small, face-to-face encounter. Here, in the smaller group, the social expectation is such that attention is expected, perhaps even demanded – if not directly and openly, then subtly.

*Propose that these 'trust-structured groups' take on group-related tasks* such as sharing expectations and impressions, formulating goals, planning activities, or evaluating group experience.

*Let the results of their discussions be announced as joint agreements among themselves.* Thus, instead of having to face the group alone, each member has one or more colleagues standing back of him. (Meeting the group with an ally increases confidence and strength exponentially. In fact, it increases so much that such small groups often become feisty and independent. This leads to a different problem, but one which is far healthier than fear and passivity born of separateness and distrust.)

*Propose certain trust exercises* that are designed to make legitimate the expression of certain thoughts and feelings which would not normally find expression except by especially open and trusting people. For instance, it is possible to ask members of a small group to share private thoughts which would be risky to share with many people. By requesting this information from an outside source (out of the group), the individual is not penalized for initiating the thought. Yet the group enjoys the benefit of sharing. For instance, the small group can be asked to answer these questions to each other: What impedes progress in your group? If you could do whatever you want, what would you do in your group? What statements made by what people have particularly impressed you? What have you reacted negatively toward? What needs to be done to improve your group as a working group? For those who wish greater risk, this question can be asked: What have you thought about people in your group that you have been reluctant to say to them?

If such questions are employed, it is important that sufficient time is given for a full discussion among participants. In addition, the leader should be available for counselling, in order to make certain that members have a resource for support and guidance.

In general, caution ought to prevail whenever the natural flow of trust development is being speeded up, either from within the group or outside of it. There is no question that it is now possible to induce increased trust from outside sources, and to do so on a vastly accelerated scale. For instance, participants in groups of three or four can be asked to share a secret they never told before, or to share something about their bodies that they do not like. They can be asked to touch each other in some way, such as holding hands, lifting participants off the ground, or blindfoldedly studying one another's faces with their hands. They may lead each other in trust walks where one participant plays blind and is led about by another. Sharing private thoughts and making contact in these ways will indeed remove certain barriers between people. But sustaining this level of intimacy may not always be easy, and, more importantly, it may not even be desired. While we have the capacity to promote rapid trust by these direct means, it does not appear, at this time, that the classroom is an appropriate place for their use. (These techniques are more dependably used in therapy or encounter groups led by skilled leaders, who are prepared to deal with the issues of 'individual timing and readiness for such actions.')

Because of the unusual power which authorities exert over groups (even though many members might deny this), the behaviour of the leader can significantly affect the group's trust status. If a teacher sets a trusting example, this somehow eloquently states that trusting is in vogue here. On the other hand, if he distrusts, this norm is easily picked up too. Rogers (1961) has proposed a model for teacher behaviour, one which may not be easy for all teachers to achieve, but which has implications for developing trust. Though he has developed this from a therapy model, he believes it has implications for education, too.

*Rogers' model*
1 The teacher behaves in a manner that is authentic and 'role-free'. He behaves as a real person – himself.
2 The teacher accepts his students, with no 'conditions of worth' attached to this acceptance. The result is a 'safety-creating climate of unconditonal regard'.
3 The teacher perceives the student's world as it is seen by the student. He feels this private world of the student as if it were his own. To accomplish this, the teacher listens carefully, fully, empathically.
4 The teacher shares and communicates these three responses (his congruence, his acceptance and his empathy) so that they are clearly felt and understood by the students.

Unfortunately, the implementation of Rogers' model for securing trust takes far more capacity than the mere will to behave in this manner. As Jersild (1955) points out, when teachers face themselves, some of them find liberal amounts of anxiety, hostility and conformity. They find that these and other personal concerns often pre-empt their concern for good teaching. For some, a 'compulsion to compete', or a need to use their 'power and influence in a blind way to serve ...(these) ... competitive needs' suggests an inability to play the mature role which is required in order to fulfill Rogers' more idealistic model.

*Self-disclosure.* Perhaps the clearest measure of trust comes from the interpersonal phenomenon of self-disclosure, the process of letting another person know what you 'think, feel or want.' While self-disclosure is the most direct means by which one person can make himself known to another (healthy children employ this directness), there is often a reticence to disclose oneself, even at great cost, for self-disclosure is not easy. It takes trust. It sometimes needs facilitation. In fact, Jourard (1964) proposes that the major skill in the art of counselling and psychotherapy is 'the art of coping with the terrors which attend self-disclosure, and the art of decoding the language, verbal and non-verbal, in which a person speaks about his inner experience.'

The terror of disclosure is so great for some people that they are unaware of their unbridled facility for remaining unknown even to themselves. (Jourard proposes that some people 'work at it ceaselessly, 24 hours daily.') Non-disclosure is further facilitated through ongoing *social norms* which enable people to remain mysteries to their colleagues without any of them realizing, sometimes, that they really do not know one another, or that this is a primary matter in their joint effort to learn together. (Students, too, often fall into the myth of believing that they know each other better than they really do.) While social norms provide protection for people's privacy (a basic need, to be sure), these norms often obscure the cost which such non-disclosing behaviour brings. One of the costs in classrooms is that students often do not disclose what they know or do not know. Another cost is the continuously defensive climate which makes disclosure a high risk matter which only fools or unrealistic idealists will undertake.

There are various degrees of disclosure, from low to high. In his categorizations of various degrees of disclosure, Greene (1964) suggests that where people talk and think in stereotypes, clichés, catch phrases, or represent themselves as having no real problems, or where the content of their statements is utterly safe and sharable with anyone at all, it is clear that a low level of disclosure is taking place. Discussion at this level is emotionally neutral, and is relatively evasive.

At the other end of the disclosure spectrum is the prospect of people sharing basic feelings which are central to their inner life, where facades are gone, and where a real person emerges, one with conflicts, problems, and/or feelings of personal confusion; these are sharable, at least to others who have earned the right through equal self-disclosure.

Between these two extremities are other levels of self-disclosure. The difference seems to lie in the sharing of one's inner world, or the safer external world, whether one will risk being vulnerable or conflict-free, or whether one speaks of highest priority concerns or neglects these in favour of minor issues which make little difference.

The development of trust within a group correlates highly as a measure of its growth and maturity. Therefore it is not surprising to find that measures which improve mutual trust in a group also increase group growth. Some of these growth indicators are as follows.

*The ability of a group to look at the ways it is functioning*, and to make good use of the observations which members are making. In the process of sharing these observations, and making practical use of them, trust can be increased.

*The ability of group members to share responsibilities interdependently*. The very process of assigning, accepting and carrying out duties which are separate but interdependent is an act of faith which breeds trust.

*The ability of a group to be sufficiently open and permissive so that its members can behave naturally* – and be themselves. This includes feeling free to share ideas, problems, wants, needs, fears, aspirations and talents.

*The ability of a group to face problems* about its own nature, such as the presence of unwholesome cliques, restrictive leadership, inhibiting controls, needless procedures and other counter-productive characteristics.

*The ability of a group to set realistic goals*, to set them with the concurrence of its members, and to change these goals where warranted in terms of consquent realities. It is hard to maintain trust in a group's destiny when its goals relate more to fantasy than reality; it is hard to trust a group which cannot adjust to its ever-changing here-and-now-demands and needs.

In existential terms, one might say that trust is a more likely possibility in a group where existential crises are as likely for one member as for any other. This holds for a teacher and for a student. They are all in this human dilemma together. If any stand apart or above, if they are not vulnerable to being tested as are the others, then this can inhibit both growth and trust. On the other hand, where human qualities are allowed to show through, particularly qualities of limitation – of skill, understanding, insight – then this enables others to call to mind their own limitations, and even perchance, to share them.

One might say, along with Gibb (Bradford, Gibb and Benne 1964) that trust comes about when there is an absence of fear, of punitiveness, of the need to be defensive. It develops in orientations marked by mutual inquiry, exploration, spontaneity, candour, honesty, interdependence and play. With the establishment of such trust, it is possible to disclose oneself in a natural manner without worrying about the consequent impression being made on others. In such a state, one is ready to learn because there is a readiness to expose oneself to the benefits of learning.

# Appendix

## A MEASURE OF GROUP TRUST (Circle appropriate figure)

| | | | | | | | |
|---|---|---|---|---|---|---|---|
| 1. | 1 | 2 | 3 | 4 | 5 | 6 | 7 |
| | Members have high trust for each other | | | | Little trust | | |
| 2. | 1 | 2 | 3 | 4 | 5 | 6 | 7 |
| | Members express their feelings openly | | | | Feelings not expressed | | |
| 3. | 1 | 2 | 3 | 4 | 5 | 6 | 7 |
| | Members discuss their feelings | | | | Feelings not discussed | | |
| 4. | 1 | 2 | 3 | 4 | 5 | 6 | 7 |
| | Members accept a wide range of feelings | | | | Narrow range of feeling only | | |
| 5. | 1 | 2 | 3 | 4 | 5 | 6 | 7 |
| | Discussion flows openly (ideas, feelings, attitudes) | | | | Very little data shared about ideas, feelings, attitudes | | |
| 6. | 1 | 2 | 3 | 4 | 5 | 6 | 7 |
| | Most important communications are out in the open | | | | Covert communications are significant (grapevine, non-verbal exchanges, passivity) | | |

| 7. | 1 | 2 | 3 | 4 | 5 | 6 | 7 |
|---|---|---|---|---|---|---|---|

Members willing to be
influenced by others

Members closed and resistant
to peer influence (or from
authority)

| 8. | 1 | 2 | 3 | 4 | 5 | 6 | 7 |
|---|---|---|---|---|---|---|---|

Members freely make suggestions about ongoing process

Avoid making suggestions
about process

| 9. | 1 | 2 | 3 | 4 | 5 | 6 | 7 |
|---|---|---|---|---|---|---|---|

Differences of opinion
are readily expressed

Differences of opinion
are avoided

| 10. | 1 | 2 | 3 | 4 | 5 | 6 | 7 |
|---|---|---|---|---|---|---|---|

Members willing to struggle
for what they want

Accept defeat easily

| 11. | 1 | 2 | 3 | 4 | 5 | 6 | 7 |
|---|---|---|---|---|---|---|---|

Members act on impulses—
are spontaneous

Speak carefully, after
forethought

| 12. | 1 | 2 | 3 | 4 | 5 | 6 | 7 |
|---|---|---|---|---|---|---|---|

Members share partially
formed ideas

Ideas presented are safe
(questions, facts)

| 13. | 1 | 2 | 3 | 4 | 5 | 6 | 7 |
|---|---|---|---|---|---|---|---|

Movement is toward
intimacy

Movement is not toward
intimacy (roles, formality,
distancing prevail)

| 14. | 1 | 2 | 3 | 4 | 5 | 6 | 7 |
|---|---|---|---|---|---|---|---|

Members respond with
empathy

Members seem closed within
themselves; their own views
predominate

| 15. | 1 | 2 | 3 | 4 | 5 | 6 | 7 |
|---|---|---|---|---|---|---|---|

Most members feel included        Few feel included

# 6

# Developing Skills for Small Group Work

*Donald A. Bligh*

## Starting a Discussion Group

### The Objectives of Discussion Methods

The major objective of discussion methods is usually to teach students to think. To achieve this the teacher must have a number of subsidiary objectives if a discussion group is to get going. Discussion methods are among the most difficult teaching techniques. They require a wide knowledge of the subject matter, an ability to attend to detail while keeping an eye on the overall view, an appreciation of different viewpoints, receptivity to new ideas, tolerance and respect for problem students, and the maturity to manage a group of students without dominating them. Consequently, not only do teachers have to learn how to teach by discussion methods, but students have to learn how to learn from them. In spite of the difficulties, many teachers are expected to be able to conduct a seminar in their first month of teaching without learning simple techniques first. If discussions are not be dominated by the teacher, then new students should not be expected to learn from them until they have learned how to listen, take notes and organize what has been said for themselves. They need some confidence in their ideas and their ability to express them. They will achieve this quicker if the group as a whole has a co-operative spirit. Thus, in addition to the major objective of discussion methods, to teach students to think, it is also the teacher's job to teach students to learn, to give them self-confidence, and to foster a group spirit. A teacher employing discussion methods is not just a subject-matter expert.

### Preparation of the tasks

The basic rule in teaching by discussion methods is 'Start with small groups, for short periods with simple tasks. Then gradually increase the size, length and difficulty'.

---

Reproduced by permission from Bligh 1973.

Some students think that discussion periods are occasions for general relaxation and 'chit-chat'. If the tone is set by making them work on a task on the first day, teaching is easier later on. As it is important at an early stage to encourage self-confidence, it is necessary to make sure that the students understand the problem and that it is one they can solve successfully. As it is also important to create student interest, the task should foster curiosity, which can be achieved if it applies the principles of the subject in a practical way. If this is not possible, tasks involving the acquisition or simple interpretation of facts are suitable. Problems that involve making fine judgements, or using theories or very abstract thought are best avoided at first.

## Individual work

If each member of the class is asked to solve a problem on their own first, with the possibility that any one of them could be asked for the answer, then each will do some work and even could make a contribution to a discussion group. This technique can also be used to break up a long period of formal lecturing. While students are working on a problem individually the lecturer can go to those who seem to require help. Such a period of individual work need not be very long, but it helps a lecturer to know his students and obtain feedback early in a course. Two minutes is often long enough. When one student is finished and is sitting idly with nothing to do, others have probably gathered sufficient thoughts to share out in a 'buzz group'.

## Buzz Groups

The next stage is to form groups of three, four or five to compare answers or what has been found out. If the class is sitting formally in rows, these 'buzz groups' can be formed by the first, third and fifth rows, etc. turning round to face the even-numbered rows. If they are sitting in a single line or a circle or semi-circle, every third person can pull their chair out and face the two on their right to form a group of three. The teacher stands where he can move unobtrusively to help any group as necessary. Unless invited to say something, it is better for him to become part of the listening group for at least two or three contributions before offering to help, than to burst in on the conversation and risk dominating it.

How long a buzz group should 'buzz' will obviously depend on the problem it has been set, but 3 – 5 minutes is suitable. If the problem is written on a sheet of paper where the group's attention is focused, discussions can be more relevant. If some of the paper is left blank, the group can write their report or solve the problem on it and so provide a permanent record of their opinions or conclusions.

## Reporting Back

The next stage is for the buzz groups to report back to the class on their findings and conclusions. Reports should be crisp and itemized. In large classes only a sample may report. The teacher may select what he wants from these reports and summarize them in a organized and coherent way on a blackboard (or on paper, in which case he would give the summary at the end of the reports) before going on to the next piece of subject matter. By this method every student has the opportunity to think about the subject and to express himself in its language. Nevertheless each student knows what is important and has it summarized in a logical form.

## Further Development of the Group

The design just described has four stages: (1) the problem set to individuals, (2) buzz groups, (3) reporting back, (4) organized summary. It can be used in either formal or informal settings with 6 – 150 students. It takes about a quarter of an hour and is very useful in the first month of a student's course. There are variations and elaborations on it which may be introduced as a transition towards the formation of the whole class into one group. A teacher may eliminate the first stage once satisfied that everyone does take part in the buzz groups and that everyone is learning from them. As students learn to listen, express themselves, be relevant, and co-operate in a group, pairs of buzz groups may be amalgamated in order to train them to work in a larger group. Such amalgamations may have 6–10 members and may be called 'horseshoe groups'. The time to amalgamate is when the students have reached some measure of agreement, but before they have come to a definite and rigid conclusion. If it is possible to amalgamate groups that optimize cross-fertilization of ideas, so much the better, but usually it is only practicable to amalgamate adjacent groups. Amalgamations save time at the reporting back stage, and it is possible to make further amalgamations until the whole class becomes one group; but groups larger than 14 require skilful handling. There are further variations which develop discussion in groups up to 30 if there is overt control by the teacher. For example, instead of asking each group to report back in turn, he can take each point raised by the first reporter, 'throw' it to the other groups and get their reactions so that there is a point by point summary of the views of the whole class. The whole class can take part because everyone has already considered the topic. By this means the transition from buzz groups to horseshoe groups to a 'controlled discussion' class can be made. Overt control can be decreased if the seating is arranged to maximize face to face interaction between students. When the class has had some experience of problem-centred groups, it is possible to curtail the time spent in buzz groups, eliminate their formal reporting back, and possibly cut them out altogether.

Part of the skill of being a teacher is knowing when to use each of these variations, to say nothing to knowing how to handle the groups themselves. The art depends on knowing the individual students and imagining them in a new situation before they are placed in it. Use of these variations requires greater flexibility in the patterns of teaching methods than is commonly practised today.

## Keeping the Group Going

Let us assume that some groups have begun to get going. There is some group feeling in the class. Individual work and buzz groups have been used in a formal situation, such as in a lecture, in order to encourage even the most shy students to say something in a small group. The students have begun to use the language of the subject and some differences in their personalities have been noticed. Let us now assume that it is necessary to start seminars, case discussion, or some other form of group teaching where a tutor will be present with a fairly small group of, say, 3 – 12 students. These classes will be different from those held hitherto, partly because they are specifically for the purpose of discussion, partly because the tutor will be a member of the group, and partly because the students will be expected to prepare beforehand.

## Choice of Groups

First the students should be divided into suitably sized groups. On the whole, the smaller the better, but usally there are administrative difficulties in obtaining very small groups. The criteria of grouping depend on the objectives to be achieved. If the objectives are a knowledge and understanding of certain facts, each discussion will be at a suitable level for the students if the knowledgeable are in one group and the ignorant in another. If the objective is that shy introverts express themselves more and noisy extroverts listen to others, it is a mistake to mix the two because the extroverts dominate the conversation and the introverts are happy to let them do so. If the introverts were put together, some of them, at least, would have to speak; and if the extroverts were put together, some of them, at least, would have to listen in the long run. If the objectives involve creative thinking or decision-making, a variety of experience and points of view is desirable. Consultations between academic staff will probably produce a more accurate assessment of students' personalities and better groupings than one person would make. Therefore, because the criteria for dividing students into groups depend upon the tutor's objectives, students probably cannot be grouped until the objectives are clear to all the academic staff consulted.

## The Physical Conditions of the Discussion Group

The physical conditions of a discussion group affect its social conditions and the roles taken by its members. Communication, and hence the harmony and learning of the group, increase if the differences in social level within the group are small. Therefore, part of the tutor's task is to play down the differences in roles. In particular he must play down his own authority and leadership if he wishes the discussion to flow freely.

Firstly, which room is to be used and what associations will it have in the minds of the students? Is it the tutor's, Dr. Smith's, a classroom, or a corner of the students' common room? Does the group regularly use the same room and can the discussion overrun time if desired? Ownership, size, regularity, noise and interruption should all be considered.

Secondly, it is necessary to consider the chairs in the room. Students will not talk to people they cannot see. If it is to be a genuine discussion, everyone should be able to see everyone else face to face. Consequently, it is important to have chairs in a circle, or nearly a circle (a 'C' or a 'U'). It is interesting to notice where people sit and, if there is a choice, the kind of chairs they sit on. The choice of a deep armchair or an erect chair may indicate the degree of ease, or perhaps the kind of relationship they wish to have with the rest of the group, including the teacher. Sometimes the person choosing the end of a semi-circle or chairs is the one who does not want to identify with the rest of the group. Other students may choose a chair they can push into a corner, where they will not be noticed or have to take part.

Thirdly, it is worth noticing the distance from one person to another, especially the teacher's distance from other members of the group. The physical distance could be symbolic of the social distance. If the teacher places himself in an erect armchair behind his desk in his own room he has taken a positon of authority which could inhibit discussion.

Many of the physical conditions affecting discussion groups may sound trivial when made explicit: nevertheless their influence is often subtle, powerful, and of great importance in creating the atmosphere of the group.

## Encouraging Students to Talk

If the general objective of a discussion group is to make students think, they must be expected to express their thoughts and to practise using the language in which those thoughts can be expressed. Therefore, the teacher's task is to encourage the students to talk – to encourage student interaction, not to display his own knowledge. Yet it is very easy for half the talking in seminars to be done by the tutor, which students often expect because the nature of school discipline prevents their early teachers from developing any other style. Because students address their remarks to their tutor and expect him to reply, there is a tendency for contributions from students and tutors to alternate. It must be the aim of the teacher to withdraw from this position. Apart from refusing to take a dominant seating position this may be done by a number of 'tricks of the trade'. If the tutor always looks at the student who is speaking it is almost as if he were saying, 'When you have finished I shall retake control'. If the tutor looks away (particularly as the student finishes) the speaker may direct his remarks to someone who appears more responsive. The tutor may look round the group for the glance, the indrawn breath or the change of seating position which indicates that another student wishes to speak. That student may be induced to contribute by the tutor's expectant look or by a slight motion of the hand just as he decides whether to risk comment. If possible the tutor should avoid using his own voice for this purpose. In other words he works for the situation in which the conversation flows from student to student without obvious control from him.

As this situation cannot normally be achieved straight away, three 'Don'ts' are sometimes suggested. (1) Don't correct or reject the first contributions even if they are wildly wrong. There is a danger that correction will seem like jumping on the students and will discourage expression of opinion. The teacher then finds himself holding the floor and future comments are put to him for approval. If corrections are made as a result of what other students say, it is easier to dissociate what was said from who said it. (2) Don't state an opinion too rigidly. Some teachers attempt to provide discussion by an outrageous statement, but this requires very skilled teaching. It has the danger that the teacher either inhibits expression of other opinions, or has to defend his own. In the first case he prevents student contributions, and in the second, half the contributions are from him. Both provoke frustration and then aggression from the students. Tolerant questioning is easier and in any case students accept the opinions of their fellow students more readily than those of their lecturers. (3) Don't answer questions that could be answered by another member of the class. Most teachers are selected from their ability to express themselves in writing and put their thoughts into words. Yet they are sometimes poor listeners. Teaching by discussion requires skills in listening and observation, while lecturing provides an opportunity to talk.

Keeping a discussion going is a task in human relations management. It is not easy and needs to be learned. Like lectures, group discussions require careful preparation if they are to achieve their objectives.

## Following the Discussion

It is not uncommon to overhear students saying, 'I don't know what I was supposed to get out of that discussion,' 'I couldn't say anything; I was lost,' 'We kept going round in circles,' or 'We kept getting off the point.' Obviously the teacher was not completely successful, yet how was he to clarify and guide a discussion without dominating it? There may be a number of ways of overcoming this conflict; I shall only describe the technique I try to use.

I work for a situation in which the students and I can all say, 'This is the question we have discussed, and these are the possible answers to it.' This requires taking rough notes and, where possible, preparing a list of answers and facts to be considered.

The first thing I do is to *decide* as clearly as possible what *the basic issue* of the discussion is. It is usually a question or problem and I jot it down as a heading in my discussion notes. In many cases it is decided before the discussion and the students have read and prepared for it – and so should I have done. In other cases the students come with their difficulties and it is important to make sure the problem is clear to the rest of the group before it is discussed.

I try not only to summarize (or ask the students to summarize) the answers to each question before proceeding to the next, but also to recapitulate the whole discussion to that point. This gives an overall view and a sense of direction to the students. Points I wish to include in my summary are noted and numbered under the heading. Thus with reference to every contribution that is made, I try to ask myself (and to persuade the students to ask themselves), 'How is this relevant to the problem?' When the discussion gets off the point I do not bring it back to the straight and narrow immediately, because students may need to get something off their chests. I want the students to discipline themselves in relevance, and, in any case, some deviations permit a broader view of the subject. But I do try to remember where the discussion became irrelevant so that we can return to that point and preserve a thread in the discussion.

Answers to a problem frequently consist of 'pros' and 'cons' which can be noted in two columns. Thus, because ideas in a discussion are not expressed in a organized sequence, taking notes involves a sorting process. Similarly, when students fail to distinguish two important issues, rather than impede the flow of thoughts on one of them, I note contributions under their appropriate question. When the distinction is eventually made (I usually want the students to make it for themselves) it is possible to remind them of what has been said and to ask to which issue each point is relvant. (This requires them to practise making the distinction they previously failed to make.)

It is often useful to know which student made what contribution. (Why?) Therefore in my jottings I draw a circle (or another shape) to match the circle of chairs. If there are 12 in the group it will look something like a clock face with me as number 6, and contributions can be labelled either with a number or letter, or with an arrow in the direction that the clock hand would point.

I also note contributions that could be used as a 'lead-in' to points not so far made, or to other issues to be discussed. These I usually mark with an asterisk and a label indicating the contributor so that I can remind him of what he said and ask a 'lead-in' question. This enables me to withdraw from a vocal role more quickly and gives at least one student a feeling of involvement with the next topic.

Above all there is a need to keep an overall view of the discussion period. This is the purpose of taking notes (not, like the students, to keep a relatively permanent record), but it is much easier if the questions and possible answers are prepared before the group meets. It is essential to remember that because discussions can range widely, they need as much preparation as lectures (although they cannot be 'planned' in the same way).

# 7

# Small Group Teaching Methods in Higher Education

*J. P. Powell*

## Summary

The proceedings of thirteen undergraduate tutorials in a variety of disciplines were tape-recorded and analysed to determine the amount of speech contributed by each member and the cognitive content of the verbal interaction. A small number of groups worked without a tutor. Tutors spoke for rather more than half of the time and when the tutor was absent many students doubled their own contributions and participation was spread more evenly. There was a marked emphasis on providing information in almost all of the meetings but in the leaderless groups this tended to diminish and there was rather more stress on argument. It is suggested that the use of leaderless tutorials be more widely adopted.

## Introduction

The application of the techniques and research findings of social psychology to the problems of interpersonal relations and learning in small instructional groups is still very much in its infancy and, although much of the enormous amount of work devoted to the study of group dynamics is of interest to teachers, remarkably little of it has been aimed at increasing our understanding of what goes on in classrooms. A recent textbook (Shaw 1971) is typical in this regard in that its subject index contains no reference to education, school, college, learning or teaching. Anyone interested in the study of small group teaching at the university level is therefore thrown largely upon his own resources, although there are some guides to the scanty literature (Powell 1971) and one excellent discussion of research findings (Abercrombie 1971).

My own interest in the study of small group teaching methods sprang largely from the seminal work of Jane Abercrombie (1960) which prompted

Reproduced by permission from Powell 1974.

me to carry out some small-scale experiments with leaderless tutorial groups, the results of which (Powell 1964) suggested that groups of this type might achieve some educational values which tend to be neglected in conventional tutorials. An early review (Bass 1950) of the leaderless discussion technique contains no mention of its use for educational purposes and subsequent applications have been overwhelmingly concerned with leadership, personnel selection and psychotherapy.

The study reported here had two main aims: to collect data relating to verbal participation in 'conventional' tutor-led groups; and to examine the feasibility of using leaderless groups in university teaching.

## Procedure

Many problems confront the investigator of university teaching methods if he wishes to tape-record class proceedings. Both staff and students tend to be wary of having their every word preserved on tape: the wife of a colleague who was in no way involved in the experiment once remarked to me: 'Are you still doing your eavesdropping?' Despite careful explanation of the purposes of my work I sometimes failed to persuade students to take part or to dispel the perfectly understandable uneasiness of some tutors. Students who agreed to work without a tutor were always given an assurance that the procedure would be abandoned if they became unhappy with it.

For a number of reasons I was obliged to take whatever groups I could get and this meant that it was impossible to obtain anything which looked remotely like a 'sample', a 'control group' or a 'sound experimental design'. If students and tutor agreed to the tape-recording and they were able to meet at times which did not clash with other recording sessions then they became part of the investigation. Few members of staff were willing to give up their teaching role entirely so the number of totally leaderless groups was always very small and was drawn either from my own classes or from Preliminary Year students completing the university's matriculation requirements. Almost all the students were male Papuans and New Guineans. After a number of technical problems had been overcome, recordings of an adequate quality for analytic purposes were obtained from thirteen groups, each consisting of between seven and eleven students.

Tutors and students were not given any instructions as to how the meetings were to be conducted although it was suggested to the leaderless groups that they could appoint a chairman if they wished. Only the students were present at the leaderless meetings. Most of the leaderless meetings had a definite topic to discuss which was prescribed by the tutor; they were also usually provided with a handout containing some questions or other stimulus to discussion. An interesting question, not taken up in this study, concerns the relationship between the stimulus materials which students are given in tutorials and the amount and quality of the subsequent verbal interaction. As far as I am aware, this important problem has yet to be tackled by research workers since no findings which bear upon it have so far appeared in the literature.

All meetings lasted 45-55 minutes and took place weekly, except for the alternating tutored/leaderless groups which met twice a week, yielding a total of seven to ten recorded sessions with each group. It is not possible to gauge accurately the effects of tape-recording: I feel that most participants became accustomed to it quite quickly but I know from remarks made by students that even at the end of a semester some of them were still inhibited by the procedure. Students were assured that nobody but myself would listen to the leaderless tape-recordings. The only alternative is hidden microphones and that would be ruled out on moral and professional grounds. Records were kept of seating positions for each meeting and at the final gathering for each series all participants (except tutors) given a sociometric test and a questionnaire. I also discussed the whole project with them at that meeting. This yielded an immense amount of data, only a small proportion of which has yet been analysed in order to establish the amount of verbal contribution from each member and the cognitive characteristics of what was said.

The participation rate for each member was obtained by the use of a technique developed some ten years ago (Powell and Jackson 1946) which requires only a typewriter, a metronome and a tape-recorder. Each group member is assigned a code-letter and the appropriate typewriter key is struck at one second intervals according to who is speaking. Blanks are left for periods of silence. In this way the verbal interation of an entire tutorial can be sequentially displayed on a single sheet of foolscap paper. Each member's participation score can then be calculated as a percentage of the total amount of speech and a mean percentage score can then be derived from these to indicate each member's level of verbal participation over the entire series of meetings.

The content of what was said in tutorials was analysed in terms of a category system (see Table 1) devised to take account of the major forms of cognitive activity which might be thought to possess educational significance at the undergraduate level. There are a large number of category systems currently in use for the analysis of classroom interaction but none of these appears to reflect the pedagogical interests of university teachers. Many of them are concerned with affective responses such as 'shows support' or 'shows hostility' while others concentrate heavily upon the moves made by teachers in initiating interaction. After a great many modifications the system shown in the table was adopted: it is far from satisfactory but most university teachers will, I hope, agree that it identifies cognitive activities which may be seen in all tutorials and which are of major educational significance. The most difficult to see in operational terms, and in my view the most important, is category A, 'arguing'. One of the central skills to be acquired by a student is the ability to develop an argument, to criticize the views advanced by others, to defend his own position, to muster reasons and justifications for his own beliefs, interpretations and claims of knowledge. A number of people worked on the calculation of participation rates but in order to avoid the risk of inter-coder unreliability all the category scores were obtained by one assitant after a number of training sessions with me in order to clarify the boundaries between the categories. Unfortunately, the poor quality of many of the early recordings limited the number of groups to which the category system could be applied.

It is well known to students, but not to many tutors, that most of the talking in tutorials is done by the tutor. Of the thirteen tutors for whom we have results their mean percentage participation score was 58.0

O    GIVING AN OPINION

       Expressing an unsupported belief, value judgement or interpretation. Agreeing or disagreeing. Expressing puzzlement.

I     GIVING INFORMATION

       Providing facts or data. Citing others or books.
       Recounting personal or group experiences. Reading from text or notes.
       Summing up.

A    ARGUING

       Opinion supported by information $(O + I = A)$.
       Criticizing views of others. Defending own position. Raising objections. Giving reasons or justifications. Developing a point of view.

Q    ASKING FOR INFORMATION

       Questions eliciting information, clarification, opinions, explanations. (NB Many apparent questions are often objections and should be scored A.)

C    CLARIFYING

       Rephrasing earlier statements. Giving examples. Elucidating quotations from or remarks of others. Explaining. Defining. 'Mulling over' the material.

P     FORMULATING PROBLEMS

       Suggesting, proposing, analysing or identifying the problem. Analysis or clarification of problem, suggestions, proposals or questions concerning how to attack the problem. (NB Exclude organizational proposals such as 'Let's split into three groups to do this.')

G    GROUP PROCESSES

       Proposals for, questions about, discussions of, criticisms of group organization, individual contributions. Expressions of friendliness or hostility towards members. (Include management questions or instructions, eg details of assignments, course planning and content. Include laughter and group noise, eg all talking or shouting at once.)

**Table 1**

Category system for cognitive activities in discussion groups.

per cent and the range was from 27.8 per cent to 74.0 per cent. It is clear from this that groups where no tutor is present have available to them, even if they are unable to make good use of it, almost double the amount of time for verbal interaction available to students in tutor-led groups. This can be seen in the data for three of the groups which had alternating tutored and leaderless meetings (see Figure 1). In the history of science group there were two students who said nothing whatever during any meeting when the tutor was present but both contributed when he was absent. In most cases the students increased their participation scores quite considerably when the tutor was absent: in some cases they said nearly five times as much. In a few cases students spoke less under the leaderless condition. It would be most interesting to know the explanation for very large increases in contributions from particular students when the tutor was not present but there are too many uncontrolled variables beneath the present data even to speculate about this. One important generalization which is supported by these results is that, as tutors tend to talk for about half of any given tutorial period, the time available for student contributions is correspondingly reduced. It would seem to follow that if we want to encourage students to discuss then we should keep out of the room!

In most cases the presence of a tutor tends to increase the total amount of speech in a discussion group, presumably because he is less tolerant of long periods of silence and frequently speaks in lengthy continuous bursts.

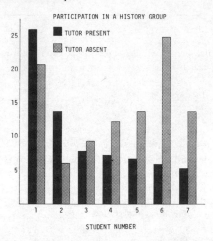

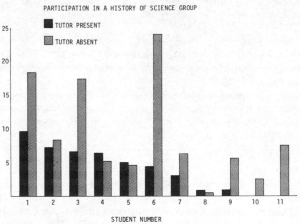

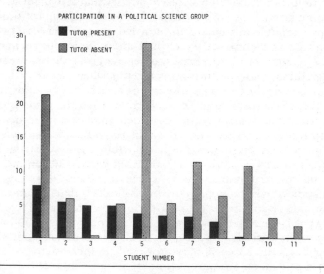

**Figure 1**

Although, taken as a whole, tutorials contain about 25 per cent of silence – one of the leaderless groups spent almost half of their time in silence – it is not common to have periods of silence continuing for longer than thirty seconds. Even half a minute appears to be interminable when one is a participant and few tutors are able to stand the strain without intervening in an attempt to get interaction under way again. This is usually self-defeating as students quickly learn that if they hold out for a while the tutor will soon come to the rescue and keep the monologue going. The tutor is also handicapped by professional norms which pressure him to keep talking since he sees his job as largely that of giving instruction. If the students fail to maintain the discussion then at least he feels that he is earning his money if he keeps 'teaching' them. Some tutors are even told by lecturers to use the time to go over the lecture material again so that it is better understood; in other words, to give another lecture. Most teachers are poor listeners: they conceive their instructional role primarily in terms of telling and explaining and this makes it extremely difficult for them to act as just another group member, although admittedly a well-informed one, with no right to consume most of the discussion time. A consequence of this is that students tend to play the part of passive listeners waiting to be told the answers by an authority figure. One obvious advantage of leaderless groups is that they compel students to adopt other roles and encourage them to emancipate themselves from their customary total dependence upon the teacher. Many teachers do not realize the extent to which students depend upon them. Anyone who is sceptical about this should try putting a notice on the tutorial room door announcing that he will be absent because of illness. All of the students will go away: it is inconceivable to them that they could do anything without the leadership of their teacher.

It is worth noting that if the average tutor speaks for half of the available time then, assuming that there are ten students in the group and that they each speak for roughly the same amount of time, that leaves each student with two minutes in which to make his own contribution to the discussion. Over an academic year of thirty weeks each student thus has a total of only one hour in which to practise his verbal skills and to express and defend his own ideas. It is ironic that those who least need the opportunity to practise these skills, the tutors, get ten times as much practice as the average student. One wonders for whose benefit tutorials are arranged!

In order to obtain an indication of staff views on what makes for a good tutorial a sample of thirty staff members at the University of Papua and New Guinea were asked to list features of what they would consider to be a good tutorial. Some forty-one factors were mentioned and a frequency count produced the seven items listed below. The most frequently mentioned characteristic was widespread participation in discussion, the second was the development of arguments and the third the asking of questions.

1 All members participate
2 Students argue among themselves
3 All students ask questions
4 All completed required preparation
5 All enjoyed the meeting
6 Discussion keeps close to the point
7 Students gain some understanding

It should be noted that respondents were not asked to rank their opinions in order of importance; if they had been so asked then the ordering may have been somewhat different, although I am inclined to doubt this. If a tutor cannot get much response from the students then he is likely to view the whole exercise as a failure. On the other hand if he succeeds in stimulating a vigorous discussion he will count this a success even though the content is perhaps of poor quality.

Let us now turn to the content of the discussions. The category system was devised in order to throw light on the general character of what is said in tutorial discussions and it must be admitted that it is a far from perfect instrument and generates more problems than it resolves. Before we can feel at all confident that there are genuine differences in the cognitive activities of groups when the presence of a tutor is the main experimental variable a great deal more work needs to be done over a wide range of subject-areas. The present results, in view of the small sample (Table 2) and the many important factors which it was impossible to control, must be treated very cautiously and viewed as little more than a collection of hints for future lines of research. The third and final stage envisaged in the present project was the evaluation of the quality of contributions in academic discussion groups: this is perhaps the most important part of the study since university teachers are primarily concerned with the content of what students say rather than the amount of it. This task presents formidable theoretical and practical problems which have yet to be cleared up but work is proceeding on them while at the same time a wider sample of groups is being recorded in order to make it possible for firmer conclusions to be reached regarding the cognitive content of discussions.

| Group | Tutor/ Leaderless | Categories | | | | | | |
|---|---|---|---|---|---|---|---|---|
| | | I | O | Q | A | P | C | G |
| History | T | 54.5 | 7.5 | 5.7 | 1.0 | 1.6 | 11.6 | 18.1 |
| History | L | 25.4 | 15.1 | 6.8 | 2.1 | 0.6 | 14.5 | 35.5 |
| History | Tutor only | 63.2 | 1.5 | 1.1 | 0.3 | 1.5 | 11.2 | 21.2 |
| Politics | T | 37.2 | 18.0 | 7.9 | 7.9 | 0.6 | 16.8 | 11.6 |
| Politics | L | 26.6 | 35.0 | 12.4 | 6.1 | 0.5 | 13.9 | 5.5 |
| Politics | Tutor only | 46.2 | 6.2 | 6.9 | 2.6 | 0.8 | 19.4 | 17.9 |
| Philosophy/History | L | 60.6 | 11.0 | 11.2 | 7.1 | 1.0 | 3.0 | 6.1 |
| Education | L | 27.3 | 17.3 | 8.5 | 23.2 | 3.9 | 7.8 | 12.0 |
| Education | T | 28.2 | 32.8 | 3.7 | 16.9 | 2.7 | 9.3 | 6.4 |
| Education | L | 23.0 | 41.3 | 5.0 | 17.7 | 3.9 | 4.9 | 4.2 |

**Table 2**
The cognitive content of discussion.

It has already been shown that there is both an increase in and a wider distribution of participation in leaderless groups compared with tutored ones. The results shown in the table suggest several other interesting points which are worth comment. Tutors appear to spend much more of their time in providing information than in encouraging students to advance and develop arguments. This may be partly explained by the fact that in those groups where the leaderless condition alternated with tutor presence the tutor was under considerable pressure to give information since it had been agreed at the beginning that difficulties remaining from each leaderless meeting could be cleared up at the next tutored meeting. One suspects, however, that many teachers see themselves primarily as information-givers; and those who do not conceive themselves in this way are probably forced by the structure of the teaching-learning situation into the role of victuallers of information.

Another feature of the data in Table 2 is the difference between the number of opinions which were offered. It may be that tutors try to control the quantity of opinion by challenging it, asking for supporting evidence, pointing out its irrelevance, and so on, whereas a student response to an opinion expressed by a peer would commonly be the offering of yet another opinion. One would expect a considerable variation in scores in this category according to the type of material being disussed: for example, one would predict a low score in mathematics and a high one in politics.

In view of the importance which university teachers attach to argument in discussion groups it is remarkable how little of what was said fell into this category. Once again, one would expect considerable variation according to subject-matter: I have often heard scientists claim that there is little point in having discussions in undergraduate science teaching because the students do not know enough to be able to contribute anything of value. (This has always impressed me as an extremely revealing and interesting assertion but consideration of it will have to await another time.) In philosophy, however, one would expect almost all of tutorial time to be consumed in argument.

## Results

Staff members involved in the experiment were asked to give their views on the advantages and disadvantages of leaderless tutorial groups. The main advantages were seen to be the following: they encourage students to be independent and to rely less on the authority of the teacher; they give students confidence in speaking out and presenting their own ideas; they afford an opportunity for the practice of leadership skills; students are more likely to raise questions which worry *them* than questions which the tutor deems to be important; students are less reluctant to reveal their ignorance to their peers; they are able to learn at their own pace; there is an increased pressure on students to undertake the preparatory reading required for a tutorial; most students appear to work harder; leaderless groups add variety to the teaching methods which are currently being used.

A number of disadvantages were also frequently mentioned: an ill-informed student might dominate the group; without guidance the topic might not be explored thoroughly; its use reduces staff/student contact and thus makes it more difficult for staff to get to know students and to identify those areas in which they need most help; some students become anxious if they cannot see the direction the course is supposed to take and if there is no expert present to correct their mistakes; a dynamic leader is necessary for success.

A number of tutors saw considerable value in alternating leaderless groups with tutored ones (as had been done with some of the experimental groups) or in arranging for the tutor to join the group for the final twenty minutes in order to clear up difficulties.

## Student Response

Many of the above points were also mentioned by students, who in addition listed a number of other considerations. Among the advantages were the following: the atmosphere is more relaxed and students feel able to speak more frankly; there is more time so everyone contributes; it gets students away from spoon-feeding and encourages independence; students learn to help one another; students can learn more from their peers and so gain a deeper understanding; the discussions are more stimulating.

The disadvantages included: we cannot tell whether what we say is correct; much of what is said is irrelevant; one student sometimes dominates the meeting; we make more mistakes than when the tutor is there; it is a waste of time if the preparation has not been done; students sometimes fool around and attendance is poorer.

There are circumstances under which students may well learn more from their peers than from a tutor since the students are all closer to the problem. A tutor often experiences difficulty in grasping just was it is that is puzzling a student since that particular problem ceased to baffle him some years ago. Students also use language which is better understood by their peers. There is also the very important point stressed in the work of M. L. J. Abercrombie (1960) concerning the gap between the mental structures (schemata) of the students and those of the tutor; the higher degree of congruance between those of the students could be expected to favour the grasping of explanations and interpretations offered by peers.

As a number of the students pointed out, the atmosphere of leaderless groups is also likely to be more conducive to learning and understanding. All the members are equals in the absence of the dominating and assessive authority figure of the tutor and this cannot but facilitate a readiness to admit ignorance and lack of understanding as well as a preparedness to challenge what is said and a great willingness to seek credentials for claims to knowledge.

Students were also asked whether they wanted more leaderless tutorials in future and if they thought they learnt more in them than in conventional tutorials: 61 per cent said that they did not want any more participation in leaderless groups but 84 per cent felt that they learnt more when the tutor was absent!

## Evaluations

It is notoriously difficult evaluatively to compare different teaching methods. Whether or not the students were justified in claiming that they learnt more in leaderless groups would be very hard to determine. There is nothing in the data which really bears upon this point except whatever can be gleaned from the distribution of scores within the categories. Evidence from elsewhere is hard to find. A recent comparison (Clement 1971) of the retention rates of student-led and tutor-led discussion groups showed that where complex material is to be learnt student-led groups are superior. Clement suggests that this is because of the greater number of student responses and the increased likelihood of individualized encoding (a better fit with schemata in Abercrombie's terms)of the material. Another study (Webb and Grib 1967) demonstrated an improvement in student attitudes and satisfactions for those in the student-led groups, without any loss of performance in examinations.

One of the major obstacles to evaluating the effectiveness of small-group teaching methods is that of devising criterion measures which are sensitive to the kinds of student developments which might be expected to result from their use. Examinations are crude but useful measures of the extent to which students have assimiliated bodies of complex knowledge but they are of little help in detecting the kinds of learning which we hope discussion groups will foster. This general problem remains unresolved but it is worth pointing out that there is an effective reply to be made to those who refuse to try a new teaching technique until it can be demonstrated that it is superior to methods currently in use, namely, that there is no evidence that the methods currently in use are more effective than any others or, indeed, that they are effective at all!

## Conclusions

Firstly, I want to suggest that the major justification for the type of investigation described in this paper, quite apart from any 'results' that may be obtained, may well be that it provides a stimulus to general reflection upon teaching methods and encourages in both staff and students a greater willingness to experiment with new approaches to common problems. The greatest value of experiments with teaching methods may thus lie in their making available a greater range of models from which teachers can choose those which appear most suited to their own subject and personality. My own experience of university teachers in Britain, Canada and Australasia has been that they very rarely discuss difficulties which they encounter in their teaching and if anyone is prepared to collaborate with them in trying out new teaching and learning procedures then this in itself will generate invaluable discussion of the central professional tasks which they face almost every day.

Secondly, I am very sceptical of the value of large-scale studies of university teaching methods which attempt to establish that one method is superior to another. These have produced very meagre results in the past mainly because they have ignored many major variables such as the teaching and learning styles of the participants and, more importantly, because they have been carried out in the absence of adequate criteria for the success of teaching and learning. It is now very clear that we need to pay much more attention to the fine grain of teaching/learning transactions if we are ever to understand the highly personal and idiosyncratic character of what goes on in classrooms. Such work makes very heavy demands upon the researcher's time and upon his resources of tact, sympathy and perceptiveness but the dividends are likely to be substantial, as the work of Parlett and King (1971) has shown.

Finally, I am convinced that we are now justified in encouraging a much more widespread use of the leaderless group technique in high education, although students do need some initial training in order to exploit its potentialities to the full. This kind of group environment affords students an opportunity to practise a variety of social and intellectual skills which are of the greatest educational significance: the articulation, presentation and defence of arguments; the complex cluster of skills and attitudes which we associate with effective leadership; the willingness to admit frankly to ignorance and faulty understanding; the ability to criticize the views of others without giving offence and to accept criticism with a good grace; engagement in serious discussion with peers without feeling the need to defer to an authority figure; the making of independent judgements which one is able to support with some degree of adequacy and confidence; the possibility of arriving at a deeper understanding of what is involved in working co-operatively and productively with others on challenging intellectual tasks of common interest.

The lecture hall offers almost no opportunites for learning to take place in any of these areas and the teacher-led tutorial, although an excellent technique in many ways, has the disadvantage of imposing a number of major constraints upon students. We now need to be much more confident and daring in encouraging students to take greater responsibility for their own learning.

# 8

# Social Procedures in Task-Oriented Groups

*Gordon Lawrence*

At the present time there is, as the authors of a major survey of small group research complained, a sad lack of theory in this whole area of small group studies which is 'shot through with idiosyncratic concepts and labels used only by one investigator and a few of his disciples' (McGrath and Altman 1966); it is a difficult area to investigate empirically due to the large number of substantive factors involved; systematic attempts to formulate sets of propositions, postulates, and hypotheses are limited. Hence we are reduced to dealing in middle-range theories, models and sensitising frameworks to explain the processes at work in small groups. What follows is an attempt to develop a middle-range, explanatory framework for task-oriented groups; based on data from problem-solving groups, sensitivity groups and laboratory groups. Task-oriented groups have been chosen because they tend to be the kind of group in which most of us are involved in our work-a-day life.

## Preliminary Concepts

Before outlining this framework a number of preliminary concepts and notions need to be enunciated.

Although we all 'know' at a commonsense, intuitive level about small groups, for social life is group life, we need to identify the common elements of all groups at a general level. Here, Goffman's (1961) definition will be followed:

A social group may be defined as a special type of social organisation. Its elements are individuals: they perceive the organisation as a distinct collective unit, a social entity, apart from the particular relationships the participants may have to one another; they perceive themselves as members who belong, identifying with the organisation and receiving moral support from doing so; they sustain a sense of hostility to outgroups. A symbolisation of the reality of the group and one's relations to it is also involved.

Just how a task-oriented social group moves towards this kind of organization it is hoped to unravel.

---

Reproduced by permission from Lawrence 1970.

The importance of the small group is that it 'is an essential mechanism of socialisation and a primary source of social order' (Shepherd 1964). By this is meant that through our interaction in small groups, particularly the family, we acquire our definitions of the world, our images of society, our notions of how the world we live in is articulated, our values and norms, and our conceptions of self. It is quite elliptical to say that we are born into a society and a culture, we are born into families which are part of a kin network and a local social system composed of other small groups. Initally, the adult members of these groups, acting as significant others, induct us into their values and the meanings they place upon the objective world. At the same time, the foundation of our identity, our self-conceptions, are laid as part of the same process. Through subsequent interaction in other social settings and groups these values and meanings will be strengthened or modified, as will our self-conceptions be confirmed or denied by others. Socialisation is a life-long process and continues well after childhood and is part of the content of any small group's processes.

At the inception of a face-to-face relationship we each have *typificatory schemes* about the other in the relationship to rely on (Berger and Luckman 1967). These schemes arise out of previous interactions and allow us to 'deal with', initially, new interactions in that the other can be apprehended, for example, as a priest and Scotsman which enables us to modify our conduct in the relationship accordingly.

When a *we-relationship* (Schutz 1953) develops, however, the typifactory scheme that the interaction has been founded on is overhauled. This is done by each in the social relationship scrutinising the subjective meaning placed upon the social action of the other. The particular values, norms, meanings and ends each subscribes to are exposed either by actual declaration or, and this is more likely, are inferred from the conduct. The end for the relationship doesn't need to be calculative and can be, quite simply, to perpetuate the relationship. Should the parties in the relationship have coincident meanings, expectations, values, and definitions of the situation, then they will have a relationship characterised by harmony; should they disagree on any of these dimensions and reject the demands made by one upon the other, one of conflict; and should they completely misunderstand one another and fail to communicate, one of anomie. Social interaction in the course of a social relationship moves within the three points of *perfect co-operation, perfect conflict,* and *anomie.* (Anomie: the sense in which this term is being used here is to refer to situations which contain no norms, what Talcot Parsons sees as 'the polar antithesis of full institutionalisation'. This can be understood as the contrary of 'society'.) Although this is a much abbreviated indication of Rex's (1961) action frame of reference, it should be sufficient to help us interpret the conduct of persons in small groups. In general terms, the action framework pays due attention to individuals pursuing different ends of 'projects' (Berger and Luckman 1976) in social interaction, and recognises that individuals have not always coincident values, norms, and definitons of the situation.

It has been necessary to outline these notions separately as they constitute the particular perspective to be taken here on the phenomenon of the small group. The pedigree of this particular perspective is, in the main, apart from Rex's action frame of reference and some of the ideas of Alfred Schutz as interpreted and extended by Berger and Luckman, heavily reliant on Tuckman's (1965) developmental model of small groups, and owes something to the symbolic interactionist framework in sociology.

## The Framework

Examining small groups on a temporal dimension, it is suggested they develop in the following fashion: they *form, storm, norm,* and *perform.* This developmental model has been proposed by Tuckman (1965) on the basis of a review of fifty reported studies of groups in a variety of settings, ranging from therapy groups through laboratory groups to natural groups. This model induced from the literature aims at serving a conceptual function as well as an integrative and organisational one. Although some criticism can be levelled at the over-representation of qualitative studies as basic data, the model would seem to stand the test of commonsense and is consistent in its general features with other developmental models and findings in the area. Here it will be used as descriptive framework, with the addition of an extra stage, *informing,* around which to build other concepts about conduct, tasks and structure.

For purposes of exposition it is a framework which can be applied to a small group of people come together for the purposes of attaining some goal and which has no structured authority system, and would certainly be applicable to an organic, problem-solving group (Davis 1967). Having outlined the framework, some qualifications will be made to ground it more firmly in reality by, for example, examining authority relations.

## *Stage I. Forming*

When a number of people come together for the purposes of *forming* a group to attain some task, the first critical issue each has to face is that of commitment. In actuality, the issue is never resolved. Overtly, the content of the interaction will be directed towards attempting to identify the task and each person in the new situation. In part, persons are identified through the task, in that by exploring the parameters of the task the ways in which the group's pooled experience might help is also revealed. Generally,there is an orientation to the task and an attempt to establish some 'ground rules' for the interaction through discovery. Tuckman points out that this general class of behaviour cuts across both natural and therapy groups but that instrumentality and expressivity of orientation will be dependent on the kind of group. The task will be directed either at others or at the goals of the group, but whichever is salient the participants will certainly be establishing what interpersonal conduct is deemed appropriate through a moment-to-moment observation of what each does and an appropriate adjustment of actions according to the observed patterns of behaviour.

Conduct, then, appears to be directed towards establishing some boundaries, what Schutz (1958) calls the problem of inclusion – to join or not to join; commitment, in our terms. Another feature of this phase is dependence on any authority in the group. Schroder and Harvey (1963) describe it as 'an initial stage of absolutistic dependence, featuring the emergence of a status hierarchy and rigid norms which reduce ambiguity and foster dependence and submission.' This authority boundary will be broken in subsequent phases of the group's life but its quick establishment is of some functional importance for the new participants in the group, as it enables self-lodging to be initiated.

## The Self-lodging Hypothesis

This acceptance of any authority may be because underneath all the talk about task, whether instrumental or expressive, there is a covert agenda for each member: the successful presentation of self and an attempt to lodge this self-concept in the interaction. This relates to the issue of commitment in that if the presentation is successful, or, perhaps, just uproblematic, then, presumably, it would be advantageous to continue the interaction.

Support for this hypothesis comes from an interpretation of a number of writers on social interaction. Goffman (1959) argues that much of our everyday behaviour is directed towards maintaining our status and sense of personal worth. Using dramaturgical analogies he analyses our everyday conduct in terms of performances before audiences by seeing us as always trying to create and maintain a favourable impression as we present ourselves to others. If we are successful in convincing our audience that we should be taken at our own evaluation, then we are contented and happy. On the other hand, anxiety, frustration, and unhappiness will be our lot if we are unable to perform convincingly.

To see all interaction as simply the presentation of self to others is an oversimplification, however, for 'at some point in the cycle of recurrent interactions the self moves from the presentational to the lodging phase' (Denzin 1969). Here it is being argued that in the forming stage selves are simply presented and accepted at face value, why typificatory schemes go unchallenged, just as any authority does. What is being said here about self-lodging begins to gel in the *storming* stage of the group's life and is almost totally resolved at the *norming* stage, but for neatness of exposition the whole process will be treated at this point.

According to the symbolic interactionist perspective it should be recognised that 'human beings interpret or "define" each others' actions instead of merely reacting' (Blumer 1967). If consensual action is to flow, then there needs to be common agreement as to the meaning of objects which the parties involved have access to. 'Once the meaning of objects have been agreed upon, conduct can flow along the lines of custom, tradition, and ritual' (Denzin 1969). One such object is the self, which is a continually evaluated object by all, and stable patterns of interaction will only be possible when selves are consensually defined. Until this consensual definition emerges, group life will be changing in character as long as the different selves are objects open to negotiation and change because of their differing interpretations.

Self-lodging is the process whereby 'persons translate crucial features of their own identity into the selves, and into the memories and imaginations of relevant others. In this way, Cooley's (1902) proposition that the other exists in "our imagination of him" comes to life. By lodging the self in interaction, and in the selves of others, reciprocal bond is created, and the firm foundations for future relationships are established' (Denzin 1969). Group life, according to this view, is a series of social selves that have been successfully lodged to form a structure.

In the initial phases of group life, this process of self-lodging takes place, it is suggested, through the individual presenting his own definition of self, his identity, to the relevant others for whom it is an object to be interpreted. Similarly, for the presenter it is an object of evaluation. The process of self-lodging is the forging of a consensual definition of the self by all the parties. This view suggests that the process is one motivational feature of human conduct. An additional hypothesis, suggested by Denzin, is that 'if valued portions of the self are not lodged, recognised, and reciprocated, a dissatisfaction concerning the encounter is likely to be sensed.' The importance of this whole idea is the recognition that human interaction is not as rational and instrumentally orientated as some believe. Unsuccessful self-lodging can prevent the person from taking up a rational standpoint. Because self-lodging relies on affective bonds between the self and relevant others, rational action can be displaced by action grounded in love, hate, jealousy or unquestioning respect.

In an attempt to explicate these related concepts systematically, the second stage in the developmental model, *storming*, has been anticipated to some extent. In summary, nothing is resolved at the *forming* stage except that a pattern of interaction is initiated on the basis of two agendas: an overt one of task, and a covert one of self-lodging by the participants. So that these two agendas can get under way a quick authority structure is thrown up uncritically by the participants to satisfy their dependency needs; in short, a crude redoubt from which the participants can foray and forage for their identity and new authority.

## Stage II. Storming

The critical issue is still that of commitment, but it is now more sharply tested and is articulated with the critical issue which will become dominant in the third stage: the issue of group authority or personal freedom. Here, it is being suggested that the problems of identity and authority are fused to a considerable extent and that they straddle, as a covert agenda, the three stages of *forming, storming* and *norming*. What is particularly in mind here is the observation of Knickerbocker (1948) that since our conception of self is acquired through interaction with significant others such as our parents who are authority figures, then our identity is inextricably bound up with our notions about authority.

This second stage is characterised by intra-group hostility, rebellion, opposition, and conflict. The evidence for this comes from a variety of observations about groups: Schroder and Harvey (1963) identify a stage of negative independence; Bion (1961) sees the basic assumption of fight/flight becoming salient; while Bennis (1964), using Bion's framework, describes the phase as one of counterdependence on any authority. All are agreed that it is a stressful period and that the participants are involved at an intense feeling level in this '"unfrozen" period of anarchic activity' (Shepherd 1964).

Why is there this period of *storming?* What is is about? Overtly, in the task area it is about ends and means. From their apparently secure redoubt thrown up at the *forming* stage the participants involve themselves in the group by declaring their differing definitions of the situation and meanings of the objects in their environment towards which action is to be directed. To use Blumer's phrase, the differing lines of action are declared. These, however, tend to be seen in for-and-against terms, as leaders will advance opposing views and be supported, albeit temporarily, by their followers. Everything is seen in crude terms and there are no gradations of meaning although this will follow.

Here, it is suggested that the *storming* which is non-rational to an observer is indicative of the self-lodging process which must generate feelings.

## Stage III. Norming

The critical issue at this stage is that of authority. (Here it is being assumed that there are no formal superordinate-subordinate relationships structured, for example, by the organisation in which the task group is set, but to this point we shall return.) The kind of authority being assumed here is that which rests on an individual's 'capacity for the kind of reasoning that relates technical requirements to transcendent values and beliefs' (Friedrich 1964). More particularly, this kind of authority relies on a rational demonstration of means to ends which can be elaborated by valuational as well as technical reasoning, and so is a quality of communication which generates 'power and influence through the consent it engenders' (ibid.).

The participants can both exercise this kind of authority and allow themselves to be subject to it on a rational basis only if the self-lodging has been successful. If the participant's identity has been successfully negotiated then freedom and authority cease to be problematic for the individual and he can truly 'hear' what others are saying without 'reading' any threat into their statements. If the individual can do this then authority of the kind suggested above can operate.

The stage of *norming* is characterised by cohesion and the concern of the members is towards integration, so emphasis is laid on mutuality and interpersonal relationships (Schroder and Harvey 1963). Certainly, there is some degree of affection (Schutz 1958), and the conduct is characterised by harmonious relationships in the main.

The content is directed towards a systematic evaluation of means and ends (Bales 1953), as can be witnessed by asking of opinions by the members and the giving of information (Klein 1961). That the discussion can proceed in a rational fashion, that there can be an open exchange of relevant interpretations, and a genuine exploration of the task and its parameters together with modes of attaining the task, is only possible if the interacting selves have successfully lodged themselves and developed an interpersonal structure. All of which, it is suggested, is a function of the hostility and conflict in the preceding stage of *storming*.

At this *norming* stage a group culture can begin to be identified as personal norms are replaced, where necessary for the social action, by some common group norms, but this does not mean that there is some monolithic belief system. Individual conceptions of means and ends for the group having been declared, a common goal is possible, but individuals have to give up their 'bits of authority' and some of their freedom in the situation if this goal is to be reached. At this *norming* stage the necessary spadework for goal attainment, that is negotiating of common meanings of the relevant objects, is accomplished.

## Stage IV. Performing

The critical issue is now that of intimacy and work, for the purpose is to pursue a collective goal. There is now at this stage a recognisable structure of functionally related roles, what Mills (1967) terms instrumental roles interlocking in a technical system. Schroder and Harvey (1963) labelled this stage 'positive interdependence' as there is 'simultaneous autonomy and mutuality (ie the members can operate in any combination, or as a unit) and an emphasis on task achievement which is superordinate to social structure' (Tuckman 1965).

Solutions to problems emerge at this stage, and in therapy groups there would be the emergence of insights yielding solutions to personal problems. All this is possible because the critical issues of commitment and authority have been resolved and the self-lodging been successful.

Here can be seen a distinct group culture which, in addition to norms, has explicit definitions of objects in the environment, and a preferential ordering among alternative objects, ideas, states of affairs, and values.

Using the criteria of a successful group outlined by Shepherd (1964), the group at this stage will have clear objectives (goals), a clearly differentiated role structure known by all the members, shared norms and values (ie ideas as to procedures and what is desirable), a clear-cut membership, each recognised as having differing skills and responsibilities to offer to the totality, and open and full communication of what is relevant information: in short, a work group.

Up to this point, the small task-orientated group has been seen in isolation, but groups do interact with other groups which constitute their environment. Consequently, a fifth stage is posited: *informing*.

## Stage V. Informing

Whether this is an appropriate label or not, it derives from Rice's discussion of inter-group exercises in sensitivity institutes, where he argues that 'for a group to communicate as a group, it has to have a "voice". For the "voice" to be coherent and understandable, not only outside the group, but inside as well, some mechanism, some "political" machinery has to be devised. This enables a group to agree on what its "voice" is to say. It also has to agree on a mechanism for the reception of communication from other groups, and on a framework of beliefs and attitudes within which it can interpret these communications' (Rice 1965).

Once a group has attained the appropriate political machinery, which is but a short move from the performance stage, then it can interact with other groups. This raises problems of hostility to outgroups and, initially, can be threatening to whatever structure has been developed within the group. Group self-determination is not only demanded, but also the forging of ideas deemed worth communicating.

## Some Reservations

In outlining this particular framework for task-orientated groups, there have been dangers of oversimplification: first, there has been an implication that groups survive and that participants move smoothly from stage to stage until they attain their goal. From observation we know that this is not so, for groups can be unproductive and can cease to exist. Using the action frame of reference sensitises us to the fact that participants can pursue different ends, and at any stage the interaction can break down, because their projects do not coincide or because self-lodging has not been achieved by a particular member. On occasion, this can mean that a task-orientated group may have to *re-storm* and *re-norm*.

Second, an assumption made in this exposition was that there were no superordinate-subordinate relationships structured in the group and that members' authority came from their own ability to convince the others in the situation that their particular choice of means and ends was rational. The reality is that there are other sources of authority, and in a natural, task-orientated group the chances are high that there will be a 'coercion-compromise structure – a status and power system' (Shepard 1965) at the group's inception. This means that choices of ends and means by participants may not be at all rational and may be highly calculative. This latter point is indicated by Burns in his criticism of rationality models of organisations. His thesis is that within organisations and task-orientated groups such as a department set in such a matrix, there are 'systems built out of the conduct (and the relationships specify) of individuals as they act in pursuit of the different ends to which they commit themselves, and find themselves committed, as members of the concern' (Burns 1969). These systems he identifies as the working organisation, the political system and the career structure which 'exist for the individual as social *Gestalten*' (ibid.). The point here is that in attempting to isolate the ends being pursued in task-orientated groups, and the differing definitions of the situation held by participants, some attempt would have to be made to identify from which system a participant was deriving his salient values as, presumably, this must affect the decision-making process.

Third, a major objection to this particular framework could be the implicit assumption that the ideal task group is one characterised by an organic approach to problem-solving. The evidence is that an organic approach to task-attainment is the only way that an organisation can innovate and cope with problems of change (Burns and Stalker 1961; Davis 1967). As important, it is also known that 'people are responsible and creative when given the opportunity' (Myers 1968); the evidence of Herbst (1962) on how effective autonomous work groups can be also confirms this.

# Conclusion

An attempt has been made here to provide a middle-range, explanatory framework for task-orientated groups in an organic fashion. Some major qualifications have been made which must be taken into account when considering task-orientated groups in an organisation. The last problem we want to examine is how can those in structured authority positions, we can call them administrators, enable others to be leaders exercising authority of the kind outlined above?

Mills (1967) uses the concept of 'executive' which may be helpful here. Briefly, the executive is someone who takes on responsibility for the total dynamic configuration of the task group but also has ideas as to what the group can become in the future, vision if you like, and so his conduct is directed towards this. To do this he has to de-commit himself by standing, figuratively, both inside and outside the group. In this way he can experience, observe, and assess the reality of the momentary situation. At one and the same time, he must be in touch with the feelings in the situation, able to examine the processes at work and able realistically to appraise the environment outside the group. If others can be led to take on this perspective then not only are the possibilities of innovative solutions to problems enhanced but also conditions for the personal growth of the participants are improved.

# 9

# Small Groups

## *M. L. J. Abercrombie*

Man is pre-eminently a social animal, and most of us spend most of our waking time interacting with other people. From the moment of birth, satisfactory psychological interaction of the infant with his mother (or any person who takes her place) is as essential for the development of his mental health as physiological interaction was previously for his viability as a parasite in the womb. Our ability to participate in many kinds of groups is conditioned by our experiences of this first group of two, and its early extensions to include the rest of the family and other people around the place. At present, this crucial development goes on 'naturally' – not haphazardly, because it is highly conditoned by tradition – but largely without conscious control; we are not, on the whole, aware of what other possibilities of behaviour are open to us as individuals, much less as a species.

Research on the way people behave in various kinds of groups may help us to behave more appropriately, not only the better to achieve the aims we already have set ourselves, but also the better to think up new aims as yet undreamed of. The need to do this, whether on the scale of intimate personal relations, or at national and global level, is clearly urgent. Impoverished by ignorance and enchained by irrational fears, few of us lead our little lives as happily, or as fruitfully, as we would wish, and all of us are threatened with extinction by the forces that split the atom manipulated with not much more understanding of what makes the cerebral cortex tick than the first man had when he split a stone to make an axe.

As we shall see, many factors affect the way each of us behaves in groups, mostly without our recognising them. People who do recognise them can do quite a lot to modify the behaviour of others. Understanding the effects of different kinds of leadership, channels of communication, and group climates, may make it possible so to manipulate a given situation that a group will work more effectively towards a prescribed goal. This kind of human engineering, like the results of any other research, can obviously serve good social ends or bad. According to the orientation of the manipulator, whether it is good or bad that a group of workers should be helped to increase its output depends on what goods it makes and for whom; and if a committee is made to work more harmoniously, whether this is good or bad depends on what kind of resolutions it passes and what activities it initiates.

---

Reproduced by permission from Abercrombie 1966.

Perhaps one of the most useful results of the study of groups, and the safest one for the ultimate good of mankind, is the possibilities it gives of extending each person's understanding of his own behaviour, and thus empowering him with better control of his otherwise automatic and unthinking reactions. Two main sources of information are available for this purpose. One derives from reports of other people's behaviour, made by more or less 'objective' or 'scientific' methods, often involving the use of control (or at least comparison) groups. Notable recent contributions summarising various aspects of this sort of work are Homans' classic *The Human Group* (1951), Cartwright and Zander's *Group Dynamics* (1960), Sprott's introduction to the more general and sociological aspects (1958) and Klein's summary of communication studies (1956).

A second source of information comes from experiencing one's own behaviour in groups which are specially arranged to make each participant more effective in his behaviour outside the group. Among others, Slavson (1956), Frank and Powdermaker (1959) and Rosenbaum and Berger (1963) have surveyed this field, and Foulkes and Anthony (1965), Balint and Balint (1955) and Abercrombie (1960) have dealt with more specific aspects. Workers in this area tend to be therapeutically orientated rather than fact-finding; they tend to be less articulate (though not less vocal) that the experimentalists, and because their material is less amenable to pigeon-holing and their results to rigorous testing, they tend to get neglected by more conventional psychologists. It is, however, being increasingly recognised that the potentialities of applying this kind of work to the education of normal people (and not only to the mentally sick or delinquent, for whom it has mostly been developed) are very great (Morris 1965).

If a legitimate aim of psychology is to give each of us better control over our mental processes, a step in the right direction might be taken if these two approaches to self-knowledge could be combined. The kind of skills the group therapists have developed might be used in groups in order to facilitate the uptake of the information that the students of group dynamics have collected, and to make possible its efficient application to subsequent behaviour. This is no light task, and the hazards involved are commensurate with the potentialities it offers for mental growth. It is not without apprehension that I venture the bold but modest step of talking about both sources of information within the same few pages; in this essay, I shall focus attention on those aspects of the study of group behaviour that seem to be most immediately relevant to this aim of increasing the range of our reactions that might be subjected to more effective self-monitoring.

Part of the potentiality that groups have of improving self-awareness depends on the perception of individual differences among the participants, and this runs counter to much common thinking about groups. We tend to concentrate on the fact that a group consists of members who are behaving alike in certain important respects, and many of the terms used, 'gang', 'clique', 'mob', 'following the crowd', 'mass movements' or 'herd instinct', have denigratory implications. We shall begin this essay, therefore, with a discussion on the ways people in groups tend to act alike.

First, however, let us be clear what we may mean by 'group'. A group may mean simply an aggregate, as a group of people waiting at a bus stop; in such a case each person has the same aim, to get on the bus, but there may be very little interaction between them, unless say, no bus arrives, or an accident is witnessed when, the commonality of their experience increasing, they start talking to each other. Many novels are histories of groups of people who have come together by chance and then interact, taking up various fairly well defined, but maybe changing roles; Golding's *Lord of the Flies* is a notable example and so is the film *Twelve Angry Men*, and Mary MacCarthy's *The Group* tells of the continuing effects of joint experience at college on the subsequent behaviour of members when the group has dispersed, and reassembles at intervals. Most laboratory studies are of a number of people in a single face-to-face meeting, or series of meetings. Field studies may be of larger, looser and more permanent groups, as in industry or housing estates.

It is clear that the term 'group' covers a large range of intensities of relationship between members; this essay will be concerned with groups small enough, and the members being long enough and in close enough contact, for each person to be aware of each of the others.

## Conforming in Groups

There is a great deal of evidence to show that people tend to conform in groups. People prefer to be with those like themselves, and having chosen their companions, become even more alike. Newcomb (1960) made a study of the behaviour of a group of seventeen men who were at first unacquainted and lived together in a students' house for a year, at the only cost of giving an hour a week to the psychologists for investigation of their attitudes. It was found that long-lasting friendships were built on similarities; rather than change their attitudes, dissimilar people would break their incipient relationships. Moreover, as time went by, friends became more like each other in, for instance, their assessments of other people. This tendency to stick to the familiar is of course very obvious in ordinary life. An example of how easily habits can be built up was provided by an experience at an international conference on group work. Small groups of people, initally strangers, had been discussing professional matters for a few days, and then it became necessary for two groups to join together. Arranging the room to accommodate the newcomers, I took care to mix up the green chairs which my group had used, with the red ones brought in from the other group's room. As the people came in, they took their familiar seats, so this manoeuvre succeeded in mixing up the groups spatially, but it did not immediately achieve the aim of fusing them. Two conversations went on for some time, members of each group maintaining their relationship by talking across members of the other group.

This tendency to adapt oneself generally to other people is consistent with the human need to avoid discomfort, and is not unexpected. What is more surprisng is that one's judgment on matters of 'fact' such as the relative sizes or weights of objects, is influenced by other people. In a classical experiment, Asch (1951) asked a group of eight people to match the length of a given line with one of three unequal lines. Unknown to one person (the 'subject') the other seven ('stooges') had been briefed by the experimenter to declare that certain lines matched even though they clearly did not. The subject was therefore faced with the extraordinary situation of a group unanimously contradicting the evidence of his senses. One-third of the choices made by the subjects were errors in the direction of the distorted opinions of the stooges (although a control group made virtually no errors). When those subjects who had made errors were cross-questioned, a few seemed to have suffered distortion of perception – the lines really had looked to them as the majority said they had looked; others suffered a disorder of judgment – they had been aware of a difference between their perceptions and those of the stooges, but had not trusted their own judgment; still others had suffered a disorder of action – though they recognised the disagreement, they had not liked to appear different from others. An experiment by Seabourne (1963) was made in more life-like conditions and illustrates some of the difficulties that may occur when people are examining goods to see whether they are up to a required standard, a task which is common in industry. People were asked to pick out of a stack of cards those which were imperfect according to certain dimensions which were assessed with a notched gauge. A subject working at the same table as others, and on stacks of cards with the same proportion of substandard cards, would reject a similar number. But if his co-workers' stacks contained a higher proportion of substandard cards than his own, so that their reject rate was higher, then his proportion of rejects went up. The extra cards which he rejected in these conditions were not randomly picked but were borderline cases of the kind that might be rejected by himself and others in normal conditions. His judgment of where to draw the line between 'reject' and 'accept, even when it was made against an 'objective' standard, altered according to the number being rejected by his co-workers, and this without their attempting to influence his behaviour.

## Dissonance Reduction

Festinger's ideas about 'cognitive dissonance' are of great value in helping to make comprehensive statements about these and other aspects of group behaviour. Festinger and Aronson (1960) state that 'the simultaneous existence of cognitions which in one way or another do not fit together (dissonance) leads to an effort on the part of the person to somehow make them fit better (dissonance reduction).' Dissonance reduction seems to be the psychological analogue of the physiological mechanisms which maintain homoeostatis in the body.

Social interaction inevitably involves some dissonance – some disagreement with people like oneself. The magnitude of the dissonance will vary with the importance of the person expressing disagreement, and with the importance of the issue over which there is disagreement. Dissonance may be reduced in several ways (just as, in homeocostatic control, if one's temperature goes up it may be brought down by several mechanisms). The person may convince himself that the person disagreeing with him is unimportant; or the topic unimportant; or he may change his opinion, or attempt to change the other person's; or he may seek support from other people.

Several laboratory experiments have been made that analyse the factors that affect which mechanism is likely to be used in certain prescribed conditons, and a remarkably interesting piece of field work also strengthens Festinger's thesis. The behaviour of a number of people who firmly believed that the world would end by a cataclysm was studied. On the night that the cataclysm was expected most of the believers gathered in the home of one member to await a flying saucer which was to rescue them. When the prophecy was not fulfilled, the group was intensely disappointed and spent some hours trying to reassure each other. They finally concluded that the explanation was that the world had been saved by their faith, which in this way they were able to retain. Other members had stayed in their own homes, and there, lacking social support, abandoned their faith. Whereas before the appointed day, the sect had made no attempt to attract public attention or proselytise, after the disappointment those who remained faithful attempted to convert new members, and gave press conferences, that is, they sought support from outside. In various ways predictable from Festinger's theory therefore, attempts were made to reduce dissonance.

Conforming to a group is only one method a person may take to reduce dissonance and whether he uses this or another depends partly on his personality. Crutchfield (1955) found that non-conformers, compared with conformers, were more effective intellectually, more mature in social relationships, more confident, less rigid, less authoritarian, more objective and realistic about their parents, and more permissive in their attitudes to child-rearing practices. Now one tends to think of such characteristics as fairly stable and unchanging, but the same person may behave more or less in these ways, according to the group climate.

# Group Climates

The classic experiments of White and Lippitt (1960) show that children behaved differently according to whether their clubs had an autocractic, democratic, or laissez-faire climate. The climate was established by the behaviour of the leaders who were trained to take these special roles. The leaders moved from one club to another each six weeks, and changed their leadership style as they did so. Thus each club, consisting of ten-year old boys roughly equated for intellectual, physical and socio-economic status and personality characteristics, experienced three different climates under different leaders. Records were made of the behaviour of leaders and boys during each meeting.

Leaders taking the autocratic role tended to give orders, to make disruptive commands which cut across the activities of the boys, and to give non-objective criticism and praise, whereas those taking the other roles tended to control behaviour rather by making suggestions and giving information. The chief single difference between the democratic and laissez-faire leadership consisted in the amount of guidance given at times when it seemed necessary; the democratic leaders were more sensitive to the child's welfare and participated more fully in the life of the group than did the laissez-faire leaders. It is an interesting comment on the flexibility of behaviour that the leaders were able to play these different roles so well. The records of their behaviour in these respects show that they resembled each other more strongly in the same role than they resembled themselves in different roles.

Summarising the main differences in the behaviour of the boys, the amount of work done was greatest in the autocratic climates and least in the laissez-faire; but motivation to work was greatest in the democratic climates, for the boys tended to go on working even when the leader had left the room. Work-orientated conversation among the boys was greatest in the democratic climates and least in the laissez-faire. Nineteen out of twenty boys preferred democratic leaders. Under autocracy, there was more discontent; the four boys who dropped out did so under autocratic regimes, though at times when there was no overt rebelliousness. In autocratic climates, the boys were more dependent on the leader, and more submissive to him, but more hostile and aggressive to each other. There was more originality, group-mindedness and friendly playfulness under democracy, and more readiness to share club property.

In this experiment is was the deliberate behaviour of the leader that caused differences in the climate of groups, other factors remaining constant. In less controlled conditions of course innumerable factors interact. In Deutsch's experiment (1949) the significant difference was made by giving different motivation to groups. Psychology students were given puzzles and human relation problems to work at in discussion groups. Some ('co-operative') groups were told that the grade that each individual got at the end of the course would depend on the performance of his group. Other ('competitive') groups were told that each student would receive a grade according to his own contributions. No significant differences were found between the two kinds of group in the amount of interest and involvement in the tasks, or in the amount of learning. But the co-operative groups, compared with the competitive ones, had greater productivity per unit time, better quality of product and discussion, greater co-ordination of effort and subdivision of activity, more diversity in amount of contributions per member, more attentiveness to fellow members, and more friendliness during discussion.

When a group works together for a long period it develops a characteristic climate which may or may not be the best for its declared aims. Attending meetings of various scientific societies one is strongly aware of different subcultures reflected in the length of papers read, whether questions only are invited, or open discussion, whether the expression of non-conformist views is encouraged or inhibited, the facilities provided for informal conversation, and the amount of food and drink consumed communally. But the function of all these meetings is to disseminate information among the members. Designing a suitable climate is specially important when strangers meet for a short time with important work to do; Fremont-Smith (1961) has fruitfully paid attention to this in organising interdisciplinary discussion among experts, and some of the complexities of arranging international conferences have been wisely discussed by Capes (1960). The main aim is to facilitate communication between members and careful attention is paid to group climate.

## Communication in Groups

There has been a great deal of experimental work on different kinds of communication networks in groups, but as good discussions of it are easily available (Sprott 1958; Klein 1956) it will not be dealt with at length here. For our present purpose, the most relevant points are that different networks are optimal for different purposes. Thus in a situation where a group of five people have to solve a problem and each has an essential piece of information, the task is done most quickly where there is a central member to whom each of the others has direct access.

In the diagram, each letter represents a person, and each line a communication link. Groups organised on the 'wheel' and 'Y' plans solved the problem more quickly than the 'circle' or the 'chain'.

```
      C                                        D   E        B   D
    /   \                                       \ /          \ /
  B       D      A—B—C—D—E                       C            C
    \   /                                        |           / \
     A—E                                         B          A   E
                                                 |
                                                 A

   Circle            Chain                       Y           Wheel
```

In the circle, no one member was regarded as leader, but in the others, C tended to be so regarded. The circle people enjoyed themselves more than the others, because all could interact, both giving and receiving messages, whereas in the other systems the peripheral members had less to do, and in the wheel they needed only to send information to C, who needed to do nothing but collect it. When the task was changed, so that the information to be sent was ambiguous, the circle did best, because all the members could receive all the messages and could sort things out, whereas in the wheel, C only received ambiguous messages which he could not check. The circle people had learned to cope with uncertainty (Klein 1956).

It is notable that most of our institutions have communication networks more like the Y or the wheel than like the circle, so that speed of performance of routine tasks may be gained at the cost of frustration and passivity for the peripheral members, and loss of adaptability at time of change.

Revans (1964) found a correlation between patterns of communication in hospitals and several indices of efficiency. In hospitals with low wastage of student nurses, slow turnover of senior staff, and rapid discharge of patients, communication between the various groups of people was better than in those with higher student wastage, quicker staff turnover and slower discharge of patients. In the former hospitals compared with the latter, the climate was more permissive and less authoritarian; the patients felt more able to question the nurses, the student nurses felt they could question their tutors, the sisters the matron, the matron the consultants, and so on. There was ease of communication upwards as well as downwards.

Although in ordinary life the main barriers to free communication are such psychological bogeys as habit, or timidity, seemingly quite trivial things like spatial relationships also play their part. Sommer (1959) found that conversations occurred more frequently between people sitting at the corners of tables, than between those sitting opposite each other, or side by side. Communication between patients in a geriatric ward were improved when moved from a row against the walls, and put around little tables (Sommer and Ross 1958). Foulkes and Anthony (1965) pay special attention to the seating arrangements for their practice of group analytic psychotherapy. Ideally the chairs should be similar, and placed in a circle. The positions taken by participants are significant – beside the therapist or opposite him, for instance, and pulling their chair in or withdrawing it from the circle.

## Groups for Changing Behaviour

Although much of the experimental work on groups has been concerned with studying differences in behaviour according to current group structure, the importance of groups for facilitating more permanent changes has been long recognised. It was found easier, for instance, to cure alcoholics, to persuade people to eat more liver or to give their children more orange juice, in groups than singly.

The various kinds of group psychotherapy are all based on the assumption that the changes made in response to certain designed group structures are not transient, but carry over into behaviour outside the group; in fact, that in a group one can learn to behave better outside it. I shall not attempt to deal with strictly psychotherapeutic techniques, but only to refer to some applications to the learning of normal people.

The value of groups for improving the understanding of social interactions by people who themselves are professionally concerned with human rela-tionships is obvious, but the potentialities of this are by no means fully exploited. There are several possible lines to follow. One is the experiencing of group processes as a model for what goes on beneath the surface in ordinary life. Bion (1961) was one of the pioneers in this; his technique (erroneously called 'leaderless') forced the group to come to terms with conflicts over the authority-dependency relationship. It has obvious implica-tions for education at all levels; modifications of it have been used for teachers in training (Morris 1955).

Another line has been explored by E. and M. Balint (1955) in their teaching of psychotherapy. In groups of doctors learning about the psycholo-gical aspects of medical practice, the participants presented current cases, and in discussion of them it became clear that their treatment of the case was conditioned by personal attitudes which were not necessarily the most effective possible. The differences of opinions in the group and the interpreta-tions made by the conductor experienced in a supportive climate, helped to liberate the participants from too restricted a personal psychological framework. The potentialities of this kind of work for training in many professions is tremendous.

## Groups for Scientists

Still another line has been taken (Abercrombie 1960) of using a group situation for helping medical students to be more 'objective', to observe more accurately and comprehensively and to draw reasonable conclusions from their observations. Postulating that one might learn to make more valid judgments if one could become aware of some of the many factors that ordinarily influence them, a teaching situation was arranged to facilitate this. The approach was influenced by the transactional views on perception, and by Foulkes' method of group analytic psychotherapy. The method differed from the more therapeutically orientated uses of groups for training in human relations, in that the discussions were not entirely unstructured, but each was focussed on a specific scientific topic – radiographs for instance, or an account of an experiment. It was also more didactic in that statements about the processes involved in perception were deliberately introduced at appropriate times, in the hope that what was learned from a specific example would be more easily generalised. Within these limits, however, freedom of discussion was encouraged, and the conversation ranged widely, permitting the linking up of reactions towards scientific material with habitual ways of behaving in everyday life and thus encouraging the transfer of training. One of the most important features was that each student was confronted with a range of different interpretations of the same stimulus pattern. These different interpretations were made by people like himself – he was not comparing his effort with the 'correct' answer as is usually the case, but was forced to consider his own and other statements on their merits, and without the guidance of authority. It would appear, for instance, that what one student took for granted as a 'fact', another regarded as an inference, of questionable validity; but then, very soon, on another issue the tables would be turned. By analysing the ideas that each student associated with his judgment, it was possible to tease out some of the factors that had caused the differences between them. It was discovered that these factors ranged from minutiae of the immediate context (eg the precise typescript layout of a report of an experiment) to generalised and deep-seated attitudes concerned, for instance, with the extent to which you could take it for granted that researchers reported their work accurately.

At the end of a course of eight discussions the participants reacted more objectively to a test than did the other half of the class that had not yet had this course. They distinguished better between facts and inferences, made fewer false inferences, explicitly considered alternate hypotheses more frequently, and were less often inappropriately 'set' in their approach to a problem by previous experience of a similar one. It seemed that the experience of the discussions had helped them to be more flexible in their reactions to scientific material, and thus to attain greater objectivity.

## 'Synectics'

We began this essay with a discussion of conformity in groups, so it is appropriate to end it with reference to one or the newest uses to which groups are being put – to help people to depart from conformity, and to encourage originality and inventiveness.

The advocates of 'brain-storming' techniques (Osborn 1953) for producing original ideas believe in the value of increasing spontaneous behaviour in groups. The participants are encouraged to express as many ideas as possible, the wilder the better, criticism must be withheld, and the need to combine different ideas together to make something new is emphasised. The practitioners of 'synectics' (Gordon 1961) resemble the brainstormers in encouraging spontaneity and a rich flow of ideas in groups, but they have in addition worked out methods for increasing the participants' understanding of what is going on. Their approach is based on the assumptions that invention in arts and in science involves the same fundamental processes which can be described, and that the descriptions can be used for teaching people to improve the creative output of both individuals and groups. Their groups consist of five or six people with diverse backgrounds and intellectual experiences, for the coming together of different analogical ways of thinking is regarded as essential. They stress the importance of such operations as making the familiar strange and the strange familiar. They recognise that the emotional aspects of the creative task are as important as the intellectual, and pay great attention to group climate.

In closing with these two examples of the use of group situations for the improvement of individual effectiveness, it may be noted that they attempt to give control of two kinds of behaviour which may seem to stand at opposite ends of a continuum. At one end is the scientist's need to see things as they are, objectively, veridically, and at the other the need to originate, to create something new. In both cases, the perception by participants of similarities and differences between their own behaviour and that of other members of the group is an important factor in learning. We are back again to conforming and non-conforming, and there would seem a promising future here for a link up with Festinger's ideas on dissonance reduction.

Although the last few years have seen an enormous expansion of interest in group behaviour, our knowledge is still fragmentary and insecure, so that those who work with groups need faith as well as humility. Since he made the first stone tool, man has won increasing control over other animals and plants. Now the urgent need is for him to win better control over his own nervous system, and for this it is essential that he should understand how it interacts with those of other men.

# 10

# Problems in Group Work and How to Handle Them

*Colin Flood Page*

Among the problems which recur in small group teaching there are three that seem to plague many teachers, and to which I shall devote this short article. The problems can be listed as follows:

1 Inadequate preparation by students
2 Student unwillingness to speak
3 Grossly unequal student contributions

## Inadequate Preparation by Students

It is a common complaint that students come to small group sessions without having done the necessary reading, so that any attempt to get a real discussion going is frustrated by the fact that only the lecturer and one of two students have sufficient knowledge of the proposed topic to carry on a meaningful conversation, and the session becomes a dialogue, or, often, an uneconomic lecture to a minimal audience. There is a tendency to attribute this lack of preparation to ill-will or indolence on the part of the students; but teachers should be chary of accepting these facile and emotive explanations. Reasonable investigation of the situation may disclose other causes, such as undue pressure from the total environment (particularly on courses which involve several departments teaching the students at the same time), or unavailability of the material that has to be read. Students may also have intelligent doubts as to the worth of what they are asked to do, or may find the recommended texts beyond their comprehension. Not all of these possible sources of failure are under the control of the teachers, but they should always ask themselves, when lack of preparation is obvious, whether they have done all they can about the items that lie within their power. Before blaming the students try to make sure:

i   That the text to be read is actually available in sufficient numbers and in sufficient time

---

Reproduced by permission from Flood Page 1972.

   ii That the students are convinced that what they are being asked to do is meaningful for them. (This objective is probably best achieved by spending time at the beginning of a course discussing aims and means, rather than by plunging without preliminaries into the subject matter.)

   iii That the recommended reading is at the right level.

The problem of environmental pressure is more difficult to deal with, and often can only be solved, if at all, by action at a higher level than that of the individual teacher. (I shall say a little about this later.) If students feel under stress, reading for small group discussions is likely to be the kind of task that gets pushed to one side – they can always hope that somebody else will have done it even if they haven't. The problem can be solved to some extent by involving students, either individually or in twos or threes, in specific preparation for specific sessions on an agreed programme worked out at the beginning of the course and known to all. Students may be willing and able to prepare for one or two meetings a term (particularly if they have plenty of notice in advance), though they find eight or ten too much in view of their other commitments.

Realistically, though, the situation may often arise when an adequate amount of prior preparation cannot be counted on. In such cases one general solution of background value is to announce the session topics as questions and not merely as themes or morsels of subject matter. Then, at the least, students may be asked to think about the questions in advance, even if they do no reading or writing, and the session can begin by exploring their tentative answers. It is also worth considering spending time at the beginning of a session providing material to be discussed later in the same session. For those blessed with good audio-visual services, short films or TV programmes may serve this function; but if such delicacies are unavailable then a good duplicated hand-out will serve. The signifcant point of all these operations is that they ensure a minimum level of shared experience from which the discussion can arise. A talk, rather than a hand-out or a moving picture, doesn't do this job so well – what the students take in is liable to vary too much and it is difficult to refer back to precisely what was said – unless you go to the trouble of tape-recording. Many teachers seem reluctant to use part of the small group time for preparation in this way, but if the aim is to stimulate a good quality of discussion then it is time well spent.

## Student Unwillingness to Speak

Some parts of this problem are patently connected with the lack of preparation already discussed; but over and above this there may be a reluctance on the part of students to make any contribution, even when preparatory circumstances seem favourable. As with the previous problem I will try to consider causes for this silence and to see how far it is possible for the individual teacher to take action to provoke speech. Unwanted silence may be connected with any, or some of the factors arising from (a) students' personalities, (b) their previous social and educational history, and (c) teachers' personalities and techniques. Though occasionally a particular combination of significant factors early in a course may make total silence predictably certain there is no reason why this should go on happening. As in many other educational situations the time element is of importance, and teachers must be prepared for a certain amount of difficulty to begin with, confident that things will come right later. Let us consider each of three sets of factors in turn.

## Students' Personalities

Teachers do not need to be expert psychologists to know that students differ profoundly in character. Perhaps in the ideal educational sytem we would be able to categorise students on the basis of their personalites in such a way as to know exactly what was the best instructional treatment to give each one. Tentative efforts are being made in this direction, but as yet we are still in the dark about the most meaningful categories and the optimum treatments. However it is important that teachers should be fully aware of the importance of character differences and should not expect the same reaction from all students to similar treatment. It should be part of every teacher's professional equipment to acquire some understanding of what psychology has to say on this extremely important subject, and to use their daily teaching experience to test out and consolidate such knowledge rather than to rest content with traditional assumptions and folklore on these matters. It is in this field that some of the most signifcant developments in teaching may be expected to take place, but the essential precondition is that teachers should accept the facts of personality differences among students and work with them rather than try to stifle or ignore them. One or two practical aspects of such differences will be mentioned later.

## Students' previous Social and Educational History

Students are not blank sheets when they enter higher education. If they come from families where open and intelligent discussion is the norm, and if their parents are similar people to their lecturers, they will not find it difficult to take part in discussion. Similarly, if they have been to schools and studied subjects in which active pupil involvement is common they will not find the transiton too awkward. But even students from backgrounds like this may take a few weeks to feel at home in the new environment and therefore be less forthcoming than might be hoped; and it is important to realise that a large number (perhaps the majority in many subjects) will have neither of these inital advantages in their make-up. They will not have come from families where reasonable discussion is frequently carried on, they may even have had little meaningful verbal contact with their families in years, and school may have been predominantly a place for taking down notes and learning as much as possible by heart. Several years of this deadening process will have depressed their intellectual enthusiasm, discouraged them from thinking, and left them with a feeling of distrust towards teachers. They have become bored with education, have some rather dead-end learning habits, and a general inclination to wait and see rather than to put themselves forward. They will wait to see, for instance, whether you as a teacher do what you say, or make impressive promises about the quality and nature of higher education and then give them the same treatment they languished under at school. They can usually talk more freely among their friends, because they feel on an equal footing; but they have a strong sense of 'them and us' which acts as a barrier to good discussion with teachers. To change their habits and attitudes is not a quick or easy task, but it is one for which the small group is the best mechanism we have.

This leads us to the third group of factors which affect student silence and with which are bound up possible solutions to the problem.

## Teachers' Personalities and Techniques

Many different kinds of people can make good teachers, because teaching is not one simple single operation, and it is unreasonable to expect any one person to be able to do all teaching jobs equally well. The intimate personal context of the small group situation is one that may be uncongenial to the person who would rather deliver a good, straightforward talk and keep students at a distance; but the majority of teachers probably enjoy small group work once they have acquired the necessary techniques, though some may have difficulty in accepting certain desirable changes in their own habits.

Consonant with what was said earlier teachers must try to create a feeling of equality between members of the group, and must strive to put themselves on the same footing as the rest in as many ways as possible. The more students feel there is a great gulf between them and the teacher the more they will incline to keep quiet. Teachers may therefore have to practise a considerable degree of self-restraint in the amount of their utterances, and try to put them forward in a manner unlikely to be damaging to the self-esteem of the other members of the group. Tape-recording of group sessions and honest self-analysis of one's own contribution may help here. It is much easier to frighten students off unwittingly than many teachers realise, and, particularly in the opening stages of a course, the delicate plant of student confidence and ease of utterance may need careful handling. Once students and teachers know each other better much more robust exchanges are possible.

Other points of technique to which teachers should pay attention are the kind of subjects with which to start off a course, and the nature of student involvement, which has already been touched on. It is better at the start to discuss matters of general interest, rather than highly technical matters, even on a technical course, in order to get participants into the habit of discussing, so that the right atmosphere and easy habits are encouraged before the difficult subject matter is encountered. Some people even maintain that to begin with it doesn't matter what you discuss provided you can get things going well. Teachers should try to follow the golden rule of starting from where the students are, not from where the teachers are. There is then a much better chance that the learners will finish where the teachers want them to be.

Student involvement in decision-making about the course is important. People are much more inclined to be active in matters about which they have helped to decide than in those in which they are just the passive filling for someone else's rigid framework. Teachers must retain overall responsibility for the general outline of courses, but they should try to make the structure they propose a supporting rather than a constricting one, and within the proper boundaries which they have established should encourage the students to help in choosing what to do. Often they may not want to, and if they do they will make mistakes; but so do we all, and students will learn more incisively from their own mistakes than from following ours. One practical way in which this principle may be applied is in the question of the order of topics within a course. What a teacher may feel to be the 'logical' order may often not be the best for the students' learning, and if they can help to arrange things in a way that feels meaningful to them participation will be encouraged in subsequent discussion.

The suggestions put forward here should all help towards that well-informed and lively interchange which is aimed at in a good small group session; but we must not deceive ourselves into thinking that we can all achieve this every time with every group of students. Things are bound to go a little astray from time to time, even in the best-regulated institutions, and especially is this likely with those new to higher education; but proper application of the right techniques will reduce the negative sessions to a minimum and ensure that newcomers get into the swing as soon as possible. One must not expect more, and there will always be the awkward customer – about whom a brief practical hint is in order, with reference to our third main problem.

Every small group teacher sooner or later becomes aware of the problem of the session-hogger – the young man or woman who, once warmed to the occasion (or even before), hardly lets anyone else get a word in edgeways, or any other way. Direct frontal attempts to stem the flow may have little effect, because this verbal profusion is often bound up with the individual's amour-propre and publicly giving in to the teacher is not to be thought of. The solution is to have a private interview with the individual at some other time and place, not announced before the assembled group, and ask him (or her) not to speak without being specifically requested to do so by the teacher. Tactfully made this request is rarely refused, and can be used to keep verbosity within bounds, especially if teachers set the example by keeping their own contributions reasonably brief.

At the other extreme is the student who says nothing, who even when asked a direct question ingeniously framed to provoke a long answer says no more than a brief phrase or a hesitant 'Yes 'or 'No' after a protracted pause. We know that verbalisation is an important aid to learning among children. It is not so important in higher education. Good learning may well be going on in the mind in the complete absence of any overt (spoken) activity. It is what is happening in the student's mind that is significant, and as yet we have no adequate way of measuring this. One is therefore often faced with the difficult task of deciding whether non-contribution on the part of the student is due to apathy or whether, on the contrary, intense mental activity is going on behind a quiet and withdrawn facade. It may well be, particularly among some of the brighter students. This is a case where knowledge of personality type is a help: quiet introverts are much more likely to be taking an active (mental) part in the discussion than silent extraverts. There is no need to push the former too much – you will find at the end of the course they have profited. The latter, however, would probably be better prodded. Apart from that, one should try and draw in the quiet member on as many occasions as possible in class decisions, and perhaps give them more than their fair share of times as official openers of the discussion.

## The Institutional Problem

I earlier referred to the fact that some of the problems that teachers face in small groups lie outside the competence of the individual to solve. Sometimes a teacher, especially a young teacher, will be asked to teach small groups in circumstances which render the positive accomplishment of a proper professional task almost impossible. The teachers, being conscientious and hard-working, will feel guilty and inadequate at not doing a good job when what they have been asked to do would be beyond the prowess of all except a microscopic minority of geniuses and saints. The institution has a responsibility to see that teachers are given reasonable physical conditions in which to conduct their (stable) groups, reasonable time-tabling, and reasonable objectives. Cases of most bizarre assignments have come to light when none of these conditions have been met, and where, not unnaturally, the teachers concerned have been at their wits end to know what to do to improve matters. The problem of general institutional pressure has also been mentioned. This pressure often arises from the best of motives. If you have five separate departments teaching the students concurrently each will ask for what looks like a sensible work load, but the total load renders the student insensible, and some subjects are bound to suffer neglect. This may create a vicious circle in which departments compete to lay burdens on the learners' backs until something breaks. The answer is more self-knowledge on the part of institutions and more strong-minded deans; but the problem is always just round the corner in academic institutions because of the character of the people who work in them. To recognise its existence and its origin is the beginning of wisdom. To translate the wisdom into practical measures for curtailing the pressure is much more difficult.

## Summary

Among the problems frequently met within small group work are those of lack of student preparation, lack of student contribution, and unequal student contribution. Overriding these are institutional problems whose solutions do not lie within the sole power of teachers. Within their own control it is recommended that they pay attention to the following points:

1 Availability and pertinence of required preparation material
2 Student understanding of the purpose of the course (and agreement therewith)
3 Student involvement in organising and delivering the course
4 Student background and personality
5 Awareness of the teacher's own personality and habits.

# 11

# Introduction to Groups to Begin

Small groups continuously change and develop. They consist of individuals who interact. The interactions reflect personal relationships. Consequently in small group teaching it is the teacher's task to develop personal relationships. Relationships change according to how people feel about each other. Hence the teacher's task is concerned with students' feelings.

Earlier in this book (Chapter 6) I tried to show how buzz groups and horseshoe groups could be used to start a discussion group. In this respect the use of buzz groups is the most fundamental small group technique. So far as feelings are concerned they provide a safe climate. There is a natural disposition for human beings to talk to each other in relaxed 'family size' groups. The buzz group technique tries to use this disposition.

You may say to talk to one other person in a trusting relationship is even more basic. Dave Potts uses this fact (Chapter 13) with his learning in pairs. Horseshoe groups (Chapter 14) are the next stage towards teaching in larger groups and eventually in the presence of a tutor.

Dave Potts has also put his finger on an apparent contradiction in many humanities courses: we want students to be personally involved, enthusiastic, confident, highly imaginative and committed towards their subject; yet at the same time we seek objectivity, detachment, judgement and reasoned argument. It is an old conflict as well known to eastern thought as to the Greeks and western society. It is sometimes described as a choice between heart and head.

As soon as you recognize that eastern thought has well tried methods to resolve this 'conflict', it is a short step for any western academic with a truly open mind to consider how the art of Zen can be adapted to academic thought.

This is what Dave Potts has done. The reconciliation between involvement and detachment requires first an understanding of oneself. It requires answering in depth questions such as 'Who am I?' To persist at depth requires both the sustained attention and the support of a partner. The questions are relevant to the search for identity experienced by many students, the feeling of a little fish in a big pond, the culture shock of leaving home and school, the feelings of alienation from the enormousness of institutions and society ...

The point is, to take Dave Pott's example, that in the academic world, when a student has an understanding of himself, he can begin to consider what he would have done if he were Maximilian (involvement) as well as display a more objective judgement and understanding of what Maximilian did (detachment). A similar reconciliation is required in the appreciation and criticism of literature. Universities and Zen are both concerned with intensive enlightenment.

# 12

# The Buzz Group Technique

*Donald A. Bligh*

Buzz groups are seldom used in college teaching. My purpose here is to encourage lecturers to consider them more often; and to suggest when they are appropriate. To this end there are two broad themes: the use of buzz groups is possible in a wide variety of circumstances; and the use of buzz groups may achieve a wide variety of objectives.

## Possible Methods

Buzz groups are groups of two to six members who discuss issues or problems for a short period, or periods, within a lesson. If used within a lecture the most common method is to ask alternate rows to turn round to face the row behind. This may be difficult in a steeply terraced lecture theatre or where high backed chairs are fixed and tightly together in rows. In that case the groups may consist of two or three members in the same row. In either situation there should not normally be more than three in the same row if those at the ends are to be able to see and here each other with ease. If it is desirable to vary the composition of the groups, those who did not turn round the first time may do so the second, while part of the front row moves across to form a group with the rest. If the seating position is uncomfortable the length of a 'buzz' period should be short.

If the problem set is one where students may have very individual viewpoints, such as are frequent in philosophy and literature, smaller groups will offer each student a better opportunity to develop his own thinking and have it considered by others.

Although discussion methods are amongst the most difficult for a teacher to learn, buzz groups are amongst the easiest and may be the basis for developing other methods. They are popular with students; they may be used in either formal or informal settings with six to 160 students; they are flexible in that they do not necessarily require elaborate preparation and may take as little as two minutes of class time depending on their objective. Consequently they may be used in a relatively 'impromptu' fashion if the need arises. Furthermore they may be adapted for a variety of objectives.

Reproduced from Bligh 1978b.

# Possible Objectives

A lecturer who thinks he may not have 'got his point across' may set a problem or task for the students to work at in twos or threes. The problem should be simple but require a knowledge of the point in question. The objective here is *clarification*. It may be achieved either by the students teaching each other, which they may be able to do more simply than the lecturer who is an expert, or by the lecturer when he demonstrates the solution afterwards.

If, in the same situation the lecturer visits those groups that seem to be having difficulty, or receives suggested solutions from the class before he demonstrates his own, he will obtain *feedback* on the effectiveness of this teaching. By choosing a suitable task, feedback on the whole lesson can be obtained quite quickly.

'I understood it at the time, but I don't now', is not an uncommon remark from students writing up experimental work or doing revision. What was required was some *consolidation of the learning and understanding* that took place. Almost any discussion situation could provide this, because all provide an active learning situation and use of the information taught, but buzz groups have a particularly important role because they may take place immediately following the inital learning situation such as a lecture and before substantial forgetting takes place. Since the students in this case understand the information, the task should be more difficult than for 'clarification'. It may require the student to relate different parts of a lecture together or to common experience.

The same kind of tasks will teach new *concepts and terminology* provided the students can only perform the tasks by using the concepts. The ineffectiveness of presentation methods alone for learning terminology may be demonstrated to the reader if he goes through three pages of a dictionary and then tests himself to find the proportion of meanings he can remember only one day later.

The ability to think is best acquired by practice. It is part of the job of the teacher to provide the opportunity. This requires the design of situations in which the student must apply, analyse and evaluate information. Buzz groups provide one such situation, although horseshoe groups, seminars and group tutorials probably allow more thorough thought if there is more time and greater diversity of opinion. Problem-solving situations may teach the *application* of information. Questions such as 'What is the difference between ...?' and 'In what way are ... similar?' require *analytical thinking*. Discussion of evaluative statements or simply listing the merits and demerits of a theory, may teach *evaluative thinking*. (The question 'What are the merits of ...?' is sometimes neglected in favour of a more destructive form of *critical thinking*. Both have their place in education. The former may be important for developing an *appreciation of research* and its difficulties.)

Imagine a lecture in psychology in which the teacher presents a list of factors causing forgetting and factors aiding memory, together with some experimental evidence and practical applicatons. He does not make his students think very much about the concepts, nor make any attempt to consolidate their learning of them. If he can make the students analyse the concepts for themselves he may be able to achieve all these objectives. For example he may form buzz groups and give them the following task: 'If you think about the concept of "motivation" as it affects memory, you will realize that I could have classified it as a factor aiding memory just as easily as a factor causing forgetting. "Interference", on the other hand, could only be classified as a hindrance to memory. Look at each of the other concepts I have mentioned and decide which is like "motivation" in this respect, and which is like "interference".

*Relevance* may be encouraged by providing a task that has definite criteria of its completion. Problem-solving tasks are usually suitable. A handout, placed in the middle of each group, with a succession of short problems each with space for their answer, will provide a physical focus of attention and criteria of relevance. However, irrelevance may spark off creative and original solutions.

If creativity is one of the course objectives, perhaps the student will first need to be taught to distinguish between problems that have definite solutions and those that do not.

Just as individual tutorials and counselling provide a confidential situation between a member of staff and a student, buzz groups provide a confidential situation between a small number of students. Yet, unlike the college refectory or the union bar, they are within the total teaching situation. They provide the immediate reaction of the students to the teacher and interaction with him is immanent. Consequently they possess unique properties in the group dynamics which the teacher can use. Buzz groups may be used to *release tensions* because everyone has the opportunity to express them. The discipline of listening to lectures prevents the release of these tensions; the energy needs to be constructively channelled; consequently the use of buzz groups is a particularly valuable technique for bad lecturers! They may be used to work off examination nerves that prevent attention to any kind of class teaching, but problem-centred groups are usually even better.

Buzz groups may also be used *to give* the flustered teacher *breathing space*. No doubt in the best of all possible worlds the teacher is never flustered; but some new teachers in higher education, thinking that they must lecture all the time, find that if a lecture starts badly they are unable to recover the situation. It is the sensitive lecturer who easily goes from bad to worse in this way. The use of buzz groups can give him time to think and recover his composure. Furthermore, group work is precisely the kind of teaching in which his sensitivity is an asset.

When buzz groups are used in this way, the objective is an immediate one in terms of class management. It is only indirectly related to the objectives of the course, but such secondary objectives are none the less important in the long run.

The same confidentiality and release of tension may *encourage the reticent student* to put his ideas into words. He is therefore more likely to be listened to, heeded and accepted by a small group. Each of these gives encouragemnt. With the prior agreement of his group, he is more likely to risk a contribution to the whole class at the reporting back stage or in a larger group. Since most forms of student assessment and selection place a heavy emphasis on verbal ability, and 'the ability to express oneself' is an important objective of most teaching, buzz groups have an important role with the sensitive student. Since his pattern of college behaviour (which may be quite different from his behaviour at home) is probably established in his first term, buzz groups may be particularly important at that time.

This conclusion is reinforced if buzz groups are used *to foster a cohesive class spirit*. While few people make a large number of friendships quickly, a buzz group places up to six students on speaking terms with each other in quite a short time. The observant teacher will be able to notice if these relationships continue outside the classroom. Assuming students do not always sit in the same seats, the network of relationships may be broadened by the frequent use of the method. The speed with which it establishes friendships is important for short and sandwich courses. It is useful for evening classes and non-vocational courses where students frequently come for the social contact as much as the social culture, and where student numbers are important. Early friendships are also important for the full-time student away from home for the first time. Signs of 'homesickness' are difficult for the teacher to observe, but the work of Student Medical Officers suggests that it is more frequent than many teachers suppose.

Thus it is important to see teaching methods in their social and emotional roles, as well as for their academic content. Buzz groups can satisfy the need for social interaction. They may not be possible in all circumstances, but they are in a great many. Most teachers will have some of the above objectives at some time, and buzz groups are an appropriate method of achieving them.

# 13

## Paired Learning: A Workshop Approach to a Humanities Course

### *David Potts*

Traditional academic discussion groups have always seemd to me to offer very limited opportunities for learning. Therefore, I have been experimenting with 'one-to-one' discussion methods.

There are many problems with traditional (one hour or so) tutorials and seminars. The tutors are not always good at leading discussions: often they give mini-lectures; or often they use questions to herd the group to a set of conclusions, the process of which the individual student rarely understands. Even with neutral chairing there is little space, on average, for each student to talk. Thus direct practice in skills of thinking and communication is low, and responsibilities to be prepared and to contribute are ambiguous.

In 1972 I visited schools and universities and informal learning centres in London and New York. In all the classes I saw, group discussions were still the norm. What eventually captured my imagination was the use of one-to-one talks.

One-to-one is where people pair up and take turn, and turn about, of uninterrupted time to talk through their problems, doing their own learning, undirected, unjudged, unadvised; where each person alternates between having the rich support of an attentive listener and having the direct responsibility of listening to others working for themselves. The most exciting use of one-to-one that I have experienced was in a three-day 'Enlightenment Intensive' run by Geoff Love through Quaesitor. Participants, in pairs, spoke in seven-minute turns, changing partners every forty-two minutes, hour after hour tackling the one question, 'Tell me who you are'. The most articulate and self-denigrating of them gradually made huge strides towards self-knowledge and an affirmation of self-worth.

Next I discovered the work of Jerome Liss on the value of attentive listening, and on the harmful effects on people's thought processes of regular interruption. I also discovered Harvey Jackins on co-counselling, and later John Heron, too; both asserted the benefits of talking-through as a learning process. Then in 'marathon' groups I found that attention spans are huge

Reproduced by permission from Potts 1977.

where interest is high and there is output as well as input. Gradually I translated these and other experiences into a programme for academic learning.

In 1973 I returned to Melbourne to help run a course in Mexican history. I asked for volunteers to participate in experimental, weekly, three-hour workshops in place of one-hour tutorials. From those who volunteered I formed two workshops of sixteen students each. The basic learning structure I used was one-to-one. Students would pair up, to take turns as talker and listener. The listener was not to interrupt at all, however silent, incoherent, irrelevant or whatever the talker might be, and was to give obvious attention. A standard pattern on a set question came to be something like this, for students A and B: A four minutes, B four minutes; A four minutes, B four minutes, A and B open discussion four minutes. (We used a bell-ringing oven-timer to measure the times.) Then we might change partners and repeat the process. Next we might form a group to share conclusions quickly before going on to other questions or exercises.

I decided students would naturally want to learn if interested enough, if their learning, personal growth, and social orientation all became linked, and if the learning was free of apprehension and if it developed step by step from their own understandings. I dropped examinations and official grading of written submissions, to reduce anxiety. But to hold the group together and guarantee some commitment I imposed quantitative requirements: attendance at workshops and submission of weekly four-hundred word journals (as constant feedback to myself on how things were going and as learning consolidation for the students), and standard essays (which I and other students read and commented upon but did not grade in any way), and occasional special exercises.

I set up the workshops specifically to meet my learning intentions, working on three main areas. First, a part of the workshops was always given over to students getting to know each other, and to develop their *awareness of* such things as their *own values, interests, needs* and *attitudes to learning and to criticism*. I spent most of the first workshops making sure everyone knew each other by name, starting from the question 'Tell me something about yourself' (always naming each other with the question), changing partners, sharing with the group, and naming and re-naming in circles.

Other questions were 'What are your main life values?' and 'What are your main hopes and expectations?' Some of these were used as lead-ins to historical material. For instance, we would then go on (in the Mexican history course) to 'What were the main hopes and expectations of the Zapatistas?', and then 'What are your hopes and expectations for the Mexican Revolution?'.

A second pattern of the questioning was to help students become more *aware of the terms or concepts* they were using. For instance we did 'What is democracy', What is understanding?', 'What is revolution?'. When we were discussing conditions of the unemployed in the 1930s (in an Australian history course) we did 'What is suffering?' and 'What is degradation'. These last two questions cleared away a lot of over-anticipation and question-begging before we looked at people's actual experiences (from written reminiscences and later from interviews).

Finally, there were the *content questions* on the reading, like 'What is the Mexican Revolution?' or 'What was the cultural impact of movies in Australia in the 1920's?' or simply 'What did you get out of the reading?'. Mostly I tried to keep questions very open, conceptual, Zen-like, looking for the heart of the matter – but I encouraged students to define their own sub-questions.

I also came to vary the formula. For instance I tried 'What would you do if you were president of Mexico in the 1920's?' and the listener would suggest what difficulties might be encountered; then partners would change roles as assessor and would be president. In my current Australian social history course we use threes to practise interviewing technique; one as interviewer, one as interviewee, and one to take notes for a later discussion on what happened.

Over the whole three hours I vary the type of questions, the type of learning objectives, and the type of structure. There is regular movement around the room with students changing partners. And we have a coffee break of fifteen to twenty minutes (when we talk about anything at all), taking it in turns to bring foodstuffs.

Obviously, then, while the one-to-one gives students great responsibility for their own learning, there is a lot of direction. The teaching function emerges in the weekly lectures, setting weekly reading lists and problems, planning the workshops (I plot a programme minute by minute), deciding the specific one-to-one questions, participating in one-to-one and group discussion, and commenting on written work. The journals give students a chance to criticise what happens, and I respond to these in planning for the next week or by direct comment in group. (Journals, incidentally, are a fair bit of work to read each week, but as they are so directly on what I am trying or failing to achieve I always find them fascinating; I read them in all sorts of odd moments quite spontaneously.)

Student responses to the workshop courses have varied from ecstatic (especially in the first weeks) to troubled. And overall the groups settle into something friendly and purposeful, which I personally enjoy very much and which most students strongly support. In four years, covering about two hundred students, I have had only half a dozen pull out immediately because they found the approach upsetting. My drop-out rate has been far below the average at my university. Admittedly I have no exams (and grading only by special request and extra work). A pass is automatic provided set tasks are done with any reasonable effort. But I demand regular attendance at long sessions and about twice the amount of written work of many other courses. Enthusiasm and quantity of work is high, and overall the standards of written submission, though still ranging from bad (in very few instances) to first class, are higher than I have previously experienced.

Since giving seminars on my teaching I have had the experience of watching other staff members try the one-to-one method with mixed success. Where my own workshops have worked better it appears to have been because of my confidence in one-to-one (not saying 'let's *try* this' but 'we are going to *do* this'), because my questions were easier to handle, because I explained to students my experiences and ideas about the method, because I trained them in attentive listening, because I insisted that they stick very rigidly to the courtesies and rules of the style (not interrupting, addressing their partners, and their sharing the information across a full circle while using names regularly), and because I used the method over long enough periods and repetitons for students to have the space and the challenge to extend themselves.

Overall, I find one-to-one has immense potential and can be mixed into a huge variety of learning structures.

# 14

# Horseshoe Groups: Including Square Root Technique

*Donald A. Bligh*

## Method

A horseshoe group may be an amalgamation of two buzz groups and could vary in size from four to twelve members. The larger the group, the shorter the time it will take to answer problems which demand special knowledge, skills, or particular procedures, because the necessary expertise is more likely to be found in the groups. If the answer to the problem is a matter of opinion, consensus will, on the average, be obtained more quickly in a small group, as there will be less variation of opinion to be reconciled (see Klein 1961). In most cases a group of six is very convenient. Groups larger than this may break into smaller conversation groups for at first short, and then for longer periods of time, unless there is a leader, or the problem supplies a sense of common purpose, or the seating arrangement creates a tightly knit group.

By definition, a discussion group is arranged so that each member may interact face to face with every other member (Abercrombie 1970). Consequently, chairs are normally arranged in a 'C' or a 'U' shape, with the opening facing either the centre or the front of the room (Figure 1). The central opening enables the teacher to stand in the middle of the class, listen to the progress of each of the groups and unobtrusively join each group to give help as needed. This is made easier if there is a vacant chair in position at the opening so that the teacher closes the circle, making it more intimate when he joins the group. The front-facing openings can be used in a similar way and have the additional advantage that the teacher may stop the discussions to explain a difficult point from there with the use of the blackboard or other visual aids. It is a useful arrangement for alternating formal teaching with horseshoe groups; and if the problems are written on the board rather than separately for each group, the students may refer to them as they go along. Provided there is a table in the centre of the U for specimens and notes, the flexibility in teaching method offered by this seating arrangement is very convenient for any teacher who possesses a variety of

Reproduced from Bligh 1978c.

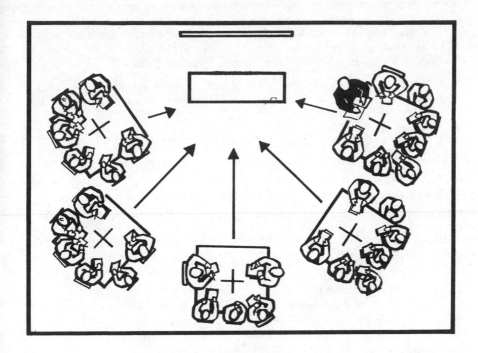

**Figure 1**
The arrangement of furniture for horseshoe groups.
The crosses on the tables represent specimens, problem sheets or overhead transparencies on
which students summarize their conclusions.

teaching skills, and who is sufficiently sensitive to student reactions to know when to change method and what method to use. The horseshoe method is a particularly good one for getting to know the students when the class is less than forty in number and is never taught in small groups at any other time.

One caution should perhaps be observed: the teacher should make sure that the sides of the U are not so long and straight that those at one end cannot see those at the other. As with buzz groups, three per straight side is the maximum, it being possible to lean forward to see past one person, one's neighbour, but not past two people.

It should be noticed that this method requires careful planning. Thought must be given to the arrangement of the furniture. Time must be allowed for introducing the problems, visiting each group, preferably more than once, and pooling the findings of the class at the end if necessary. 'Introducing', 'visiting' and 'pooling' each require different teaching skills (eg clear, succinct and interesting statement of a problem; sensitivity to both individual and group reactions; astute chairmanship).

The preparation of the problems often requires considerable thought if they are to develop student thinking in a specified direction. Figure 2 illustrates a series of problems given to student teachers of physical medicine. The objective was to make them aware of philosophical assumptions in the

1. Is it true that you/students/patients can sometimes *choose* to do one action rather than another?
2. Does choosing involve selection from various possibilities?
3. Is it a scientific assumption (an assumption made by scientists) that all *physical* events in the universe are completely caused (by what has happened before?)
4. Is this assumption valid?
5. If some processes/events are completely caused and some are not, which are not?

6. Are all human actions physical processes?
7. Is all neural activity some kind of physical process?

8. Are all human actions completely caused?
9. If 'No' to Question 8,
      (A) Which is not?
      (B) Is it possible to have physiolocial theories?
      (C) Is physiotherapy possible?
10. If 'Yes' to Question 8,
      (A) Is there a possibility of a person not doing what he in fact does?
      (B) Can a person choose to do one thing rather than another?
11. Does having 'professional/moral' standards or principles assume it is possible to choose one action rather than another?

12. If 'Yes' to Question 11, is there a conflict between having professional/ moral standards/principles and believing scientific evidence?

**Figure 2**

A series of problems given to physiotherapists in horseshoe groups. The problems were progressively presented in five stages.

treatment of patients. Formal lectures and group tutorials had not achieved this with previous students, who had failed to see the relevance of philosophy. Horseshoe groups succeeded. The reader is invited to place himself in the position of these student teachers, answer the questions, compare his answers with those of another person and find the reasons for any disagreements there may be. These reasons may either be assumptions themselves, or point to assumptions. If assumptions were not made explicit in the discussions, it was the teacher's role to elicit them on his 'visits' and during 'pooling'.

## Objectives

The major objective of teaching using horseshoe groups is that the student should think. Whether the precise kind of thinking is analytical, creative, evaluative or applies general principles depends on the problem given.

A second objective is to provide an opportunity for 'feedback' from the class to the teacher.

There are five kinds of problems that can be set to a horseshoe group and it is easier if these are introduced, broadly speaking, in the following order.

There is the task to search for information and introduce an element of *selection and organization of the information* that is found. This may be set with the objective of teaching facts and their organization, but it may also be set with the objective of teaching how to *find facts* and how to *use available literature* of the subject. This second objective is very important for students at the beginning of a course, and may be suitable for buzz groups whose members know each other fairly well. In this latter case the groups should feel free to go to the library or other sources of reference during the period, and come back at a certain time to report their findings. I shall call this type of horseshoe group 'mini-syndicate', since it only takes part of one lesson and no formal written report is required. A lively method to acquaint up to thirty students with relevant literature available in the college library is to borrow about one hundred books for the duration of the lesson, arrange them about the room, and set problems which may be answered by using specific references given on the problem sheet. If reporting back is delayed until the following week and the books have to be returned at once to the library shelves before the students have finished their task, they usually use the library catalogues to complete it. This method is more effective than giving a bibliographical handout for an essay, because their appetite is whetted, they know what they are looking for and there is allegiance to the group to finish the job. Syndicate method itself may also be introduced by this means.

If one has a larger group and is more concerned with the first objective, especially the organization of facts, it saves class time to set *specific* reading before the lesson so that the students are expected to arrive having both read and selected appropriately. Much of the lesson is then concerned with organization and the consequent understanding of facts from different viewpoints.

It may be that not many lessons need to be spent on this kind of objective at university level as university students have often learned the skills in the sixth form, but in technical colleges and other institutions in higher education with less able students, a considerable part of a course could possibly consist of teaching students how to find out information. These skills are essential to any other kind of independent work on which so many professions depend.

The groups may be asked to work out a *problem that has a correct answer*. The term 'problem' should here be interpreted very widely. It may consist of interpreting facts or identifying the cause of some phenomenon of the specific subject of which students have some previous knowledge from lecturers or pre-reading. Hence this kind of horseshoe group is normally used in conjunction with other teaching methods. It requires a knowledge of facts and use of the general principles of the specific subject.

The usual objectives of this kind of discussion are to *consolidate* the knowledge of general principles, to teach how to *apply* them and to teach students how to *relate* their knowledge of facts to principles. These three objectives are relevant to all levels of education.

Using over two hundred subjects, Gore formed two experimental classes to compare the effectiveness of lectures and of horseshoe groups of three or four students each given job sheets (1962). In addition to the usual sources of information, films and visual aids were available for the horseshoe groups on request. Changes in group membership were permitted. The job sheets were also given to the students in lecture classes, but they had to be done outside lecture time. The performance of the horseshoe groups was significantly superior on tests at the end of the course, on delayed tests of retention of information, and on the answers to the job sheets themselves.

One may also ask the groups to work out a *problem with a number of possible answers*. For example, there may be a number of interpretations, causes or explanations of a given set of facts. In many ways this kind of discussion has the same objectives as those mentioned above in connection with working out a problem that has a correct answer. But since there are a number of possible answers, it has the additional objective that students should *be aware of*, and *understand, different points of view*; and the form of the discussion is often quite different from that where there is a correct answer. Where there is a correct answer, the form of the discussion will converge towards that answer. Anything that does not do so may be eliminated by the participants as irrelevant or incorrect. Where there are a number of possible answers the discussion will have a number of possible strands running at the same time. Consequently the task of the group will be much more difficult. If the students do not do so, the teacher must relate the alternative answers either when he visits the groups or when they report their conclusions at the end. He must try to preserve a balance between the different answers that are put forward. This requires an open, clear and flexible mind. The teacher must make sure that the answers are laid out clearly side by side either on paper or on the blackboard so that the differences and similarities can be understood easily.

A fourth kind of problem may *require* the students to make an act of *judgement*. Once a number of possible answers are laid out before the students, they can then decide which is best. For example, they may be asked to evaluate a theory, in which case there may be a judgement commonly accepted by the experts in the field, which the teacher wishes the students to infer by the same reasoning.

In so far as there is an accepted answer, the discussion techniques here may be similar to that in which there is a correct answer, although the criteria for the judgement are much wider because they will often involve the use of principles, such as the principles of scientific method, which are outside the empirical science. These principles are frequently not those that can be looked up in a textbook before the lesson. They are principles of reasoning which the teachers cannot necessarily expect the students to have learned from lectures or reading before they come to the class. Consequently they often require a questioning technique to make the students think behind their everyday judgements. This involves posing a number of questions that crystallize and polarize the central issues so that the answers by the students will form a closely reasoned argument. The best questions are those with Yes/No answers but these take a lot of thoughtful preparation (see Fig. 2). In this respect the technique is more subtle than when there is a correct answer.

Horseshoe groups have a very useful function in *revision and preparation* of students *for* essay *examinations*. They provide an outlet for pre-examination nerves that seems relevant to the student, while the presentation of yet more information in lectures only provides more to be anxious about. The urgency

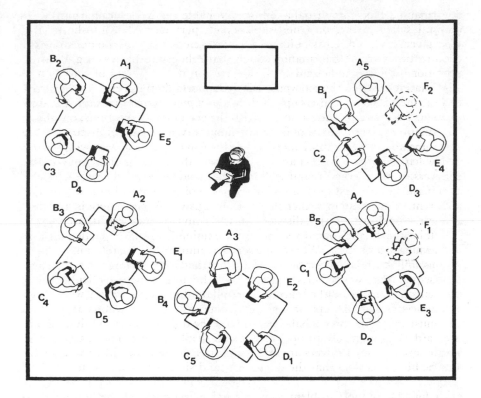

**Figure 3**

Square root or cross-over groups. When, as in this case, the total number of students is not 9, 16, 25, 36 or some other number with a convenient square root, extra students (F1 and F2 in the diagram) will have to accompany a colleague. This means that they will therefore not be forced to concentrate so hard in their first group.

of the pre-examination situation enables horseshoe groups to be used with larger classes than at other times. The limitation in size is usually dictated by the furniture, space and general physical provision rather than by the number of students. The problems set require the group to plan answers to examination questions in about fifteen minutes each. The teacher may present a specimen plan, conduct a brief pooling of the group's ideas, or, if there is time and the groups have been given different questions, visit each group to improve their 'model answers'. Used in this way horseshoe groups are particularly good for helping students see the breadth, and possible interpretations of questions, and to suggest ways of organizing the answers. They provide a suitable opportunity to discuss examination technique.

Teaching with horseshoe groups is useful, but the problems, their answers and the general organization of the class require thoughtful preparation and a variety of teaching skills.

A technique I find increasingly useful I have called the 'square root technique' (Figure 3). It is a way of recomposing groups into what are sometimes also called cross-over groups. Make the size of horseshoe groups roughly the square root of the number of students. For example if I have 38 students in a class I might form four groups of six and a couple of groups with seven. I have cards, or write out slips of paper, labelled A1, A2, A3...A6, B1, B2..., through to F6. I issue one card to each student (the two extra above 36 each share with another student) such that one group has all the A cards, another all the Bs, and so on.

It is then possible to recompose the groups simply by saying 'if your card has a "1" on it come to this table. If it has a "2" on it go to that table', and so on. This ensures that each student (with the exception of the two extra above 36) will find himself in a new group none of whose members was in his previous one.

This system can be used in a number of ways. It can ensure the concentration of every student. Each one may be required to report the conclusions of his first group; each one may become a group reporter and, if forewarned, the system will ensure that there are no passengers in the first groups. They must sit up and take notice in order to prepare their report.

The system makes plenary pooling unnecessary. It will be clear that this technique ensures in principle that every significant contribution to the A – F groups will be relayed to the new groups, the 1 – 6 groups. Thus formal reporting back, an activity known to have small benefits to learning compared with the time consumed, is rendered unnecessary.

The system breaks the ice in the second group. By making sure that everyone says something at the beginning of the second group, silent students are obliged to speak. But they are not strongly obliged to defend what they say if the opinions reported were not theirs. Having once spoken, even shy students are more likely to speak again.

It increases the number of inter-personal contacts. In the example given, each participant meets five other people in his first group (ie $Nn - 1$, where n is the number of participants) and five in his second. If there had been 36 people in the class each having to meet 35 others it would take seven horseshoe groups for each student to meet every other (ie $\sqrt{n} + 1$).

It widens the range of views received. Obviously an increase in the number of inter-personal contacts is likely to increase the variety of opinions considered. In short courses and conferences I find it is often necessary 'to mix up groups and stir well together'. Otherwise participants from one district or professional group will stick together, team up in the same small group and meet few other people. The square root technique makes them all stand on their own feet. Without mixing they don't meet many new ideas because they have met half their group before and the others are silenced by a clique.

# 15

## Introduction to
## Groups for Creative Thinking

A common problem for teachers in arts and social sciences is that students tend to be conventional in their thinking. They conform to what they think is expected of them. They seem to be afraid to express an unconventional opinion which they will then need to defend in discussion. Independence of mind, creativity and original thinking are suppressed. Brainstorming is a technique to cultivate these skills.

A characteristic of the conformist student is that he has conventional thinking habits. What Edward de Bono (Chapter 16) calls 'lateral thinking' is the opposite. Lateral thinking is a deliberate process related to creativity, insight and humour. It can be learned. It consists of generating new ideas, breaking away from old thinking habits, reorganizing information and using it in new and possibly provocative ways. Lateral thinking is intuitive and may proceed in leaps, while conventional deductive thinking is commonly sequential, proceeding one step at a time.

de Bono implies that behind students' conventional thinking is an attitude towards knowledge. It is that any item of knowledge is either correct or incorrect. Methods of teaching in schools perpetually reinforce this attitude. But, especially in higher education, we frequently want students to take risks with ideas. de Bono suggests that it is more important for ideas to be effective than correct. For example, ideas are often more effective, in the sense of being more useful, when they are not rigidly classified. Yet while an unconventional classification of concepts may be useful, it may be unjustifiable and in this sense incorrect. It is part of the attitude of a lateral thinker that he explores the least likely solutions to problems as well as the most probable ones.

Creativity is not some inborn mystical talent. It can be learned. The process has certain common ingredients. One is the *generation of alternative solutions* to a problem. 'Any particular way of looking at things is only one from among many other possible ways.' We need to encourage students to explore these other ways by reorganizing the information available to them. A second technique is to encourage students to *challenge assumptions*. No belief should be sacrosanct. The difficulty for many students is to recognize the assumptions that are commonly made. The thinking pattern that prevents students from challenging assumptions is their tendency to judge statements too quickly as correct or incorrect. For this reason de Bono emphasizes a third element of the creative process, the *suspension of judgement*. It is possible to consider an idea for some time before making a judgement of its correctness, alternative ideas are more likely to obtain consideration.

When considering the causes of an historical event, the factors in an economic situation, or the forces creating a geological feature, many students can analyse and list the component elements of the situation. What de Bono calls '*fractionation*' consists of dividing, grouping or arranging the elements of a situation in a new way. It is not trying to find the 'true' component parts of a situation. Fractionation does not have to be a complete analysis of a situation, nor do the component parts have to be without overlap. Essentially one is looking for new criteria and dimensions, for similarities and differences.

Another technique recommended by de Bono is what he calls '*reversal*'. 'In the reversal method one takes things as they are and then turns them round, inside out, upside down, back to front .... It is a provocative rearrangement of information. You make water run uphill instead of downhill. Instead of driving a car the car leads you.' Reversal does not have to be realistic or plausible. Fear of being ridiculous is one cause of rigid conventional thinking.

Brainstorming is a teaching method in which all these techniques may be practised.

A second technique using similar principles was researched and developed by SES Associates at Harvard University. Called Synectics, it is illustrated in Chapters 17 and 18

# 16

# Brainstorming

*Edward de Bono*

Brainstorming is a formal *setting* for the use of lateral thinking. In itself it is not a special technique but a special setting which encourages the application of the principles and techniques of lateral thinking while providing a holiday from the rigidity of vertical thinking.

Brainstorming is a group activity. Nor does it require any teacher intervention.

The main features of a brainstorming session are:

- Cross stimulation.
- Suspended judgement.
- The formality of the setting.

## Cross Stimulation

The fractionation technique and the reversal technique are methods for getting ideas moving. One needs to move to a new arrangement of information and then one can carry on from there. The new arrangement of information is a provocation which produces some effect. In a brainstorming session the provocation is supplied by the ideas of others. Since such ideas come from outside one's own mind they can serve to stimulate one's own ideas. Even if one misunderstands the idea it can still be a useful stimulus. It often happens that any idea may seem very obvious and trivial to one person and yet it can combine with other ideas in someone else's mind to produce something very original. In a brainstorming session one gives out stimulation to others and one receives it from others. Because the different people taking part each tend to follow their own lines of thought there is less danger of getting stuck with a particular way of looking at the situation.

During the brainstorming session the ideas are recorded by a notetaker and perhaps by a tape recorder as well. These ideas can then be played back at a later date in order to provide fresh stimulation. Although the ideas themselves are not new the context has changed so the old ideas can have a new stimulating effect.

---

Reproduced by permission from de Bono 1977.

Although the ideas in a brainstorming session are related to the problem under discussion they can still act as random stimuli for they can be far removed from the idea pattern of the person listening to them. The value of random stimulation is discussed in a later section.

# Suspended Judgement

The value of suspended judgement is that it reduces fear of criticism. The brainstorming session provides a formal opportunity for people to make suggestions that they would not otherwise dare make for fear of being laughed at. In a brainstorming session anything goes. No idea is too ridiculous to be put forward. It is important that no attempt at evaluation of ideas is made during the brainstorming session.

Attempts at evaluation might include such remarks as:

'That would never work because...'
'But what would you do about...'
'It is well-known that ...'
'That has already been tried and found to be no good.'
'How would you get that to...'
'You are leaving a vital point out of consideration.'
'That is a silly, impractical idea.'
'That would be much too expensive.'
'No one would accept that.'

These are very natural remarks but if they are allowed then the brainstorming session is useless. Not only is one forbidden to evaluate the ideas of others but also one's own ideas. It is the job of the chairman of the session to stop any attempts at evaluation. He must make this quite clear at the start of the session.

Thereafter he need only say: 'That is evaluation', in order to put a stop to it.

The other type of evaluation which must be guarded against is the evaluation of the novelty of an idea. The object of a brainstorming session is to produce *effective* ideas. Usually this means new ideas otherwise one would not be holding the session. But the purpose of the session is not actually to find *new ideas*. During the session a long forgotten idea may be resurrected and found to be very effective.

The evaluation of novelty might include such remarks as:

'That is not new.'
'I remember reading about that some time ago.'
'That has already been tried in America.'
'That was the way it was done years ago.'
'I thought of that myself but threw it out.'
'What is so original about that idea?'

To counter such tendencies the chairman has to say, 'Never mind how new it is, let's have the idea and worry about its novelty later.'

# Formality of the Setting

Lateral thinking is an attitude of mind, a type of thinking. It is not a special technique, much less a formal setting. Yet the value of a brainstorming session lies in the formality of the setting. The more formal the setting the better. The more formal the setting the more chance there is of informality in ideas within it. Most people are so steeped in vertical thinking habits that they feel very inhibited about lateral thinking. They do not like being wrong or ridiculous even though they might accept the generative value of this. The more *special* the brainstorming session is the more chance there is of the participants leaving their inhibitions outside. It is much easier to accept that 'anything goes' as a way of thinking in a brainstorming session than as a way of thinking in general.

Within this formal setting one can use all the other techniques that have been described so far for restructuring patterns and also those techniques which are yet to be described. One can try dividing things up into fractions and putting these together in new ways. One can try reversal. One does not have to apologize for it or even explain it to the others. The formality of the session gives one the licence to do what one likes with one's own thoughts without reference to the criticism of others.

# Format for Brainstorming Session

## Size

There is no ideal size. Twelve people is a convenient number but a brainstorming session can work very well with as many as fifteen or as few as six. Less than six usually becomes an argument and with more than fifteen each person does not get enough opportunity to contribute. If there is a larger group then it can be broken down into smaller groups and notes can be compared at the end.

## Chairman

It is the chairman's job to guide the session without in any way controlling or directing it. He has the following duties:

1 The chairman stops people trying to evaluate or criticize the ideas of others.
2 The chairman sees that people do not all speak at once. (The chairman must also pick out someone who has been trying to say something but is always outspoken by a more pushy character.) The chairman *does not* have to ask individuals to speak. They speak when they want to. Nor does he go round the circle asking each in turn for ideas. If however there is a prolonged silence the chairman may ask an individual for his thoughts on the matter.
3 The chairman sees that the notetaker has got an idea down. The chairman may find it necessary to repeat an idea or even to summarize an idea offered by a participant (this summary must be approved by the person whose idea it was). The chairman may be asked to decide whether an idea

is already on the list and so does not need listing again. If there is any doubt or the originator of the idea claims it to be different then it must be listed.

4 The chairman fills in gaps by offering suggestions himself. He may also call on the notetaker to read through the list of ideas already recorded.

5 The chairman can suggest different ways of tackling the problem and the use of different lateral thinking techniques for trying to generate different ways of looking at the problem (eg the chairman may say, 'Let's try turning this thing upside down'). Anyone else may of course make the same suggestions.

6 The chairman defines the central problem and keeps pulling people back to it. This is a difficult task since apparently irrelevant flights of fancy may be very generative and one certainly does not want to restrict people to the obvious view of the problem. As a guiding rule it may be said that any single flight of fancy is allowed but sustained divergence so that one comes to be considering a totally different problem is not allowed.

7 The chairman ends the session either at the end of a set time or if the session seems to be flagging – whichever is earlier. The chairman must not run the risk of boring people by extending the session indefinitely if it seems to be going well.

8 The chairman organizes the evaluation session and the listing of ideas.

## Notetaker

The function of the notetaker is to convert into a permanent list the many butterfly ideas that are put forward during the session. The task is a difficult one since the nebulous ideas offered must be reduced to manageable note form. Moreover the notes must not only make sense immediately after the session but some time later when the context is no longer so clear. The notetaker has to write fast for sometimes the ideas follow one another very rapidly. The notetaker can ask the chairman to hold things until he can catch up. The notetaker may also ask whether a particular summary of the idea is acceptable (eg Shall we put this down as, 'More flexible traffic light system'?).

The notetaker must also assess whether an idea is new enough to be added to the list or whether it is already covered by a similar idea. If in doubt he should ask the chairman. It is better to put down duplicate ideas than leave out different ones, for the duplicate ones can be removed later but the omitted ones are lost forever.

The notes must be in a form that is immediately readable, for the chairman may ask for the list to be read out at any stage. It is not a matter of carefully transcribing shorthand some time after the end of the session.

It is useful to tape-record a session as the playback may set off new ideas by repeating early ideas in a new context. Nevertheless, even when the session is so recorded it is still essential to have a notetaker. At some time a summary list has to be made even of a tape and there is also the need to read out the list during the session.

## Time

Thirty minutes is quite long enough for a session. Twenty minutes would be enough in many cases and forty-five minutes is an outside limit. It is better to stop while people are still full of ideas than to carry on until every last idea has been forced out. The temptation to carry on if the session is going well must be resisted.

## Warm up

If the members of the group are not familiar with the technique (and perhaps even if they are) a ten-minute warm up session is useful. This would deal with some very simple problem (bathtap design, bus tickets, telephone bells). The idea of this warm up session is to show the type of ideas that may be offered and to show that evaluation is excluded.

## Follow Up

After the main session is over the participants will continue to have ideas on the subject. These can be collected by asking each participant to send in a list of further ideas. If copying facilities are available then the list of ideas generated during the session can be sent to each participant with instructions to add any further ideas of his own on the bottom.

## Evaluation

As indicated above there is no attempt at evaluation during the brainstorming session itself. Any tendency to evaluate would kill spontaneity and convert the session into one of critical analysis. Evaluation is carried out later by the same group or even by another group. It is important that some sort of evaluation is carried out even if the problem is not a real one. It is the evaluation session that makes a worthwhile activity of what would otherwise be a frivolous exercise. In the evaluation session the list of ideas is sifted to extract the useful one. The main points in the evaluation are as follows

1 To pick out ideas which are directly useful.
2 To extract from ideas that are wrong or ridiculous the functional kernel of the idea which may be generalized in a useful way. (eg In a brainstorming session considering the problem of rail transport one idea put forward was that trains should have tracks on their roofs so that when two trains met one could pass above the other. The functional idea here is fuller utilization of the same track or better use of carriage roofs.) The idea of using a magnet to pull apples from the trees would be considered as finding a means to bring apples *en masse* to the ground instead of picking them individually or as pretreatment of the apples in order to make them easy to pick.

3 To list functional ideas, new aspects of the problem, ways of considering the problem, additional factors to be taken into consideration. None of these are actual solutions to the problem but merely approaches.

4 To pick out those ideas which can be tried with relative ease even though they may seem wrong at first sight.
5 To pick out those ideas which suggest that more information could be collected in certain areas.
6 To pick out those ideas which have in fact already been tried out.

At the end of the evaluation session there should be three lists:

- Ideas of immediate usefulness.
- Areas for further exploration.
- New approaches to the problem.

The evaluation session is not just a mechanical sorting, for some creative effort is required to extract usefulness from ideas before they are discarded or to spot an idea which looks as if it ought to be discarded but can in fact be developed into something significant.

## Formulation of the Problem

While any problem can be the subject of a brainstorming session the way the problem is formulated can make a huge difference to the success with which it is tackled.

Too wide a statement of the problem may bring about a variety of ideas but they are so separated that they cannot interact to bring about that chain reaction of stimulation that is the basis of brainstorming. The statement of a problem as 'Better traffic control' would be too wide.

Too narrow a statement of the problem restricts ideas so much that the session may end up generating ideas not about the problem itself but about some particular way of handling it. The statement of a problem as 'To improve traffic lights' would not lead to ideas about traffic control by means other than traffic lights. It might not even lead to ideas on better traffic control by traffic lights for attention might focus on ease of manufacture, ease of maintenance and reliability of traffic lights quite apart from their functional importance.

It is the chairman's duty to state the problem at the beginning of the session and to repeat this statement frequently in the course of the session. If it should prove to have been stated badly then he – or anyone else in the group – can suggest a better way of stating it. A suitable statement of the problem mentioned above would be: 'Methods of improving traffic flow given the present arrangement of roads'.

## Practice

The classroom is divided up into groups of a suitable size for a brainstorming session. Each group elects its own chairman. If there is any difficulty about this then the teacher makes a suggestion. The notetaker is also selected in each group. It may be useful to have an auxiliary notetaker who can relieve the first one halfway through the session.

The general principles of the brainstorming session are explained with emphasis on the following points:

1 No criticism or evaluation.
2 Say anything you like no matter how wrong or ridiculous
3 Do not try and develop ideas at length or make speeches, a few words are enough.
4 Give the notetaker a chance to get things down.
5 Listen to the chairman.

A warm up problem is then given to each group and they have a ten minute warm up session. At the end of this session they go straight into the main session for thirty minutes.

The teacher may sit in on the groups in turn. It is better not to be too intrusive. Few comments are made at the time but mental notes are kept for discussion afterwards. The only thing which justifies an intervention is any tendency to evaluate or criticize.

At the end of the sessions the groups come together again. In turn the notetakers from each group read out the list of ideas. The teacher may then comment as follows:

1 Comments on the actual session stressing perhaps the tendency to evaluate or the tendency to be too timid.
2 Comments on the lists of ideas. These could point out the similarity of some of the ideas, the originality of others.
3 Comments on the tone of the ideas. Some of the suggestions may have been quite sensible others quite ridiculous. If the suggestions do tend to be too solemn the teacher might point out that at least some of the suggestions during the sessions should be outrageous enough to cause a laugh.
4 The teacher then adds some ideas and suggestions of his own concerning the problems that have been discussed

In going through the lists of suggestions the teacher may pick out some of the more outrageous ideas and proceed to show how they can be useful. This is done by extracting the functional principle of the idea and developing it further.

The general impression that should be encouraged is that the brainstorming session is a generative situation in which one should not be too self-conscious. In practice there is a tendency for some students to show off and try to be deliberately humorous if they know that their suggestions are to be read out to the assembled class. One has to deal with that situation as best one can without denying people the right to be outrageous. One way is to ask the person to explain the idea further.

Suggested problems for use in brainstorming sessions might include:

The design of money.
The lack of sufficient playgrounds.
The need for examinations.
Mining under the sea.
Providing enough television programmes for everyone to see what they

want to see.
Making the desert fertile.
Heating a house.

In each case what is being asked for is a way of doing it, a better way of doing it, a new way of doing it. These are merely suggestions and the teacher ought to be able to generate further problems.

# Evaluation

Evaluation sessions should not be held on the same day as the brainstorming sessions. The evaluation sessions are best done in front of the whole class and each idea is considered in turn for its direct or indirect usefulness.
One can have different categories into which each idea is placed. These might be:

   Directly useful.
   Interesting approach.
   For further examination.
   Discard.

An alternative to this general evaluation is to write the brainstorm lists on the blackboard a few items at a time and get each student to evaluate the items with votes. At the end the different evaluations can be compared by seeing how many 'votes' each item gets.

In this context the evaluation session is a necessary part of the brainstorming session but not an important part. Evaluations tend to be critical analysis and vertical thinking. Emphasis should be directed much more to the brainstorming session itself than to the subsequent evaluation.

It is important in any attempt at evaluation not to give the impression that the outrageous ideas were only of use in the brainstorming session but not of much practical use anywhere else. Such an impression would limit suggestions to the practical and the solemnly sensible which though worthwhile in themselves would never lead to new ideas. One of the most important functions of the evaluation session is to show that even the most outrageous suggestions can lead to useful ideas.

# Summary

The brainstorming session is of value as a formal setting which encourages the use of lateral thinking. The brainstorming session has a value as a group activity in which there is a cross stimulation of ideas. Otherwise there is nothing special to a brainstorming session that could not be done outside it. Some people equate creative thinking with brainstorming. This is to equate a basic process with one relatively minor setting which encourages the use of that process. Perhaps the most important part of the brainstorming session is its formality. When one is first getting used to the idea of lateral thinking it is helpful to have some special setting in which to practise it. Later on there is less need for such a setting.

# 17

# The SES Box Step Method for Creative Problem-solving

*SES Associates*

## Why Problem-solvers Need the SES Box Steps

All businesses have problems that have resisted solution. Solving such problems is the key to industry leadership and high profit margins but this requires problem-solvers who can see old problems in creative, new ways.

SES Associates originated the synectics method for creative problem-solving as part of their work in their Harvard University Laboratory. Since then, they have refined synectics into a simple easy-to-learn set of 'Box Steps' which quickly and efficiently reveals new viewpoints on old problems.

## Why the Box Steps were Developed

Successful problem-solvers always have been able to see old problems in new ways. However, such intuitive problem-solving is time-consuming and inefficient – new ideas strike infrequently and unreliably. Therefore, over forty years ago SES personnel began to search for the actual mechanisms of thought by which new ideas are produced. Once they had identified these mechanisms, SES developed ways to teach them to people with problem-solving responsibilities. The goal was to reduce creative problem-solving inefficiencies so that new ideas could be produced at will.

## How Creative Ideas are Produced

Although there are many different theories about how to think creatively, all of them agree that new ideas are the result of new connections. For example, most people know that Samuel Morse was the inventor of the telegraph. Less well known is a basic problem Morse faced in the development of his invention, a difficulty so serious that it almost ruined him financially. He was absolutely unable to send a telegraph signal more than a few miles. No matter how much Morse increased the power of the original signal, the strength of the received signal was not proportionally increased. No solution was forthcoming until one day when he was travelling on a stagecoach from New York to Baltimore. He noticed that at regular intervals the stage stopped at a post relay station where the tired horses were replaced (the source of the word 'relay' in electrical parlance). Accordingly, Morse set up stations at appropriate distances along his telegraph line where more power was added to his signal just as it was getting too weak.

   SES has found ways to teach people to generate the kind of new connections Morse used to solve his telegraph problem. Morse had to wait for an accident to happen – it was by chance that he travelled from New York to Baltimore by stagecoach. On the other hand, the mechanisms of the SES box steps enable people to make an accident happen: to generate connections which solve problems in creative ways.

# How the Box Steps Work

In addition to the fact that new connections are required to produce new ideas, the SES box step method includes other elements crucial to successful problem-solving.

## Paradox: The Way to Identify the Essence of a Problem

The Morse example is typical of all problems that require creative solutions. Although Morse's problem included a great number of elements (size of the wire, strength of the original signal, etc.) it boiled down to one contradictory phenomenon: an increase in the original signal did not produce a proportional increase in the distance the signal would travel. After studying hundreds of examples, SES has concluded that the reason any problem is difficult to solve is because it contains a paradox, a conflict or contradiction that cannot be resolved unless a new connection is made. Thus, the SES box steps employ paradox for identifying the essence of problems.

## Analogies and Metaphors: The Source of New Connections

Morse made a creative connection between tiring horses and his weakening telegraph signal. The stagecoach analogy provided him with a new perspective by which to view his problem. Without success Morse had been examining the phenomenon of electrical transmission in depth. He needed to go outside the area of the problem and by accident he found an analogy which gave him a creative, new viewpoint. On the other hand, the design of the SES box steps enables problem-solvers purposefully to generate the kind of analogies and metaphors which produce creative, new ways to view old problems.

## *Equivalent Thinking: The Key to Using Analogies*

Once Morse was aware that the stage coach system was like his telegraph system, implicitly he applied the idea to the elements of his problem. To do this he had to find equivalents: the horses pulling the stagecoach were like the electrical power carrying the telegraph signal; the tired horses were like the weakened signal; and the fresh horses were like adding power to his signal. It was lucky that Morse hit on those equivalents. The box steps do not depend on mere luck. They are designed to show problem-solvers the crucial equivalent between a problem and a new analogical connection.

## *Where to Use the SES Box Steps*

The SES box steps have been applied to a wide range of problems – from new product development to sales, from personnel management to strategic planning. Any problem that has resisted solution is ripe for the creative power of the SES box steps.

## *How to Learn the SES Box Steps*

SES has devised a one-day Box Step Problem-Solving Workshop in large groups. Since the workshop employs real-world client problems and is designed to establish a functioning climate of constructive innovation, it includes: consultation time for selecting workshop participants and establishing overall goals for the SES programme; materials for before, during, and follow-up; and follow-up visits to ensure carry-over. Sometimes the workshop is conducted on client-location.

---

### Problem Description—

Measure the volume of the King's new crown to make sure it is pure gold.

| Step 1—Paradox | Step 2—Analogue |
|---|---|
| The crown is a heavy, solid object that can not be measured | HIS BODY ENTERING THE BATH: his body is as irregular as the crown and can not be measured. |

| Step 4—Equivalent | Step 3—Unique Activity |
|---|---|
| Irregularly shaped crown will displace a measurable amount of water. | His irregularly shaped body displaces a regular amount of water. |

TTD–G

### New Idea–

Fill basin with water. Put in crown. Measure overflow. Compare volume of overflow with volume of a piece of pure gold that weighs the same as the crown.

---

## Problem Description–

How to save space when shipping potato chips from a factory that is far away from points of sale.

| Step 1—Paradox<br><br>The more compact the package the more the potato chips are crushed. | Step 2—Analogue<br><br>DRY LEAVES: they act just like potato chips. |
|---|---|
| Step 4—Equivalent<br><br>Soften chips so they conform to each other. | Step 3—Unique Activity<br><br>Wet leaves conform to each other and can be packed tightly. |

### New Idea–

Make the potato chips the same shape so that they will conform and can be stacked.

---

## Problem Description–

How to explain the origin of infection.

| Step 1—Paradox<br><br>Established theory says that infection comes from within but no soldier became infected until wounded. | Step 2—Analogue<br><br>FERMENTATION OF GRAPES: unless crushed, grapes turn into raisins. |
|---|---|
| Step 4—Equivalent<br><br>Skin must be cut to allow infection to begin. | Step 3—Unique Activity<br><br>Grapes must be crushed to allow fermentation to begin. |

### New Idea—

His epoch-making theory that derived from this Equivalent was that germs were carried by air.

---

### Problem Description—

A large organization wants its employees to develop the habit of meeting informally to share ideas. All attempts to bring about this behaviour, however, have been too formal and organized to produce the kind of informal cross-fertilization that used to occur before the organization became so large.

| Step 1—Paradox | Step 2—Analogue |
|---|---|
| Unless gatherings are 'unorganized', they won't work. | HERRING GULLS: they surround a fishing boat in an 'unorganized' gathering |

| Step 4—Equivalent | Step 3—Unique Activity |
|---|---|
| Offer convenient, excellent food at reasonable prices in an unorganized way. | The gulls are drawn by 'accidental', first-class food. |

### New Idea—

Serve gourmet food in the organization's cafeteria.

---

# 18

# SES Synectics and Gifted Education Today

*W. J. J. Gordon and T. Poze*

From kindergarten to college, most classrooms contain students who learn at different rates. Some students, for diverse reasons, operate at a low level of achievement. The average students have some of the same needs as the low achievers, but are better able to learn. The few gifted students have no trouble learning content.

Teachers need ways to educate all levels of students without boring the fast learners and without swamping the slow learners. However, before discussing a strategy which has demonstrated this capacity, let's examine what learning is and what various levels of students can and cannot do.

Learning is a combination of focusing, connection-making, and application. To learn, students must respond to subject matter by focusing on important points, internalizing those points, expressing their comprehension, and sometimes creatively applying what they have learned. Effective internalization takes place when students connect the subject matter to something they already know about. The basic tools of learning are analogies which serve as connectors between the new and the familiar. They enable students to connect the facts and feelings of their experience with the facts that they are just learning. Good teaching traditionally makes ingenious use of analogies and metaphors to help students visualize content. For example, the subject of electricity typically is introduced through the analogue of the flow of water in pipes. However, the SES synectics procedure for developing students' connection-making skills goes beyond merely presenting helpful comparisons and actually evokes metaphors and analogies from the students themselves. Students learn how to learn by developing the skills to produce their own, as opposed to teacher-derived, connective metaphors (Gordon 1961).

When there is a breakdown, either of focusing or connection-making, learning is blocked and slow students suffer from such blocks. Sometimes average students can focus on the important elements of the content and sometimes they can't. Thus their learning is accidental and inconsistent. The gifted students are fast, reliable learners. Giving explicit skills for focusing

Reproduced by permission from Gordon and Poze 1980b.

and analogy-formation (connection-making) to slow learners is the difference between those students being able to learn and being unable to learn. These same skills increase the learning reliability of average students because they operate purposefully, not accidentally.

As for gifted students, they learn wonderfully anyway so what can these skills do for them? Although they are fast learners, their connection-making is subliminal, not at a conscious level where they can use it. When their foci and connective analogies are explicit, on the other hand, advanced students can use them as the basis for creative extension. This is impossible when their process is implicit and they are not aware of their connections, because the foci and analogues are unavailable for conscious manipulation.

When gifted students use explicit tools, they can speculate creatively. They cannot do this when their connections are subliminal because their implicit analogical connections reside in their subconscious and are unavailable to them. When the process operates consciously and explicitly, their analogues become conscious elements which can be built-on purposefully in imaginative ways. This facilitates the production of new ideas which serve to displace boredom and disenchantment. Of course, certain average students and slower students will gain entry into the creative realm of comprehension and expression since analogy, the mechanism of comprehension, is the same as the mechanism for expression. The same analogy that is used to comprehend and internalize given content is used to express that comprehension in the student's own terms (Gordon and Poze 1974). The fact that these skills can be applied to a wide range of learning abilities means that teachers can employ a single teaching strategy to attain their goals. Thus, gifted students gain creative fluency while other students increase their learning effectiveness.

## Case History

The constructive potential of these skills quite naturally came to mind when there arrived at the SES (see Chapter 17) office a letter from a teacher named Harold Foster. Experienced in teaching biology at various grade levels, he is an educator of the highest integrity who is thrilled when his students understand subject matter in depth and saddened when they do not.

My class is a stereotype of a cross-section of students – slow learners of various kind – no damaged brains, but some pretty poor learners. Then there is the big bunch in the middle – the average ones, whatever that means. Sometimes they are down with the slow learners and sometimes they are up with the real sharp people. And, of course, there are the advanced students, the truly gifted ones. My poor students simply can't seem to grasp concepts. My average students are unreliable. And my gifted students are reliable as far as they go. They can abstract the content and present it to me with elegant recall of an amazing number of details, but they can't seem to get beyond the text.

It is safe to say that none of my students is in any way reliable when it comes to focusing. By focusing I do not mean the mere compression of details. I mean identifying the core of what is important. Even the advanced ones are poor focusers. They cover up this lack with excellent recall. But to tell you the truth, I don't know how to teach them to focus except to do what teachers always do – tell their students: 'Pick out the most important points in the content and underline those sentences.' As for how to distinguish important from unimportant points, that's where the SES technique may be able to help me.

Later Mr. Foster visited the SES Cambridge office and went into more detail about the exact difficulties his students were having. He used the example of the symbiosis unit he was using. He reported that he first assigned the appropriate chapter in the biology text, then outlined that material for his students, and finally gave them a quiz. He showed the staff his synopsis.

SYMBIOSIS: the association of two unlike organisms for the mutual advantage of both. For example, a lichen is made up of alga and fungus. The fungus gives the alga a structure and enough moisture to keep it from drying out. The alga produces carbohydrates which feed the fungus. Under the climatic conditions in the arctic where lichens are commonly found and are important ecologically, neither the fungus nor the alga can survive independently. Each of the two parts is dreadfully weak by itself. The alga would dry up and blow away and the fungus would starve.

A reading of the students' responses on the quiz clearly demonstrated the learning problems his students were having. His slow learners, at best, wrote about two plants living together. The average group's answers went a little further and showed an awareness of the fact that in a symbiotic relationship, such as a lichen, the fungus and alga help each other. His gifted students recalled the details of the synopsis well enough to repeat the content as a whole, but they lacked sharp focusing. Furthermore, the responses of his advanced pupils were so much alike and so close to the text that Mr. Foster questioned whether they had internalized the content in a useful way.

In addition, there was none of the creative activity that he wanted his gifted students to experience in order to disperse the boredom that inhabited their minds. They became bored and frustrated when dragged down by lesser lights – to say nothing of their talents being lost. Mr. Foster believed that gifted students should remain in the same classroom with students who were less advanced but of the same emotional and physical age. Therefore, he felt that it was crucial that their creative extension and enrichment activities be an integral part of their regular classroom work.

In the course of Mr. Foster's visit, the SES staff discussed with him their research findings with implications for his situation. He was shown the data from the SES Title I programme in 1975 which proved that focusing and connection-making was painfully lacking in slow learners. In that programme the target population was successfully retaught certain simple skills for making purposeful connections. The students' learning process was restored in a matter of 30 hours once they had practised an explicit connection-making rather than an accidental one (Gordon and Poze 1979). By the same token, the same skills increased the reliability of average students because they became able to act purposefully instead of accidentally and subliminally.

Mr. Foster attended an SES workshop, after which he met with the SES staff in order to lay out a clear classroom campaign. It was agreed that as a focusing device he would start out by looking for the *paradox* within the content, and would explain to the class as a whole how this was accomplished. At the core of every concept is always a resolved paradox. For instance, the concept of natural selection contains the paradox that the survival of the fittest is based on genetic mistakes. And the concept of immunization contains the paradoxical notion of safe attack (ie a small amount of the given disease is an attack which is benign) (Gordon and Poze 1980).

Mr. Foster developed a complete instructional procedure for applying what he had learned in the workshop. First the paradox at the core of the symbiosis content would be identified. Then he would present his students with an analogue drawn from material familiar to all of the class members and observe the results when they made connections between the analogue and the content. Finally, to make certain that the gifted students were given an opportunity for creative thinking, all students would produce their own analogues and make appropriate connections. For the slow learners this activity would serve as additional internalization.

When Mr. Foster returned to his school he told his class about the concept of paradox and presented the examples of natural selection and immunization and discussed the notion of a core paradox. Then, as a review of the symbiosis content, all students developed and wrote down their paradox choices and explanations.

The following three paradox descriptions were developed by students who were fast learners.

> *Double weakness makes for strength.* This is because the alga and the fungus are both weak sisters by themselves, but put them together and you've got dynamite.
> *Both parts must be deficient for combined strength.* If each, the alga and fungus, did not have a special weakness, they could not combine for strength.
> *Two weaknesses make strength.* Apart, the alga and fungus are weak; but their weaknesses are needs for each other that bond them into a strong organism.

The following pair was produced by the lower level students. They were able to evoke interesting paradoxes but note how general and vague their ideas are.

> *Two wrongs make a right.* The alga and fungus are two organic wrongs which make a right when joined.
> *Two strong weaknesses.* The greater the weakness of each, the stronger the result when the two come together.

The slow learners took more time to grasp the process for deriving a paradox and their paradox statements were not as sophisticated as the others, but it was a surprise to Mr. Foster that they did so well. They told him that the paradox, once they understood how it worked, gave them 'something to hunt for in the reading instead of just hoping that the "sense" of the content would jump out of the page.'

Next the students chose from among the paradoxes that they had written up. They settled on the description, 'Both parts must be deficient for combined strength,' because it was the most specific. A week later, in accordance with the SES plan, Mr. Foster gave his class another quiz in which he asked them to put the essence of symbiosis into their own words. Where previously the slow learners had failed to express the essence of the concept, now all of them were able to state the paradox. However, they could not go beyond the abstract, original paradox statement. The average student tended to state the paradox exactly and then produce a few, halting, space-filling expansions. The gifted students stated the paradox verbatim and expanded by recalling elements of the content and integrating them into the paradox form.

The paradox technique had enabled the students to focus on the core of the content, but now they all needed to link that content to something within their experience. In the SES workshop, Mr. Foster had mastered the skills for accomplishing his goal by making analogy to the paradox. He proceeded to do this for the symbiosis/lichen content. He looked for a simple mechanical thing that would be familiar to all his students. The classroom was in a school in the White Mountains of New Hampshire within sight of the Cog Railway on Mt Washington. What about that piece of machinery? Certainly every student would remember from the class trip how each cog of the locking wheel driven by the engine fitted into the proper notch in the rail as the system works its way up the mountain.

Mr. Foster simply presented his analogue without describing any of the parallels between the cog railway and lichens because he wanted his students to experience making their own connections. He simply stated, 'In symbiosis in lichens both parts must be deficient for combined strength. How is that like the Mt Washington Cog Railway we visited on the class trip?' The following are examples of student responses:

> The engine needs to get up the incline without slipping back and the track supplied that need – a slip-proof base. The fungus will slip into death without the alga's carbohydrates and the alga will blow away without the fungus' structure and moisture.
> The cog on the engine's drive-wheel is made by biting off the rest of the wheel's rim and thus is a weakness. And the track has bites out of it at regular intervals all the way up. But together they make a working system. The combined weaknesses of the fungus and alga also make a working system – the lichen.

At this stage, the responses from both slow and advanced students were not very different – especially when compared to the next stage where each student made up his/her own analogy. The reason for this is that the very use of a connective analogue, by itself, lends a tone of clarity and sophistication to expression even if the associations are quite simple. All students' responses manifested a true understanding of the content. The improvement from the slow learners' previous understanding and the new comprehension shown by their cog-railway/lichen connection was enormous – as was the case for most average students. The gifted students showed a new crispness and organization to their recall of details.

Mr. Foster was delighted with the learning progress of his slow learners and his average students. In fact, they had attained the learning goals he had set for them. His advanced students successfully had used the cog-railway analogue as a conceptual organizer. However, they had not yet begun to operate inventively because they were not yet producing their own analogies. Since he did not want to set these gifted students apart from the rest of the class, he followed the SES advice. He instructed the whole class to use five minutes to think up and write down a parallel analogy to the paradox description of symbiosis drawn from their own intimate experience.

Making up their own analogies had different results depending on the student's position on the learning spectrum. For the slower students, the connections between symbiosis content and the analogue illuminated and internalized the content, and gave those students a sense of self-reliance and confidence in being able to fit and apply to their own world the content that they were studying. The following two responses, which are typical, demonstrate this first-rate grasp of the symbiosis idea:

> It's like a man and his hunting dog. The dog aids his master in getting food and the man gives the dog shelter. The dog is like the alga and the man is like the fungus.
> In a car, the generator needs the battery to get things started the way the fungus needs the alga. And the battery needs the generator to keep feeding it the way the alga needs the moisture that the fungus gives it.

The gifted students made connections that went beyond internalizing the content. They generated responses that creatively extended the content in terms of scientific and poetic speculation. Here is a typical response from a gifted student:

> I see ways in which the baron and serf in feudalism are like the fungus/alga relationship. The baron was definitely strong enough under peaceful conditons but in a state of war the baron needed the serfs for his army and the serfs needed the baron and his knights to protect them from enemy barons. The alga requires the structure of the fungus as the serfs relied on the safety of the baron's castle. The fungus requires the carbohydrate supplied by the alga as the baron required the food grown by his serfs. Of course, in the final analysis the barons were the bosses even though there was a mutal need ...I wonder which is the boss of the lichen? Alga or fungus? Whose need is greater? And how do they get together in the first place? First one then the other or both at the same instant? Or are they born together? Or does one find the other like a lonely lover? (Gordon 1980).

You can see how that student extended his analogue more specifically, produced speculative questions, and developed a poetic expression.

Another form of creative extension to which Mr. Foster was introduced at the SES workshop was personal analogy, a process in which students imagine being something else. It is the epitome of individualized analogies. Based on empathic identification, it involves simple feelings and is a relatively primitive skill that all students can master easily for clearer grasp of content and for clearer expression. Gifted students, on the other hand, employ personal analogy for imaginative extension that ranges from scientific speculation to creative writing (Gordon and Poze 1968). For example, here is one of Mr. Foster's gifted student's personal analogy responses to the symbiosis paradox, 'Both parts must be deficient for combined strength'.

I'm a feisty alga part of the lichen. I hate being so dependent on Fungus. I wish I could figure out how to go it on my own. But can I make it? I bet that wisenheimer Fungus is beginning to suspect something. I better get ready to jump whether I want to or not. But I do want to. If I did stay and Fungus died what would I do? Then I would really have to jump for it. Could I ever get Fungus going again? Or me for that matter? I suppose that each of us has its own type of seeds. Could there be such a thing as a combination seed? Wouldn't that be great? One seed that sprouts two different plants.

That student used his personal analogy to create some speculations about the function of the symbiotic parts of a lichen – speculations which led to further investigations and study. Now let us take a brief look at the response of a student who was by the same symbiosis content to write a kind of short story.

I'm Alga, running around in my kitchen – the one that Fungus built for me. I am throwing together a complicated carbohydrate supper for him. And there he sits; fat and happy and scratching his belly, while I sweat away. Boy, does he make me mad! Who needs him? I'm the one who carries the load around here. If I were not slaving in this hot kitchen that Fungus would starve to death.

'Listen Fungus,' I say. 'Let's get something straight. Here I am looking your dinner and there you sit on your bottom doing nothing. Why don't you make youself useful? Clean up the place or something. Go build me a screened-in porch or something. I'm sick of doing everything around here. Who needs you, anyway?

Fungus shifts his body around in that fat way of his and speaks in that slow drawl. 'Come now, Alga old man,' he says. 'Without me you wouldn't have a place to hang your hat. You'd just blow about in the wind.'

I can't help recalling that it was good old Fungus who built my nice kitchen, and in fact the whole house we live in, but I am too upset to let that slow down my anger.

'All right,' I say, 'But I want to settle who's boss around here, you or me. And settle it right now.'

'Why in the world does there have to be a boss?' asks Fungus in that sticky voice of his.

'That's what makes our relationship so unique. There's no boss because we need each other so much.' 'I know that,' I said. 'But who needs who more?'

'Isn't it enough that neither of us could exist without the other? What more do you need?' and Fungus talks to me the way he would to a baby.

I mumble my answer so that I can't be understood. I see the point that Fungus is making, but I don't stop trying to figure out how to get to be boss. After all, that is the American way, isn't it?

Both of those examples start from the same content premise and are based on the correct grasp of the symbiosis concept. Each departs in a different though equally imaginative direction and demonstrates the possibilities for creative extension that are open to gifted students.

# Summary

Harold Foster had to deal with the problem of effectively instructing his slow learners while making sure that his gifted students were kept interested by practising creative thinking.

In a situation where the content is not being learned satisfactorily, the patent need is for a procedure by which the content can be understood. The first step toward this end in the SES procedure is organizing the core content material by identifying the paradox within it. The second step to to produce a close and practical analogue to that core (Gordon and Poze 1975).

In a gifted situation where no learning problem exists, there is the need to extend students' imaginations into inventive speculation, which is the basis for the creative arts and sciences. The first step, the paradox procedure, is not crucial for the gifted, but it does help expose an explicit and distinct focus. The second step is crucial since it produces a stretched and aesthetic analogy which goes beyond the content and reveals it in a fresh and vibrant way. This new-insight process underlies all creative activity and gives students the skills for being creative adults.

The procedures by which the paradox and analogue techniques are used depend on teachers' insight into their students' needs (Gordon and Poze 1972). For gifted students, of course, SES teachers emphasize the highly creative, highly personal analogues. However, from time to time, teachers will want all students to experience drawing on their inner selves to create original analogues.

For students who are not prepared for such creative extension, the metaphorical approach to learning serves the practical didactic purpose discussed previously in the article. However, SES synectics teachers allow for general class discussion of all concepts under consideration at a learning level as well as a creative level. Gifted students are interested in the particular learning analogues by which other students internalize given content, and the creative extensions of the gifted students intrigue the rest of the class. Since all students are responding to the same content, the class performs as a whole. However, there is an extremely important concomitant to this procedure. Participation in this activity by certain students who previously have not been identified as being gifted will reveal hidden talents.

# 19

# Introduction to
# Groups for Project Work

Universities take great pride in the fact that they do research. There is also a popular belief that their research and teaching are symbiotic. Yet at undergraduate level any attempt to teach research techniques or give research problems is remarkably rare. Research students are selected on the basis of timed examinations which may well demand very different skills from research. True, final-year students are often given projects, but, since these are usually done individually so that it is very difficult for tutors to give everyone adequate introductory guidance, research competence tends to be something that students must develop for themselves.

I believe university teachers and others underestimate the ability of students to teach each other. Naturally, the assignment of individual marks for joint projects can be difficult, but why should a difficulty in assessment be allowed to divert anyone from one of the unique functions, the teaching of research?

More and more research methods are also being taught in schools, colleges, polytechnics and other institutions. The chapters in this section show how research can begin to be taught using the power of the group. They do much more. Paul Black shows in Chapter 20 how joint projects can begin to cultivate independence, improve personal relationships, personal involvement and an appreciation of group work in undergraduate physics. Gerald Collier (Chapers 21 and 22) introduces the syndicate method, which can be used to teach students team work, committee procedure, how to seek information, complex problem-solving and inter-disciplinary thinking. Although with younger students the tutor must constantly check that an assignment is carried out jointly, with all students committed to every part, syndicates give mature students an opportunity to use their experience, which they are usually very enthusiastic to do.

# 20

# Group Discussion

## *P. J. Black*

An important part of the final-year Honours physics course in Birmingham is seven weeks of the course devoted full-time to activity known as Group Studies. The reasons for establishing this course and a detailed account of its first year of operation have been given elsewhere (Black, Dyson and O'Connor 1968). Students complete the lecture programme of their final year by mid-February and take the final written examinations on formal lecture work in that month. They then work on group studies for the last two weeks of the Easter terms and the first five weeks of the summer term; this work is assessed by continuous assessment and the only formal examinations after the group studies period are two general papers which are on a wide variety of problems ranging over the whole of undergraduate physics and which do not call for intensive revision.

These arrangements provide a context in which a student can concentrate almost exclusively on one activity. Students choose to work on one of four broad topics, so that each topic offered will attract a group of about twenty who will work with four lecturers. Within each group, work is undertaken by small sub-groups each concentrating on particular aspects of the topic in open-ended experimental projects and in background study; in addition the whole group comes together to study the common theme, to interrelate the various special projects and to receive and discuss reports. The main initiative for the progress of the work lies between the small sub-groups (each with about five members) and the meetings of these as a group of twenty, and the detailed pattern of activity varies according to the individuals involved and the topic studied.

Although students earlier in their course have experienced small group teaching, in tutorial groups of various kinds, the group work in this exercise is a new experience. This is because such work is now central to the whole activity rather than peripheral; a typical group study, if it has a timetable at all, might list one background lecture and one open discussion meeting of the large group per week, and two or three other large group meetings at special times during the seven weeks – eg for final reporting at the end. The initiative for determining most of the working timetable lies with the sub-groups. In the first meeting of a sub-group, the lecturer will usually take a lead by proposing some problems which revise basic ideas relevant to the topic studied. Discussion of these ends in assignment of work and selection of a time to produce this work – usually within about two days.

At the same time students will start to do some elementary experiments concerned with the topics they might investigate. The first two weeks might proceed in this way, with an intensive pattern of background study together with preparatory experiments. An important criterion for selecting the main group study topics is that each should demand the use and inter-relation of basic physics already learnt in different contexts in previous undergraduate courses. Problems set for students are important in this first phase in promoting discussions in which the understanding of these basic topics is exposed and developed. In the second of these two weeks the sub-group is presented with proposals for various projects, and has to select problems to be investigated as the main study and to discuss the design of the projects so chosen.

This is a formative stage of the group: the agenda and the pace of work are partly set by the staff member, and partly by the necessity to complete certain tasks by the end of the Easter term, since an important feature of the group study is that a substantial amount of written work has to be done during the Easter vacation. The frequent meetings and the co-operative work in the laboratory help the formation of the group, but the outstanding influence appears to be the assumption of responsibility: when the sub-groups face the need to make decisons about their own line of work for the five weeks of the third term the members are forced to take more seriously both their study and their relationships within the group. The better students quickly realise that they do not know the topic well enough to be able to make choices and construct plans, and this gives a new bite to their questions and leads to more intense and longer group discussions in which initiative begins to pass from the member of staff. A sub-group of about five students may also have to decide whether to work on one project together or on two or three, splitting into trios or pairs as required; these decisions are left to the group.

The work in the five weeks of the third term may form a distinct second phase. Students return having completed work over the vacation which includes a background essay on the project topic and a short design study for the particular experimental investigations to be undertaken. At this stage the sub-group is told that it has to present a report to the larger group about its plans for its projects, and the staff member will say that although he is available to answer questions students should meet amongst themselves to plan their presentation. There will not be more than a few days available before the full group has a meeting, typically lasting three or four hours, devoted to the presentation of plans by students. At this stage the sub-group acquires a 'public' presence and although overt competition between sub-groups is not an outstanding feature, the need to ensure that the public appearance of the sub-group's work bears comparison with that of other sub-groups is a significant stimulus. At the same time, the main experimental work commences. This commencement involves further choices at the intellectual and personal levels. Problems arising out of the work will be raised, by the students amongst themselves, and in formal and informal sub-group meetings with staff. The staff member at this stage has ceased to direct, but has an important role in asking questions to help the group to foresee problems or to make them aware of the need to think more critically about assumptions underlying their investigation procedure. The decision mentioned above about dividing project work amongst the members is now implemented and working patterns are formed which usually persist until the end of the work. When several students are working together on the one experiment then, provided that the lecturer is not directing them, a leader will usually emerge. Students adopt roles within the group which reflect their different abilities, and seem to be content to work together in the pecking order so established. The experimental work often involves long hours spent in observation and recording and sub-groups also organise rotas amongst themselves, which can face the staff member with a need to supervise students working into the late evening. Each sub-group member may also be expected in this period to give a short talk to a sub-group meeting about one special aspect of their field of work. The final task of the sub-group is to report to a meeting of the whole group on the results of the work. The sub-group decides how to sub-divide this task and some sub-groups go to great pains, preparing large charts or projector transparencies, to aid the presentation; thus 'public' presentation is a significant climax for the students and leads to an accelerated pace of work in the closing weeks.

Weekly meetings of the larger groups are also held during the seven weeks. In several groups, there has been an attempt to conduct these as completely open discussions about any problems which students or staff may care to raise. There is an almost overwhelming diffidence and uncertainty in such meetings and long silences have to be tolerated at the outset. Students are far more reluctant to expose their thinking in a group of twenty than in the sub-group of five and staff find the need to keep silent a more taxing one – they could all too easily convert these sessions into a series of staff monologues. However, in some groups, staff restraint and the pioneering attempts by a few brave students are rewarded in that after a few meetings lively debate amongst both students and staff is established. One feature of such meetings is the revelation, in and to the group, that staff can make mistakes, contradict one another and suffer the exposure of their own misunderstandings. Students are told of the importance of making mistakes: one group established a maxim that every member ought to contribute at least one stupid remark per week. However, success with these larger sessions is variable; in one group, degeneration into a series of sporadic staff monologues led to student reaction and the formation of a student committee which asked to be allowed to run the discussions – a request which was readily granted. Subsequent discussion was more brisk because at least some students felt responsible and came prepared.

It is not easy to summarise or to describe accurately the main characteristics or effects of group studies. The broad pattern has been in operation since 1966, and although topics for groups have been modified or completely changed, and the staff involved have changed, the original pattern has been maintained. Staff were apprehensive at the outset because it was clear that success would be very dependent on a positive response from the majority of students. The response has always been far more than adequate; student enthusiasm is a consistent feature and questionnaires about the whole final year regularly place this activity at the top of any popularity poll. The only exceptions to this are that a few students, typically two or three in a group of seventy each year, contract out and do very little work. On one occasion in five years, severe strains arose in one group because of continual criticism of arrangements and equipment, mainly by one student who was both able and highly critical and who attracted support from one or two fellow-students.

Staff reaction is also very favourable even although the need to see small groups very frequently leads to a substantial increase in time devoted to teaching. Because they have both to communicate fresh ideas and enthusiasm for projects and to join in a struggle for understanding (rather than give the same old answers) it is important to them that the group study topics be changed regularly. No one topic has been repeated without radical modifications for more than three years, and the particular experimental project tackled by students within a topic are seldom repeated. Staff frequently say that one outstanding feature is the frequent and intensive contact with a sub-group that is working full-time on a common task.

Because of this the staff come to know the strengths and weaknesses, both of intellect and personality, of their students in a way that is not possible in normal tuition; this is partly because normal tuition is ancillary to a course where the focus and initiative come in lectures or laboratories which the tutor does not attend. The second feature is the development of groups during the seven weeks; both large and small groups change quite remarkably. Some of these changes – greater involvement in the task, more readiness and confidence to speak, better relationships amongst students – are common to other group exercises, but develop here at a faster pace, and develop with staff who cannot effect such a development with tutorial groups of the normal kind which meet less frequently. Other changes seem to be peculiar to the task-orientation of the group; one of these is the emergence of different and interacting roles amongst the members. Occasionally, a student who at the outset adopts a role which he has clearly played with colleagues in the past (eg he might be the clown, or the simple man for whom all but the most elementary theory is an absurd abstraction) can be seen slowly to change it under pressure of events since, in participation in the task and in discussion about decisons concerning that task, such a role becomes unnecessary and less rewarding. Finally students frequently report, in questionnaires filled in at the end of the course, that the work 'helped them to know what scientific research was like'. This has two aspects; superficially, the pattern of work has several features, including the concentration on a task, the learning and discussion of theory because it affects decisions about a problem, and the working to deadlines for results rather than storing up for future examination responses, which are, and were planned to be, very like activity in a professional research or development group. But the deeper signifcance may be that students become more aware of their strengths and weaknesses through the experience of close interaction with their peers on a task. There have been a few examples of students changing career intentions because of the experience, including some very good students opting for research which they had previously rejected.

Many of the characteristic features arise because the exercise is one form of concentrated study, which has very similar properties to those of other forms recently described by Parlett and King (1971). These authors discuss the use of concentrated study to cover normal sections in the curriculum, whereas a group study is more open, and can build on greater maturity and experience, because it comes at the end of a degree course. These differences enhance the status of group discussion within the work. It may be that group work is more vital and rewarding in this work than in normal undergraduate teaching because its central role is explicit and evident and because it has become the focus of a scheme of inter-relationships in learning activities which gives students more freedom and more responsibility.

# 21

# An Experiment in University Teaching

*K. Gerald Collier*

## Context

One of the major problems of higher education throughout the west is that of weaning the student from dependence on instruction and building upon his powers of critical judgment. The Hale Report put it thus 'The aim...of the undergraduate course...should be not only or even primarily to equip the student with knowledge, but also, and more importantly, to teach him to think for himself and work on his own' (Hale Report 1964). An invitation to myself to take up a post as Visiting Professor at Temple University, Philadelphia, for six weeks in June-August 1965 provided the opportunity for testing the value of a particular teaching method in meeting the above problem. My assignment was to teach two classes in the 'Foundations of Education' Department, one a course on educational sociology, the other on 'education and values' In view of limitations of time and space I shall refer only to the former, a class of forty students, of whom thirteen were men. The great majority were qualified teachers working for Masters degrees, with a sprinkling of undergraduates and doctoral candidates; ages ranged, approximately, from 20 to 50.

The six-week course was concerned with five major concepts. The first was that of social-class differentiation in western societies, with some of the evidence on variations of habits and attitudes from one social layer to another. Attention was given to the influence of social class on children's aspirations and achievements and the implications of these facts for teachers working in different districts.

The second concept was that of values as a binding (or divisive) force in a society for organization. This was exemplified, at the national level, by the evidence for some continuity of social criteria through American history, while at the level of immediate personal response a critical study was made of such current ideals as the 'meritocracy' and 'good human relations'.

The third theme was the classification of authority-structures in industry, based on a case-history of changes in a particular firm and some study of Burns and Stalker's 'organic' and 'mechanistic' types of organization.

Reproduced by permission from Collier 1966.

TTD-H

The fourth concept was that of planning for change and innovations, and the fifth the convergence of these principles of social analysis in the school system, with some conclusions regarding the roles of teachers in contemporary American society and the place of different patterns of authority in the school system.

The course opened with the showing of a film, 'Twelve Angry Men'. In this film Henry Fonda takes the part of a single dissentient in a jury sitting at a murder trial. As a constituent of the 'syllabus' the purpose of the film was to provide a vivid example of racial and social-class prejudice in action, together with the emergence and exercise of a particular type of authority.

The usual method of teaching such a course, whether in England or in the USA, is for the lecturer to give a series of lectures followed by plenary or small-group discussions and accompanied by various assignments of reading and writing. This was the expectation of most of the students in the class; few had experienced any alternative. Most of my own teaching in higher education has been based on this pattern. But although I think I have had some success in stimulating discussion in seminars of ten to fifteen men, I have been struck with the perennial complaints from lecturers at the difficulty they have in persuading students, not merely to argue a case but to express personal convictions and a thought-out point of view. In addition, certain experiences in other contexts, of what I shall refer to as the 'syndicate' method of organization, have impressed me with the vigour of the discussions and the personal 'involvement' of the members. One such experience was in running courses with heads of secondary schools; another was in a course for business executives run by a team from the Harvard Business School. My object at Temple University therefore was to see if the syndicate method could be adapted to the teaching of a straighforward academic course, with the reservation that if it broke down I could at once revert to my customary pattern.

## The Syndicate Method

My method was to divide the class into small groups ('syndicates') of five or six students, to carry out joint assignments based on reading, discussion and writing. I had my class daily, with a loss of two days, for periods of eighty minutes. Thus the total of 'contact hours' was thirty-seven – roughly equal to one and a half hours a week for a normal academic year.

The class was given ten assignments or 'phases'. These varied in length and type of content and were handled in several different ways. Either written or oral reports were made by one or more syndicates, which on several occasions also sat as a forum to answer questions. For the eight assignments of which written reports were handed in, I summarized these the following day in a lecture, correcting misconceptions and extending beyond the students' material in directions I regarded as important. Plenary discussions were also held at appropriate points throughout the course. A final examination of one and a half hours was set.

As I see it, one effect of several years of largely authoritarian instruction between the ages of 10 and 16 is to establish in students' minds not only an assumption that education is the imparting of information and techniques to pupils, but also certain attitudes which make it difficult for both students and lecturer to escape from the habits of instruction and memorization. (It may well be that the 'high-flyers' of English grammar schools, the potential winners of first-class and upper-second-class degrees, suffer less in this respect because their ability enables them to avoid the grind of rote-learning at O level.) The syndicate method, if efficiently used, should create a different relation between the lecturer and student and enable the student, by argument with his peers, to fortify his own ideas and interpretations before confrontation with the lecturer's authority. If assignments were suitably prepared, the student would be led to argue out the significance of the books read, in terms of the varying interpretations of the members of the group. Thus he would become more personally 'involved' with the material of the course, and in consequence work with more zest and read with more profit.

In this context the showing of the film – a very moving and well acted production – served two further purposes. It gave the members of the syndicates, who were mostly unknown to one another, a vivid shared experience as the basis of their first assignment and of a number of references in later phases. It also provided the opportunity to establish at the outset an expectation of relating the theoretical discussions in the syndicates to personal experience. This is an expectation which is often inhibited by the verbal emphasis that prevails in western educational systems.

## Assumptions and Purposes

The assumptions and purposes stated above may be set out as a series of hypotheses:

1 The dominant patterns of teaching and learning between the ages of 11 and 16 (and frequently over a considerably longer period) tend to establish two assumptions in the pupils: (a) that the main function of the educational system is to impart information and techniques to the pupils; and (b) that the characteristic relationship of teacher to student is one of command; the teacher orders the pupil to carry out various instructions, to acquire certain information, to practise certain skills.

2 The usual forms of teaching in higher education – lecture, discussion, and seminar – tend to be interpreted by the student in terms of the assumptions stated above. Efforts by teachers at this stage to prompt students to 'think for themselves', to develop a judgement and critical insight of their own, are accordingly often frustrated.

3 The effect of the syndicate form of organization is to cut across the assumptions stated in (1) since (a) the students are now placed in a situation where in the first instance they form views derived from their reading and experience and from discussion with their peers, rather than from the teacher; (b) the students form bonds within their syndicates which give them some support in the face of the teacher's authority; and (c) the relations are no longer controlled by the naked confrontation of the teacher with a number of separate individuals and can thus become more easily personal and informal.

4 By limiting the number of members in a syndicate to six the relationships that form are likely to result in the personal 'involvement' or

'commitment' of all members in the preparation of material and forming of views, and thus to create a positive concern and appreciation towards the lecturer's views. (It should perhaps be added explicitly that students' rejection or neglect of the teacher's authority *in matters of conduct and discipline* must be sharply distringuished from their attitude to his authority *in his subject.*)

5 Hence the members are likely to work with greater energy and get more satisfaction; to read with a clearer awareness of what they want to find out; to learn to express their views more effectively on academic matters; and to derive an intellectual stimulus from the clash of opinions in the small group. Hence academic knowledge should not decline, while power of judgement should improve. With this, the bearing of the academic study on new situations and personal experience, in areas appropriate to the subject matter, should be more clearly perceived.

Set out in this form, the exercise throws up a number of questions:

i *Internal relations of syndicates*
Do the syndicates exert undue pressure on individuals to conform in their views? Can individuals be catered for who do not easily work in groups? Is it possible to arrange the membership of the syndicates so as to avoid serious personal incompatabilities? How far, in the experiment described, was the personal involvement of the student (to the extent that this took place) due to the sharing of a somewhat vivid experience at the very opening

ii *External relations of syndicates*
To what extent do syndicates spontaneously compete with one another? Is this beneficial or otherwise? What are the most effective methods for feeding back into the work of the class as a whole the findings of the separate syndicates? Are there any circumstances in which a lecturer will continue to dominate the class in spite of the system of organization?

iii *Academic achievements of members*
What standard of academic knowledge was achieved during this course as compared with normal courses? To what extent did the students develop their powers of judgment and imaginative insight in this course as compared with normal courses? How are erroneous or injudicious views formed in a syndicate to be corrected? To what extent does the effectiveness of the method depend on the skill with which the assignments are designed and the readings selected? Can the syndicate reports be used for the assessment of individuals? If so, how? If not, will the quality of reports decline? To what extent can (should) one envisage syndicate organization replacing the lecture/discussion pattern as the core of a curriculum?

At the end of the course, two checks were made on the influence and effectiveness of the method. Certain questions were set in the final examination which required the interpretation of certain features of the course; and an anonymous questionnaire was answered by all students attending the penultimate day of the course, after the final examination had been sat.

The evidence collected throws light on parts of the hypotheses and on some of the questions. Findings derived from American experience are not necessarily valid in any other society; for that matter, findings derived from one lecturer's experience with one class in one university are not necessarily valid for other teachers or classes. Nevertheless, the data are of considerable interest, particularly as no discussion was given to the principles underlying the class organization until after the examination and the questionnaire had been completed. The following material, gathered from the students' answers to examination questions and to the questionnaire, is presented in relation to particular hypotheses and questions.

The two examination questions most closely concerned were:

Qu.5 Compare the influence of a syndicate on its members with the influence of an adolescent peer-group on its members, in regard to: (a) conformism; (b) integrity; (c) intellectual stimulation; (d) academic work.

Qu.6 Analyse the organization of (this course), in regard to (a) authority structure (or faculty/student relations); (b) relation of the course-work to your personal and/or professional experiences; (c) the development of an independent attitude on the part of the students to the material offered by the lecturer.

## Hypothesis 1

'Few professional courses which I have taken have actually attempted to *teach* anything. They attempt to tell the pupil. I have been *told* not to *tell* but to teach. The method in this course actually teaches. The emphasis upon individual efforts and discovery was new to me in the College classroom. Before, I and my class mates were lectured to (or at) and told to memorize the few sections of a book. In effect, we are used to having knowledge pass from the lecturer's notebook to the student's notebook without going through the mind of either. Fortunately, the organization of this course provided for discussion and lectures of summation and guidance. This was what I had always been told to do as a teacher, but I had never experienced it as a professional student.' (Student J)

## Hypothesis 3a

'The adolescent peer-group makes conformity one of the premises upon which it is built, and continues to thrive. It is essential that the teens and the group have the same likes and dislikes, otherwise they can look forward to the quiet solitude of ostracism. ...In a syndicate such as of the type used in this course, it is *not* necessary for the group to think as one. Of course, general agreement is nice, but it is not essential; no member will be ostracised if he takes a dissenting opinion from that held by the syndicate in general. ... I wouldn't say that the people in our syndicate were stubborn; they weren't. I would say that when any of us was quite certain that he (or she) was right about something, he stuck to his opinion. However, we always tried to keep open minds to empirical evidence that would either confirm our opinions more solidly, or even give valid cause for doubting them.' (Student HE)

'When we 'hashed' over a question in our syndicate, there was always someone (usually me) who didn't agree with the group. This gave me a chance to express my views as opposed to the others. There wasn't the usual conformity one finds in the other classes – here we were in small groups 'hammering' out answers to specific leading questions. And we were able to raise questions about other groups as well .....' (Student HO)

'The organization of this course has provided for the development of individual attitudes since group work was provided. Individuals could be free to express themselves and freely choose what material they wanted to read. The groups could divide the material presented and later bring it together after careful consideration by individual members. Since the quantity of the material covered such a wide scope, independent attitudes almost had to emerge as different members would experience different books and personal experience.' (Student J)

'This course, more so than most, demands independent thinking on the part of each student. As the material was offered by the lecturer, by reference reading and by group reports, there was a need to analyse our personal attitudes, beliefs, values, etc., and then to evaluate and constantly re-evaluate these attitudes, beliefs, and values. ... Also, as conflicting reference material came forth and conflicting views arose in the class, independent thinking and then independent attitude was naturally the resultant.' (Student Y)

## Hypothesis 3b and c

Question 3 of the questionnaire asked: 'Do you consider that the relations formed between lecturer and students during this method of working differ in any way from those formed during a lecture/discussion course?' To this question eighteen students replied that they thought that relations were 'closer' or 'more personal' ('the lecturer got to know us better as individuals'; 'I feel this syndicate method created a warmer feeling between teacher and students'), while six said the relations were about the same and thirteen made various other comments.

'Here again I feel that class developed their own attitudes concerning the material. This seemed evident in the freedom of expression that was frequent. There was disagreement, yes, but again in what seemed a good academic climate.' (Student B)

'In this course I believe that we have an organic...authority structure. We have a leader who co-ordinates our work and guides our thinking and planning, yet the hierachy has become blurred as in an organic structure. We are, therefore, allowed much individual or small group autonomy which in Thelan's thinking makes for a good authority set-up. Also along Thelan's line of reasoning, the leader interrupts this autonomy only when it is in danger of becoming erratic. There is good rapport with the group and their leader and thus a good climate for productive work has been established. ... In my way of thinking (the professor's) statement about an independent attitude on the part of the students to the material offered by the lecturer would pertain to the rather autonomous situation under which we have worked in this course. In other words, we are not bound only to the lectures, but we have an opportunity to do individual research. The condition, I would think, is very conducive to a good climate of intellectual activity.' (Student SE)

'The way in which ideas and concepts were exchanged during class periods is an example of organic organization. The free interchange of ideas in syndicates is the best example of this. This group work fosters inter-dependence and smooth relations, and in this fashion exemplifies how a group organization can foster participation.' (Student J)

'Definitely the lecturer was the primary authority. ...(He) became a sort of 'guide' to the students. ...He delegated work to be done by his subordinates (students). But here information was able to go up, down, sideways, and in all directions – for assimilation.' (Student HO)

## Hypothesis 4

'Much of the class time was spent in small group discussion to which the members of the group developed loyalty (this was expressed by members of our syndicate) and felt a responsibility to do their part and even to explore further books and relate class work to work previously taken. As a result an independent attitude was developed by many of the students who went out and purchased some of the suggested books or read part of them in the library, going beyond the minimum standards set by the professor and the group.' (Student C)

'When one works alone he may tend to procrastinate some of his school work, but because everyone else did their work, no one wanted to feel badly by not doing his.' (Student D)

'The syndicate as a whole feels that academic work must be completed in the best possible manner. It is felt by members of the group that a sloppy job will reflect back onto the whole syndicate, and that the syndicate will feel that the person who did the sloppy job had let them down. For this reason, most syndicate work, even if done individually is superior to plain individual work.' (Student F)

## Hypothesis 5

(a) *Hard Work*. Two questions from the questionnaire are relevant. Question 4 read 'Do you consider that you have worked harder/less hard/about the same as in a lecture/discussion course?' Twenty-two replied 'harder' and two 'less hard', while thirteen said 'about the same' or were undecided. A number of those who replied 'harder' added something to the effect that 'it seemed less hard because of the circumstances'. Another question asking whether members had derived more or less satisfaction from the course than the normal lecture/discussion course, or about the same, gave twenty-one reporting 'more', eleven 'less', and five other responses. Taken together these figures suggest that the students worked harder on account of their involvement with the group and its work but felt less pressure and more satisfaction on account of the correlated improvement in motivation.

(b) *Effective use of books*. Question 5 in the questionnaire read 'Do you consider that you have used books more or less effectively or about the same?' Replies were: 'more' twenty-five; 'same' ten; 'less' two. One respondent commented, 'at first it was as I usually did – but now I am much more critical and seem to know what to look for'.

(c) *Intellectual stimulus*. 'This group...has stimulated all of us intellectually. So many more ideas and concepts are brought out when discussing in an informal situation than being alone to think or in a large group. ...Someone was always there to refute or elaborate on someone else's ideas in a frank, positive, manner.' (Student B)

'There was so much more information gotten, talked over, argued out. ... Our syndicate may not have had the most 'ability' in the class, but we sure achieved as much as was possible. ...So this experience into group work (and my first sociology course) was a real awakening.' (Student HO)

'Members of syndicates, by working together, learnt more and, in my own case, worked harder than if the course had been organized in an autocratic manner.' (Student J)

'Intellectual stimulation within the syndicate is exceedingly high. This is due to the cross-exchange of ideas, debate, and the attempt to reach a conclusion. Members are willing to volunteer information, read and discuss in order to gain increased insight into material at hand. ...We are attempting to reach a goal and there is co-ordination and co-operation within the syndicate.' (Student L)

'Lipset's work was a catalyst for much of my thinking. This entire course has triggered in me a want and motivation for research, references, and critical thinking, which is developing for the first time.' (Student DR)

(d) *Academic achievement, with question C*. Question 1a in the questionnaire asked, 'Do you consider that you gained more or less from the syndicate method of working than from the usal lecture/discussion course, or about the same, in regard to academic content?' The replies were 'more' fourteen; 'same' fifteen; and 'less' eight. The following is a relevant comment from the examination answers.

'Because of the positive aspects of our syndicate, we felt we produced much more than had we answered the same questions on our own. The academic work we did was of a higher degree because we worked together; stimulating and motivating each other as we went along.' (Student D)

## Questions of Management

One more of the more refractory problems is that of reporting back. For various reasons several different methods were used. On the two occasions when every syndicate handed in a written report on an assignment the work was covered very thoroughly but a considerable number of man-hours were spent on writing and typing and it would certainly have been quite impracticable to cover the ground of this particular course if every syndicate had produced a report on every phase, given that most students dispersed at the end of the class for other commitments. With three phases written reports were handed in by two syndicates which also, after I had summarized the reports in a lecture, acted as a forum for a plenary discussion. In three further phases there were two oral reports followed by a plenary session with forum. In one case a single syndicate made a written report and in another an oral report, serving afterwards as a forum. A question in the questionnaire on methods of reporting showed seventeen individuals expressing a preference for one or two syndicates handing in a written report; of these, seven suggested that these syndicates should also report orally. Eight preferred written reports by all; seven asked that all syndicates should prepare oral reports on every assignment. I had the impression personally that if two syndicates were reporting on a topic they tended to vie with each other in thoroughness, and this seemed a valid incentive. If, however, only two syndicates are reporting, a possibility arises that the other syndicates may not prepare the assignment in sufficient detail to learn from the two that have specialized in that phase of the material. There is undoubtedly room for further experiment here.

Another question that needs attention is that of assessment. In these courses I based the final grade on the performance in the final examination, modified in the light of contributions to the plenary discussion and to various syndicate discussions I happened to attend. Some students complained (in the anonymous questionnaire) that the syndicate reports should also have been taken into account. A more serious question is that of the criteria by which the students are assessed. A few individuals remarked that this was the point at which the course became authoritarian and the final decision rested firmly, yet without unambiguous published standards, in the hands of the lecturer. The situation was made more difficult for the students by the very fact that more than once I castigated the fact-mongers and stressed the importance of judgement and insight. I made a point of explaining the basis of every criticism that I made on the syndicate reports. But clearly this was inadequate. In an English college of education I have made a practice of reading scripts of different quality to students with an explanation of the way in which grades have been awarded. Discussion amongst examiners for post-O Level work in the humanities often reveals the unsureness of the criteria at work, once one has got away from actual correctness. A major question lies here (Collier 1962).

## Acknowledgment

I would like to express my thanks to Prof. J. E. McClellan and to my students at Temple University for their ready co-operation.

# 22

# Syndicate Methods

*K. Gerald Collier*

An article by the present author was published in 1966 on an experiment in
the use of 'syndicate' methods, conducted by him in an American university
(see Ch.21). Since that time evidence of disaffection or 'alienation' among
students in higher education has become widespread and irrefutable. The fact
that the primary purpose of a student's occupation is study suggests that
disaffection may be connected with unsatisfactory courses of study, and the
rather thin evidence supports this view. It seems likely that formal lectures,
and seminars of the German type, presume a high degree of motivation in the
student; they are not designed to generate involvement and often have little
influence on personal motivation. The generalization is not well supported by
evidence, since unless viable alternatives are available investigators are
scarcely likely to spend time and money measuring involvement. With the
primary object, therefore, of exploring further the potential of 'syndicate'
methods for generating involvement, the present author conducted additional
experiments during the six-week summer session at Temple University,
Philadelphia, USA, in 1968.

Two classes were involved, the first on 'Introductory sociology of
education' and the second on 'Discrimination of values in education'. The
students numbered thirty-one and thirty respectively and were mainly
practising teachers working for a Masters degree in education. Ages ranged
between 22 and 50.

In addition to the above material the author has also been concerned with
experiments on the use of syndicate methods in teaching religious knowledge
to students in a college of education (Bede College, Durham) and some
material from this source will also be used. In particular a small group of four
students met, in October 1968, the present author and the lecturer concerned
in the experiments of 1966-7, to look back at the impressions that had been
received. This will be referred to as the 'recall' group.

The pattern of work has been the following. The class has been divided into
six 'syndicates' of five to six students and the syndicates have been provided
with assignments consisting of three to four questions with appropriate, quite
specific, references. The members of a syndicate distribute the reading

Reproduced by permission from Collier 1969.

between them and use the lecture periods for discussing the views that emerge and building these into a written report on the assignment. Dissenting opinions may well be included. The lecturer summarizes the reports in a formal lecture, extending and amending where necessary, and following with a plenary discussion. Assignments of special importance in the course are worked by all syndicates; others are worked by two or three syndicates on behalf of the class as a whole. During the syndicate discussions the lecturer circulates among the syndicates. In a course of twenty-six sessions of one hour twenty minutes most syndicates have completed six assignments. (This is not the only way of organizing syndicate work but it is the form the present author has found most effective in bringing about the desired academic motivation.)

The main lines of argument and report were set out in the article of June 1966; the present paper brings forward additional evidence and raises further questions.

## Students' Satisfaction

Questions given to the two Temple classes asked whether the student 'had gained more or less from the syndicate method of working than from the usual lecture/discussion course, or about the same', in terms of 'satisfaction', 'stimulus to thinking', 'personal interest in the subject', and 'meaningfulness of an academic course'. The replies showed, respectively, forty-three 'more', three 'same', seven 'less'; fifty-one 'more', one 'same', four 'less'; forty-four 'more', six 'same', five 'less'; thirty-six 'more', eight 'same', ten 'less.' These figures support the results obtained in the 1965 experiments and are strongly supported by the personal impressions gained during the class work itself, where the intensity of involvement is often astonishing to staff or students who have not previously experienced it. This view is also powerfully supported by the recall group, among whom one remarked 'I would defy any normal student to go through this work without getting involved'. They remarked also on the intellectual stimulus received. Distinctions need to be made between the involvement, the satisfaction, the intellectual stimulus and so on, and indeed the questionnaire is open to various criticisms, but the prima facie case is unanswerable. However, problems and anomalies remain (some of which are mentioned later in this article) and further investigation is needed.

## Active and Passive Languages

A subjective impression worth recording is that students working in this way write more cogently than in the normal courses, and the recall group felt much the same. They considered that clarification was much better achieved in peer-groups than in seminars. It may be that this is due to the students having assimilated more effectively into their own personal thinking the material they have read, and thus that engagement in the syndicate discussions results in a more vigorous translation of book material into their own 'active language', ie into terms of their own vocabulary, of their own experience, of the shared concerns of the syndicate. If so, this could be a valuable by-product of the method. It could also, however, lead to more frequent misinterpretation of the book material. In any case the matter needs investigating.

## Integration of Curriculum

Much is spoken and written about the need to integrate the different parts of the curriculum and many ambitious projects have been launched. Unfortunately most of these neglect the indispensable condition, that students should find themselves obliged, by the nature of their exercises, to make the cross-references and cross-comparisons which lead to integration *within their own minds*. In all the experiments of syndicate work here recorded it has been found practicable from time to time to juxtapose readings from very contrasted sources, and thus to build into the discussion, and into the students' thinking, the integration of varied material. Although the topics handled in these courses were not designed for this particular purpose, the experience suggests that this approach to the organization of studies may have special significance for inter-disciplinary courses. (The recall group thought that the varied backgrounds of the syndicate members had produced a similar effect). General studies curricula have never made much headway in English universities, and are rather widely questioned in American universities, but the increasing concern over excessive specialization in England may well lead to a search for effective modes of inter-disciplinary integration and in this context syndicate methods may be very useful.

## The Gap between the Generations

A frequent complaint among students over recent years has been the irrelevance of the material offered by lecturers, to the students' outlook and concerns. In part this has been due to the highly specialized nature of the usual academic curriculum. But in part it is due to inadequate 'feedback' from students to lecturers. One of the significant features of the syndicate approach is that the lectures themselves derive from the reports of the syndicates. It is true that the assignments and the readings may be subject to the charge of irrelevance, and indeed the phraseology and concepts of the lecture. Nevertheless the element of 'feedback' is built into the system and it is impossible for the lecturer whose eyes and ears are open to remain unaware of the concepts and difficulties of these students. The recall group again corroborated this comment on their work.

## Relation to other Types of Small Group Work

A fair amount of experiment has been conducted in recent years on the organization of small groups in higher education. Field work, for example, has been carried out on a small group basis in various subjects – geographical, sociological, education, biological. Groups have been of various sizes. In such cases, however, the work carried out has rarely been tightly related to systematic academic studies; it is essentially illustrative of a few general principles and thus forms only a small fraction of the work entailed in the course.

Some tutorial work also is conducted with groups from one to four students. Here the groups do not have the degree of independence possessed by the syndicates. Not that this is total independence; but it enables these students to work out their views in very large part before they hear those of the lecturer.

The experiments here described appear to be distinctive in uniting a considerable degree of independence for the groups with a systematic course of academic study.

## Composition of Groups

In the 1965 experiments few adjustments were called for in the membership of the groups, which were based partly on the previous acquaintance of some members of the classes and partly on the accident of seating. In the 1968 experiments there were four groups (out of the twelve) where some degree or other of difficulty was experienced. One was in the sociological course and three in the 'values' course, and it may be that the material of the latter tended to accentuate temperamental or emotional differences between members of the class. The point, however, remains that not all groups work effectively together at once; they may need quite a lot of assistance and encouragement. In small group work with children sociometric tests have been very useful for grouping children already known to one another, and the recall group noted that students were already acquainted. The university students in the Temple classes had not met before. It may be that some kind of preliminary acquaintance is needed. Even at that there can be no guarantee that the individual joins the group which would for him be most stimulating and rewarding. Clearly, further experiment is needed.

## Assessment

In the 1965 experiment it was taken for granted that the final examination was entirely in the hands of the lecturer, and a few students, in their final comments, noted the inconsistency between the continual open interchange and collaboration of lecturer with students during the course and the absoluteness of his judgment and authority in the final examination. In the 1968 experiments the question was raised by the lecturer and explicitly discussed. It seemed impracticable to record individual grades for the syndicate work but the lecturer agreed to state the grade level of the reports, with his reasons, and to circulate specimen questions, in order that students might appreciate his criteria of judgment. These criteria still, however, remained his own, and this responsibility seems inescapable.

Yet a certain uneasiness remains. It was not practicable to permit books to be brought to the examination room, as many of the books used had circulated on loan. The recall group thought that the situation would be greatly eased if every individual had to write one or two essays during the course for (say) half his final assessment. But the real problem lies in the absoluteness of the lecturer's authority as examiner. In the development of human societies absolute authority has usually been tempered by the sharing of the authority with elected representatives. Is it indispensable for the examiner's authority to be unchallengeable?

## The Spectrum of Teaching and Learning Methods

It may be supposed from these two reports on syndicate work, that this method is being presented as a panacea. This is not so. At the present time the formal lecture and the group discussion (of one tutor with ten to fifteen students) are generally regarded as the standard methods of teaching in higher education. Individual tutorials are used intensively in a few institutions. Closed-circuit telvision is now not merely enlarging the audience but making practicable both the wider utilization of persons with a flair for exposition and the improvement of their presentation through the expertise of a 'Learning Resources' centre. Programmed instruction is greatly extending the scope and effectiveness of private study and the organization of field work is increasingly based on the independent action of small well-briefed groups.

But none of these methods make adequate provision for *generating motivation and involvement in relation to systematic academic studies*. It is in this respect that syndicate work appears to have a vital part to play. It also seems to have a useful potential in certain other areas discussed in this paper.

Even, however, within this framework of thought about methods of learning and teaching, it may well emerge that many individuals find some methods more congenial and more effective than others. Many students find syndicate methods little short of a revelation; others are not happy in them. What is needed in all branches of higher education is a full spectrum of teaching styles and a tutorial or counselling system which will enable students to find the courses that best meet their needs.

# 23

# Introduction to Case Discussion

## The Main Features of the Case Study Method

In the case study method students are presented with a real-life, or realistic, practical situation. It is usually complex and frequently requires knowledge from several disciplines. In this it contrasts with a great deal of academic teaching where only simplified or theoretical examples are considered. Complexity is minimized. Yet 'on-the-job' situations are frequently complex. Hence there is a place for the case study method in most forms of vocational training.

There are two common kinds of case: those requiring a decision or consideration of an issue; and those needing an appraisal, evaluation or judgement. Decision cases usually pose a problem and demand consideration of alternatives before a decision is taken. In appraisal cases students are often required to evaluate the wisdom of a decision already taken.

## The Objectives of the Case Study Method

There are no objectives that only case study method can achieve but it is particularly valuable in teaching professional skills such as those required in medicine, teaching, social work, law, engineering, management and business studies. It is particularly relevant to teaching decison-making in an inter-personal context. These professional skills include:

1 Analysis of a complex case (and this will be considered in more detail in Chapter 25).
2 Evaluation and judgement.
3 Personal involvement.
4 Selection of evidence.
5 Recogniton that some evidence is missing or required, and this includes asking pertinent questions.
6 Handling information, including the possible use of statistical techniques or other calculations.
7 The ability to defend ones' judgement against criticism.
8 Powers of criticism, yet appreciation of the viewpoints of others.
9 The case study method can also be used to harness the expertise of group members. This is particularly relevant on in-service courses or when

there are mature students. Where there is varied experience it is a method that may be used for students with contrasting levels of ability. Its practical relevance makes it one of the more rewarding methods for students.

# The Teacher's Skill when using Case Studies

A case may be presented to individual students, to one or more groups of students without the continuous presence of a tutor, or to a class or group led by the teacher. Indeed two or more of these techniques may be used in the order mentioned. Preliminary individual consideration fosters personal involvement and subsequent motivation. The importance of each student arriving at his own personal opinion should be emphasized. The fact that the case study method may or may not employ the continuous presence of the teacher shows its transitional position between a tutorless and tutored discussion groups. Clearly the presence of a teacher will make a big difference to how students behave. The skill of the teacher is to minimize this difference. This is not easy.

A second major teaching skill lies in how the case is presented. There can be few general rules for him to follow. It is usually advisable to give students some warning of what will be expected from them. It may be better to start with a small case not requiring lengthy discussion or delicate handling. The information needs to be presented either clearly or realistically. These may not be the same thing. While clarity may be more important while students are learning how to study cases, realism will probably be more important later.

One of the most difficult teaching skills in the case study method is the preparation of case material. For this reason the next paper (Chapter 24), adapted from a note by Robert T. Davis, gives some suggestions.

Davis's suggestions were written with reference to business administration: the reader should translate terms to suit his own circumstances. For example for 'executive' or 'manager' may substituted the name of any decision maker – social worker, doctor, teacher, engineer, designer, etc. In most cases the 'reader' is a 'student'.

The observations and suggestions on preparation to teach a case (Chapter 25) are summarized from a memorandum 'Case instruction for the beginning instructor' by Robert Merry. He assumes both that the teacher is always present during case discussion and that he has a very controlling role. Keegan's advice is for students, but it may also help teachers new to case study methods to picture the way their students could work rather than concentrating on their own role.

# 24

# Some Suggestions for Writing a Business Case

*Robert T. Davis*

## Sorting out the Parts

...Effective writing is hard; it requires tedious, careful work. And this generalization applies to writing business cases as it does to writing novels or company reports. In my experience a good case often goes through three, four, or even five rewritings before it is acceptable. Unfortunately, there is no alternative to effective writing other than practice in writing itself. This is indeed a tiring and exacting experience.

### Getting the Facts in Mind

Let us consider three basic questions ordinarily involved in the planning stages of writing a case:

    a What is the major case issue?
    b What are all the pertinent facts needed...to reach a decision?
    c What additional information [should a student (the reader)] require to analyse the issue?

### What is the Major Issue?

Before preparing his initial outline the writer should know exactly the issue or the problem that must be solved. As evident as this first step may appear, many poor cases are prepared because the writer has not fully understood the fundamental issue. The result is a case without direction, filled with superfluous data, and as useful to the reader as a Tibetan yak.

    Closely related to this step of problem identification is that of recognizing the subordinate issues bearing upon the primary question. For example, in a hypothetical case involving the problem of training company salesmen there might be such secondary, though related problems as:

   a A core of 'old-time' salesmen unwilling to be trained.
   b A financial limitation that limits the scope of any training programme.
   c A group of field sales managers presently incapable of training salesmen because they are primarily 'supersalesmen' themselves.

Unless these sub-problems are presented, the reader cannot expect to analyse the problem effectively or make any useful recommendations.

## What Facts Does the Decision Maker Need?

Probably the writer's most difficult problem is that of including all of the relevant data that the decision maker concerned would have at his disposal. And, as indicated earlier, there are many other facts that may not be as pertinent but which would be included if the case were to be realistic. But how does the writer know whether his presentation is complete? The only test is that of asking yourself this question: Does the reader have the information needed for a 'self-contained' case analysis?

The essential facts may be presented in various ways. For instance the writer may include such vital statistics as the sales and profit figures, the number and kind of salesmen, the makeup of the product line, the specifics of the market, and the competition. Other pertinent facts, depending upon the major problem, may be non-statistical. Some cases require detailed information about various executives and other people in the organization. Other cases call for data pertaining to company policies and past experiences.

Regardless of the proper 'mix', the case writer must include whatever material will make the situation as complete for the reader as it was for the business executive.

As good a method as any for correctly identifying the pertinent facts is to think in terms of the specific major and minor issues. Case material should be gathered and presented in terms of these issues so that each issue has 'around it' a set of related facts. Thus, to use our earlier illustration, if one of the subordinate problems in the training of salesmen relates to company finances, the case writer will want to include balance sheets and profit and loss statements.

## Other Information Needed by the Student

The case writer must include more than 'the facts important to the decison maker involved' because most students will have no specialized knowledge. Most students discussing a case are outsiders. For example a student has none of the background information that a business executive takes for granted. So to his first list of relevant facts, the case writer will add enough background material to bring his reader into the company environment.

It is not easy to distinguish between facts needed by the decision maker and background data needed by the outside observer. If the case writer himself is an outsider he can usually tell what is missing by trying to analyse the case. But, if the writer is a company executive, he must consider the supplementary material to be included with care.

Certain common background material comes immediately to mind for this writer, although such material does not constitute an exhaustive list. Generally, however, I would want to know something about the company, its location, its products, its competition, its history, its organization (at least in brief), and perhaps its prospects. Without such fundamental knowledge I could not think constructively about any specific operating problem, no matter how limited in scope.

So much for the prewriting aspect of case presentation. Now what about the nagging question, 'How do I present material?'

# Getting the Facts on Paper

…It seems to me there are several specific points worth considering when we talk about that elusive technique called 'presentation'. I would like now to concentrate on eight of these points.

## Starting the Case

Although practitioners do not all agree, it would appear reasonable that the case writer start his case with a statement of the problem. Such an introduction does several things. Not only does it whet the reader's appetite and made him want to read more, but it gives the reader a point of reference to which he can relate the rest of the case. This early 'sense of direction' will give meaning to what follows and, we hope, provide the reader with the initial stimulation for later problem analysis. A good case will 'sell itself', a poor one will kill whatever motivation the reader may have had.

## Providing the Background

Having aroused initial interest, the writer will probably find it best to launch next a description of the company, its products and markets, any pertinent history, and perhaps the organization. By making such a presentation early in the game, the writer helps the reader to learn the important background information before worrying about the details of the major issue. The easiest mistake for the case writer to make at this point is that of overwriting. A balance is needed between informing the reader and putting him to sleep. It is essential, therefore, that the case writer beware of the temptation to let his words run away from him during this 'background' phase of the writing. Intelligent brevity is a valuable asset.

## Introducing the Significant Facts

We have discussed the problems of accumulating data relative to the major and secondary issues in the case. Effective presentation of these data requires that the case writer group his facts into some kind of logical order. Because this grouping depends upon the nature of the problem, there can be no 'always applicable' outline plan. I have found the generous use of subheadings throughout the text to be helpful to myself and to the reader. Thus, in one case relating to the compensation of salesmen, I made use of the following subheadings: Introduction, The Company and its Products, The Field Sales Organization, The Saleman's Job, Performance of the Salesmen, Compensation Alternatives. Such an outline is relevant, of course, to but one particular case; but perhaps it will suggest a technique you might use profitably.

In some cases, effective presentation is built around the chronology of events. The reader, in these instances, is carried along from the past to the present and then left with the current problem.

There is one weakness, nonetheless, to a rigidly structured case. Such a case tends to steer the reader too drastically, giving him a sense of sureness not at all available to the original [decision maker]. Direction of this kind, moreover, may imply to the reader that there is but one acceptable solution to the problem – in fact the very pointedness of the case almost dictates the 'required' reasoning. As a consequence, some case teachers prefer a very loose case, reminiscent of the writings of James Joyce. Again, to be practical, it would seem wisest that we concentrate here on the structured or carefully organized case presentation.

## Personal Opinions of the Case Writer

How easy it is for the case writer to intersperse his case with personal opinions. But such writing is misleading and hardly useful to the student. Watch out, therefore, as a *reporter of facts* that you do not become an editorial writer. It is the function of the case writer to present the situation, not to interpret it or pass judgment upon it.

For example, if I were to write a case and say such things as 'the company's products were not well suited to the market', 'the salesmen were generally good performers'; then I would be writing personal opinions. But it is another matter if I reported; 'The manager considered the treasurer to be an egotistical boor.' Opinions expressed by the executives (and other company employees) may be highly significant and should ordinarily be included.

## Past or Present Tense

Generally, it has been our experience that cases are better written in the past than in the present tense. Thus, instead of saying that 'the company manufactures and distributes automatic extenders which it sells through jobbers,' we would write that 'the company manufactured and distributed automatic extenders which it sold through jobbers.'

There are two reasons for this widespread use of the past tense. The company is somewhat protected from censure if the practices described are not implied to be current. And the teaching life of a case is lengthened if the material is not assumed to be completely 'last minutes.' As a result the student can concentrate on his major task of analysis, whether the problem is current or not.

## Length of a Case

I know of no hard and fast rule relating to the proper length of a case. I have seen them range from a single page to well over 200 pages – the latter being as hard on the instructor as it is on the reader. But as a rule of thumb, much like the banker's traditional working capital ratio of two to one, I would draw a line somewhere between eight and ten pages. If a case runs over ten pages, it has been my experience that the reader does not do an effective job of decision-making. An appraisal case, to be sure, might run longer than ten pages. An issue case, however, seems to diminish in effectiveness as it grows in length.

## The Inclusion of Statistics

Because facts and figures are ordinarily essential to proper case analysis, we cannot leave them out of the presentation. If not handled properly, however, data of this kind may clutter up the main presentation and hinder the reader's analysis.

Ordinarily, statistical data should be presented in table or chart form, with the tables and charts numbered consecutively. the writer can place these exhibits in the body of the text or separately at the end of the case. The latter technique is probably more common. Whichever procedure is followed, however, the writer should refer specifically to these exhibits at appropriate places throughout the text.

If there is additional material, somewhat apart from the main body of the case or too long for inclusion in the text, the writer may include such material as appendices (numbered by letter from A).

## The Company's Solution to the Problem

Finally, in an issue case, the writer should not ordinarily include the company's solution to the problem. Indeed, this is the major task for the reader. On the other hand, should the company have considered several possible alternatives (before deciding upon a course of action) the writer might well list all these possible solutions without tipping his hand as to what the company actually did. But do not list alternatives that have no relation to the case facts already presented. If you find that some of your alternatives seem to come 'out of the blue', then the chances are that you have omitted some important background material, in your earlier presentation.

In addition to diluting the reader's own analysis, the inclusion of the company's solution implies that the company made the correct decision. Such an assumption may be unfounded.

# Proofing the Case

And now we come to the final stage of case writing, that of proofing the case. Did we do as fine a job as we think? The ultimate test will come when the case is assigned to a group of students and then discussed. This can be a sobering experience. Before that ultimate test, however, you should go through a few simple steps that may give you more peace of mind.

First, read the case aloud and ask yourself, 'Does the case read well and clearly?' You can pick up lots of your writing faults by subjecting your material to this oral treatment.

Next you must ask yourself, 'As an outsider, could I make an intelligent recommendation based upon my presentation of the situation?' In effect, you want to know if the case is really a replica of the situation faced by the business executive. If certain facts are missing, that is all right, provided the executive himself did not have these facts at his disposal. The surest way, at this point, to satisfy this question of completeness is to write out your own analysis of the problem. Then you can compare your recommendations (and reasons for reaching them) with the facts in the case.

And finally, but by no means least, we come to the question of company release. Will the company allow this case, in its present form, to be used for educational purposes? It has been my experience that most companies are quite willing to have many of their problems written up, provided, of course, that a major executive reads and corrects the final draft. In reality, this problem of release is taken up with the company at the time the case writer initiates his field work. If there is any hesitation at this introductory stage, I would not attempt to pursue the case writing any further.

Many times a case will be released if it is properly disguised. Accordingly, if faced with such a problem you can make whatever name and setting disguises are appropriate. Figures may be changed by applying some constant 'fudging' factor, such as 1.3 or 2.1. Disguised cases are seldom, if ever, less useful than undisguised cases. The primary consideration with a disguised case is to keep the important relationships unchanged so that the reader has the opportunity of learning from the business experience just as the original executive did when he first tackled the problem.

# 25

# Preparation to Teach a Case

*Robert W. Merry*

To any case method instructor the importance of his preparation for class is fully apparent. To the new teacher, however, it may come as something of a surprise that his task in preparing for a case class is more arduous than that of the students and more arduous also than that of a lecturer. If he were lecturing, the teacher would be the one to determine what material he would present and in what order he would present it. In embracing the case method, however, he has surrendered his sovereignty and yet undertaken to maintain control over the discussion. It would be a mistake for the new teacher to assume that he had only to read and reread the case and then go into class and ask one or two leading questions. Rather he must be so thoroughly conversant with the case that he is ready to deal with any angles which the class may introduce, to modify his approach at any time, or suddenly to change his outline in accordance with new ideas which may not previously have occurred to him.

Case teaching is a highly individualistic art, and the methods and approaches of one teacher seldom can successfully be appropriated by another. Every seasoned teacher develops an approach of his own. Each new teacher has to do likewise, and there are no general rules for him to follow. The teacher about to teach a case class for the first time, however, may be slightly at a loss as to what form his preparation should take.

The first step in the teacher's preparation of a case is to master the facts. The teacher needs to go over the printed case again and again, making outlines, marginal notes, and written summaries of essential details. If there are figures in the case, he will make many calculations, not only the ones which he himself believes to be correct but also others, which he anticipates that the students may put forward as appropriate and significant. He will scrutinize the apparent issues to make sure that they are the real ones. And if there are important subordinate issues, he will recognize that some questions probably will have to be settled before others. He may find it helpful to develop a conceptual framework which will show how the several pieces of the puzzle fit together.

Up to this point, the teacher's work on the case has roughly paralleled that

Adapted by permission from Merry 1954.

of the students. The task has been to acquire a thorough familiarity with the facts, the figures, and the issues. Now the teacher may find it advisable to make a fresh start. In some instances he will at this stage need to consider the specific learning objectives toward which he wishes to point the case discussion. And here some appraisal outline is appropriate. With an eye on the position of the particular case in the course outline, the teacher may wish to lead the students to emphasize some issues more than others. Also as a specific aspect of this consciousness of a course outline there is the frequent desirability of providing a transition from the case discussed at the preceding class meeting.

After these preliminaries the teacher needs to view the case itself as a whole, assessing it in terms of the principal areas for exploration and discussion, considering the relation of one to another and devising key questions to lead into each of them. He may wish to give considerable care to the wording of these questions. By foreseeing the various avenues of connection the teacher can be better prepared to effect transitions from one issue to another, as well as to guide the class into the critical areas for discussion.

Next he will note the answers that the class probably will offer to these key questions on the basis of the materials in the case, and the reasonable answers he will follow to their logical conclusion. Where weighing of considerations is involved, he will list the pros and cons and undertake to balance them. And in each area he will make the pertinent mathematical calculations. By these means he will develop what may be termed a teaching outline, which probably will differ markedly from his initial analysis of facts and figures and which may well cover several pages of foolscap.

In the classroom the teacher who is teaching by the case method for the first time may be inclined to adhere closely to this detailed teaching outline. He has put a great deal of thought into developing a programme for the class meeting, he has followed through all the lines of argument which he thinks the students may reasonably offer, and he is pretty well convinced that the class discussion ought logically to develop according to his script. If the discussion should deviate from the course which he has laid out, he will be tempted to try, by narrow and specific questions, to set it back on the path in order to make sure that every point in his outline is accorded proper consideration.

In actuality, rigid adherence to a predetermined line of development may make for a discussion notably lacking in freshness and spontaneity. If, as they are put forward by the class, arguments and observations on the case are forced into the teacher's own outline, the students may soon be deterred from presenting an independent development of the case. To narrow questions they will give narrow answers, and the quality of the discussion will deteriorate rapidly.

After he has experienced the disappointing class discussion which results from an attempt at rigid control, the new teacher may resort to a procedure which involves almost no control. He will put to the class at the outset the major question to be discussed and will permit the students to bring up whatever points they choose, in whatever order they see fit. This procedure also entails difficulties. There is the danger that several important aspects of the major issue of a case may be overlooked if the students move on too rapidly to another issue. The discussion of one issue may be superficial or unsound because its development depends on another issue which has not yet been discussed. The treatment of points at random, following no logical system or pattern, is likely to have the result that at the end of the hour a student has no clear concept of an appropriate analysis of the case.

Something between these two extremes of tight control and no control at all is ordinarily called for. And the new teacher may find that he can most readily achieve this objective if he can free himself from close reliance on his notes. Having worked out his detailed teaching outline, he may do well to put it aside in favour of a mere list of the critical areas – such a list as may fit on an index card or two, which the teacher may glance at during the class hour simply to make certain that no important areas have been slighted. For the details of development he will rely on the thoroughness of his own preparation.

The teacher's preparation frequently will need to go beyond the bounds of the case itself. Many cases include a considerable body of technical detail, which may relate to an industry, a process, a machine, an institution, an instrument, or the like. Usually enough facts are given to convey the significant data. Sometimes, however, student request more information; and they may ask for an explanation of terms used in the case which are not clear to them. The teacher needs to anticipate student questions of this type and to make provision for them, certainly by taking steps to become well informed himself and also, wherever possible, by arranging for showings of industrial movies or for demonstrations, or by making available for inspection the items of merchandise or pieces of equipment which are under discussion.

In planning his strategy the new teacher ought not to overlook the potentialities of the chalkboard as a teaching aid. He will turn to it naturally to set down figures. But he will find it useful also for such things as listing the pros and cons brought out by the class, or jotting down notes as to major areas for discussion, or developing steps in a programme of action to carry out a decision. When analysis of a case entails calculations, these very probably will need to be put on the board. Ideally the teacher will proceed by getting the students to tell him what figures to write, not by standing at the board and transcribing his own computations. But it will help him to make a quick mental verification if he has his own calculations before him. Hence he will do well to have with him the papers on which he has done his figuring. He may wish also to put on the board, as they are brought up in class, a series of headings which will indicate the major areas of discussion. These need not conform precisely to the teacher's own outline, but they are likely to approximate the headings noted at some point in his outline. Hence it may be useful for the teacher to devote some care to the phrasing in his own notes, and perhaps to underline in red the principal captions in the list to which he has reduced his teaching outline.

Among the papers which he carries to class the teacher may also want to include some notes from which to make a summary at the close of the class hour. Generally, however, the teacher should not be dependent on his notes.

In a course which has previously been taught according to the case method, or in a large course divided into sections and taught by several teachers, the notes of other teachers persumably will be available. After he has completed his independent preparation of the case, the new teacher may find it reassuring to refer to these. They may suggest fresh lines of approach or new ideas, and to this extent they will be useful. The new teacher may also achieve a feeling of greater self-confidence if he talks over the case with other teachers. The point can scarcely be overemphasized, however, that no teacher, under the case method, can effectively substitute another's notes for his own. Experience suggests also that notes prepared in an earlier year cannot be re-used intact. Fresh preparation is essential each time. Old notes are useful for reference, and they may serve to recall to mind certain calculations which need reworking or certain difficulties which developed on an earlier occasion. But modifications will almost always suggest themselves, and fresh study and new analysis are essential each time the case comes up.

Nevertheless, for purposes of facilitating future use of the case, the teacher may find it advantageous to develop the habit of jotting down some notes as soon as possible after the end of the class hour, touching such matters as any corrections needed in the case, possible changes in the appended questions, new lines of thought or different methods of calculation brought out by students, a possible change in the position in the outline, and so on. Such notes should be included in the case folder, to be reviewed by the teacher when he next organizes his case outline for a term and when he comes again to the preparation of the specific case.

# 26

# A Note on Case Preparation for Students

*Warren J. Keegan*

I. A general problem-solving model: an approach to the analysis of a case:

1 Define and identify the main problems and issues in the case. Determine the secondary issues as well.

2 Identify relevant facts and data and appraise how they bear upon the issues. Read through any written material quickly to get a 'feel' of what it is about or what the basic issues may be. Then re-read more slowly and begin to note down facts and quasi-facts supplied and their relationships.

3 Identify any facts of data not known which may need to be taken into some manner of account or which ought, if it is possible, to be ascertained or estimated.

4 Summarize key assumptions about the situation.

5 Identify the causes of the problem. In particular look at the background environment or circumstances in which the problem or case arises.

6 Identify alternative courses of action and appropriate ways of analysing the facts and data relevant to a decision about which course of action to take.

7 Determine the consequence of each action alternative.

8 Weigh and decide among alternative courses of action giving full regard to the conclusions suggested by facts and analysis, and to your own judgment regarding the 'best' choice.

9 Develop a plan of implementation.

II. The approach to analysis suggested above is universal – it is applicable to analysis for class discussion assignments as well as written assignments. The only additional element to a written assignment is that it should include a formal summary-conclusion.

III. You are encouraged to join fellow students in forming study groups for the purpose of analysing cases. In study groups and in class discussions:

Adapted by permission from Keegan 1977.

1 Try to understand thoughts, ideas and points of view introduced by your classmates, and relate your own ideas, analysis, etc. to the evolving discussion. Take note of both the strengths and weaknesses of each point. Few situations are black and white.
2 Try to build up on what has already been said and relate your contributions to it, or if you feel the discussion and approach to the problem are wrong, suggest an alternative.
3 Try to relate the views of others to your own in a logical fashion. Identify different assumptions, faulty steps in the logic, errors in analysis, etc.
4 Do not introduce a new topic until the one under consideration has been adequately considered.

IV. Although discussion and study with fellow students is encouraged for written as well as class discussion assignments, written assignments are, of course, expected to be prepared without assistance of any kind.

# 27

# Introduction to Subject-Centred Tutorials

The subject-centred group tutorial is the most used and most abused group discussion method. For many teachers it is the only method. If you talk of teaching by discussion, they assume you mean a subject-centred group tutorial. They assume that the conduct of the discussion is under the direction of a tutor rather than the responsibility of the group as a whole, that discussion should focus upon academic topics rather than the perceptions, feelings and interpersonal skills of group members, that the topics should be chosen by the tutor, and that there is more than one student.

But group tutorials can be student-centred and individual. When there is only one student – an individual tutorial – the student and the tutor nonetheless form and behave as a group, albeit a rather special group, a dyad.

The first chapter in this section, on teaching styles (Chapter 28), is one of very few on the individual tutorial, in spite of the long use of that method at Oxbridge. The reader should bear the different styles in mind in reading subsequent chapters. Chapter 29 by Peter Frederick emphasizes the questions and tasks students are set to get the process of learning by discussion started. Fawcett Hill, discussed in Chapter 29, considers the structure of the discussion as a whole. Since he assumes there is some initial reading or presentation for discussion, he is primarily concerned with seminar teaching. Yet to have a model for the structure of a seminar leaves me unsatisfied. One problem in using seminars, and indeed all group tutorial teaching, bugs me. How can I push students' curiosity intellectually towards the brink of the unknown? To teach for breadth is one thing; to teach for depth is much more demanding. It is helpful to read Professor Broady's chapter (31) with this problem in mind.

# 28

# Tutorial Styles

*The Royal College of General Practitioners*

Any teacher must know what it is that he wants his trainee to learn; a competent teacher helps the trainee to see what needs to be learnt; a good teacher creates in his trainee a wish to learn those things which are appropriate, even if neither has identified them previously.

All learning is the result of an interaction between the learner and the material being learnt. If a teacher is present, there will also be an interaction between the learner and the teacher. If other learners are present, there will be interactions between them. In many of the learning situations in general practice, particularly those involving contact with patients, there will also be an interaction between the teacher and the subject of the lesson. The trainee will be able to learn and form his attitudes as a result of any of these interactions, but in particular from that between teacher and patient. The extent to which all four interactions can be used depends chiefly on the teaching style adopted.

Broadly speaking there are four styles which a teacher may adopt:

1 Authoritarian.
2 Socratic.
3 Heuristic.
4 Counselling.

## The Authoritarian Style

This might be called 'tell and sell'. It is the style to which most teachers and many trainees will have been exposed already. Questions may be encouraged and answered, but usually to elucidate points that the teacher has already made. The teacher assumes the authority of his position and it is often implied that questioning him questions his position and that this will not be tolerated. It is a good style for conveying facts, but possibly less good than the learner reading or looking at pictures. For instance:

Trainee – I am puzzled by this rash of Jimmy's. What is it?

Reproduced by permission from Royal College of General Practitioners (A Working Party) 1972.

Teacher –    *That is pityriasis rosea. You should be able to get a history of a herald patch. It needs no treatment. One usually sees it about this time of the year.*

# The Socratic Style

This is teaching by question and answer. The teacher always asks and the trainee always answers. It is essential that each answer be the trigger for the next question and that the teacher only provides new facts when the trainee demonstrates an area of ignorance. The style permits the teacher to define and provide only the information needed by the trainee. It seems to be an inherent ability and is not easily learnt. Many teachers who claim to use the style in fact use it to enforce certain trains of thought and only provide answers when the train of thought is not followed rather than when ignorance is uncovered. This then becomes a form of authoritarian teaching. An instance of socratic teaching would be:

Trainee –   I am puzzled by this rash of Jimmy's. Will you look at it?
Teacher –   Tell me about it first
Trainee –   He is aged fifteen. He feels quite well. He's had the rash for two days.
Teacher –   Does it itch?
Trainee –   I didn't ask.
Teacher –   *Well, you really ought to in future. Why do you think I say that?*
Trainee –   I suppose because allergic rashes itch. I rather think that it doesn't itch because, if it did, he would have told me.
Teacher –   *Perhaps. If he doesn't itch and he isn't ill, what rash could it be?*
Trainee –   I can't think.
Teacher –   *Do you know what a 'herald patch' is?*
Trainee –   Yes, it occurs in pityriasis rosea.
Teacher –   *Did Jimmy have one?*
Trainee –   I don't know. I didn't ask.
Teacher –   *I think that you will have to learn that the history is as important in making the differential diagnosis of a rash as it is in any other sign or symptom. Shall we go and have a look at Jimmy now?*

# The Heuristic Style

This is 'find out for yourself', a style which helps to establish the independence of action and willingness to take responsibility which are implicit in our original job definition. It encourages learning by doing and demands that free interchange between teacher and trainee which is particularly suited to the vocational training situation when some knowledge is shared by them both and each have some knowledge which is not shared. For example:

Trainee –   I am puzzled by the rash on Jimmy's body. Will you look at it?
Teacher –   *Let's see him together, but, before we do so, what has Jimmy told you?*
Trainee –   That he's had it for two days and that it doesn't itch.
Teacher –   *What do you conclude from that?*
Trainee –   That it's not an allergic rash.

Teacher –     Good. How old is he?
Trainee –     Fifteen.
Teacher –     Is that any help in reaching a diagnosis?
Trainee –     Not really.
Teacher –     Let us go and see him together. (They go to see the patient.) Describe the
              rash to me.
Trainee –     Some of the patches are pink and some are darker, nearer a
              buff colour.
Teacher –     What about their size and shape?
Trainee –     They are irregular in outline and they vary in size.
Teacher –     Are they raised or not?
Trainee –     Not raised.
Teacher –     Right, irregular macules then of variable colour. Have you asked Jimmy
              if they all came up at once?
Trainee –     He says they came up suddenly in the past two days.
Teacher –     What is the distribution?
Trainee –     Mainly on the trunk and flanks and upper arms.
Teacher –     Is there any scaling?
Trainee –     A few patches show it.
Teacher –     Try scraping the scales off.
Trainee –     They come off from the centre out.
Teacher –     Any bleeding points left?
Trainee –     No
Teacher –     This is pityriasis rosea. You should be able to get a story of a 'herald
              patch'. Jimmy, did you see any rash at any time about a week ago?
Jimmy –       Yes, this one.
Teacher –     (to trainee) – Read about pityriasis rosea; see what the differential
              diagnoses are and think out how what you did established the correct
              diagnosis in Jimmy's case.

Before considering the counselling style of teaching, which is likely to be
unfamiliar to most teachers, let us consider some of the implications of what has
been said so far about teaching styles.

We tend to learn and to do as we have been taught, and we tend to teach as we
have been taught. The authoritarian style is suitable for achieving the recall of
factual knowledge, such as the facts about pityriasis rosea, and it may be used in
demonstrating manual skills. To ensure that manual skills have been acquired
the heuristic style must be used. Having been shown or had described the
multiple-pressure method of smallpox vaccination, the trainee will still have to
do it, especially if his ability is to be assessed. Similarly, the scraping of the
scales of pityriases should be done, if it is to be remembered. The teacher could
certainly use the socratic style to encourage the acquisition of facts, but it is best
employed in achieving the use of knowledge and skills. Those teachers who do
not possess the largely innate skills of the socratic style must rely upon the
heuristic style to achieve this. The trainee will often possess both knowledge
and skills that the teacher does not. If the teacher is able to face this with
honesty, he will readily adopt the heuristic style when it is called for.

In covering these three styles we have only covered the first three, the more
concrete, of our categories of educational objectives: knowledge, manual
skills and the use of knowledge and skills. What of the remaining two? These

more abstract objectives, interpersonal skills and self-understanding, cannot be taught in an authoritarian style. They may be reached towards, but they cannot be completely achieved by the socratic or the heuristic style. This is because any change in the learner's attitudes stems from all the sets of interactions which take place in learning/teaching situations. To help the trainee in this area of his learning the teacher must be aware, simultaneously, not only of the trainee's interactions with the situation, but also of the interactions taking place between himself and the trainee, between the trainee and his peers, and above all between the teacher and the situation. The teacher had to find out what the trainee knew about the condition pityriasis rosea, and to understand what a general practitioner ought to know about it. To help the trainee to gain interpersonal skills and self-understanding, the teacher should know what he feels about the situation in which he is learning and what he thinks the teacher feels about that situation. Above all he should know what he, the teacher, feels. To teach those skills of practice which reflect attitudes, the teacher will need to possess parallel skills in teaching. These categories of objective will be best achieved by the counselling style of teaching. The skills needed will be best acquired by experiencing counselling situations.

## The Counselling Style

The style of a teacher stems in part from his personal perception of learning/teaching situations and of his role within them. The authoritarian sees this as giving factual knowledge, the socratic teacher sees it as developing the critical faculty in his trainee, and the heuristic teacher as showing the way in which learning can take place. The authoritarian sees problem-solving situations through which he will guide the trainee; the heuristic teacher also sees problem-solving situations, which he and his trainee will work through together, so that the trainee learns the methods of solution.

The counselling style is a development of this last view; it is less directive than the other three styles and its aim is that the trainee shall understand the interactions that are taking place between him and the material being learnt. It always requires the teacher to understand his own interaction with the material so that he can use it. The teacher will also use the interaction between the trainee and himself and the trainee will sometimes have to understand this interaction. The teacher must not be authoritarian and should point out those occasions when his trainee asks him to be so. For instance:

Trainee – I am puzzled by the rash on 15-year-old Jimmy. Will you look at it?
*Teacher –* *What puzzles you?*
Trainee – Well, I don't recognize the rash
*Teacher –* *Is Jimmy by himself or with his mother?*
Trainee – By himself
*Teacher –* *What did you tell him when you came in to me?*
Trainee – That I wasn't certain what the rash was
*Teacher –* *What did he say?*
Trainee – Well, he looked a little worried and asked 'was it serious,'

*Teacher –*   *And what did you reply?*
Trainee –   That I did not think so.
*Teacher –*   *Did you have any idea in your mind that it might be something serious?*
Trainee –   Well, no. I knew it wasn't psoriasis and I was pretty certain that it wasn't a seborrhoea.
*Teacher –*   *What did you think it was?*
Trainee –   Well, I think it's pityriasis rosea, but I've never seen it.
*Teacher –*   *What was it you were anxious about then?*
Trainee –   Well, secondary syphilis is a differential diagnosis from pityriases.
*Teacher –*   *Well, that would be serious, wouldn't it?*
Trainee –   Yes.
*Teacher –*   *How are you going to confirm that it isn't syphilis?*
Trainee –   I hoped that you would be able to tell.
*Teacher –*   *You mean by recogniton*
Trainee –   Yes.
*Teacher –*   *But I would have to make sure, wouldn't I?*
Trainee –   Yes
*Teacher –*   *How am I going to do that?*
Trainee –   Well, I suppose you'll have to ask him if he has exposed himself to the risk
*Teacher –*   *Why didn't you do that?*
Trainee –   Well, it's a difficult question to ask
*Teacher –*   *Was it a necessary question?*
Trainee –   I thought so.
*Teacher –*   *We can discuss why you thought so later. What are you going to do now?*
Trainee –   Could you ask him?
*Teacher –*   *I could. Should I?*
Trainee –   Well, no, I suppose it's going to be pretty threatening to Jimmy if you just pop in and ask him that question.
*Teacher –*   *Was it because it was threatening that you didn't ask him?*
Trainee –   Yes, I suppose it's really not a necessary question. I just wasn't certain what the rash was at first and, to tell the truth, I thought of syphilis first and pityriasis second.
*Teacher –*   *OK. Do you still want me to see if I recognize the rash?*
Trainee –   Well, Jimmy's going to feel pretty odd if I've been talking to you all this time and you don't see him.
*Teacher –*   *Right. Let's see Jimmy and we'll discuss the whole thing over coffee.*

The example demonstrates the refusal of the teacher to make ex cathedra statements or to respond to his trainee's perception of the teacher as knowing all. It also demonstrates the attempt to have the trainee understand his own behaviour. Like any learning/teaching situation this one gives the opportunity for many levels of understanding to be discussed. Shared learning/teaching situations are one example of the use of interpersonal communication for a specific purpose; the doctor-patient consultation is another.

Personal perceptions of his role stem from the self-image of the teacher. It is possible for any teacher to acquire a facility in the use of all four styles of teaching although the style he adopts will always be coloured by his own preference.

# 29

# The Dreaded Discussion ... Ten Ways to Start

*Peter Frederick*

> The only privilege a student had that was worth his claiming, was that of talking to the professor, and the professor was bound to encourage it. His only difficulty on that side was to get them to talk at all. He had to devise schemes to find what they were thinking about, and induce them to risk criticism from their fellows.
>
> The Education of Henry Adams

The conspiracy of silence is breaking up: we are learning to talk more openly about our joys and fears as teachers, our achievements and frustrations in the classroom. And it is about time. Most teachers, though certainly not all, find the greater openness liberating. 'You mean that happens in *your* class too?!?' As I have listened to my colleagues — in many departments and institutions — talk about their students and their classrooms, the one fear and frustration mentioned more than any other, as for Henry Adams, was in leading a discussion. No matter how many articles on technique we read, or workshops we attend, or learning theorists' justifications of the value of student participation we struggle through, the dreaded discussion continues to bother us more than any other part of our daily teaching lives. First-year seminar and discussion-based core courses continue to develop. Pressure not only to 'do more discussion' but to do it well, reinforced by student evaluations and faculty development centres, do not go away. We are learning, alas, that to walk into class and hold up one's copy of the assigned text, asking, 'How'd you like it?' does not necessarily guarantee an enthusiastic, rewarding discussion.

We need, first of all, to acknowledge our fears in facing discussion classes: the terror of silence, the related challenges of the shy and dominant student, the overly-long dialogue between ourself and one combative student, the problems of digression and transitions, student fear of criticism, and our own fear of having to say 'I don't know' to a question. Worst of all, perhaps, is the embarrassment of realising, usually in retrospect, that 'about half way

---

Reproduced from Frederick 1981.

through the period I lapsed, *again*, into lecture.' I suspect that our fears about discussion (and our lapses) have a great deal to do with the issue of who controls the classroom. Although psychologically rooted, the control issue is best dealt with as a nitty-gritty practical question of how to plan and how to begin.

My first assumption is that an effective discussion, like most anything, depends upon good planning. Although I prefer using discussions whenever appropriate, I believe most of all in employing a variety of learning approaches, in part because different students learn better (whatever that means) in different ways. We ought to be able to choose from among a repertoire of approaches: lectures, films, laboratory experiments, open-ended discussions, tightly-directed structured experiences, simulation games, guided design, and other classroom options. We also vary what we do depending on the content goals of any given class period. Particular goals suggest particular strategies for learning, and we would like to be able to choose an approach with confidence. Planning, then, involves clarity of goals, several methods one feels confortable with, including a variety of discussion strategies, and the wisdom to select methods and strategies appropriate to our goals.

The purpose of this article is to provide a basis for confidence in choosing 'to discuss' by describing very precisely several different ways of starting a discussion. Like Henry Adams, we 'devise schemes' to find out what our students are thinking. My particular schemes are guided by the following assumptions and principles about discussions:

- that because we have much to learn from each other, all must be encouraged to participate

- that it is important to devise ways in which each student has something to say, especially early in the class period

- that students should be expected to do some (often highly structured) thinking about a text or issue before the discussion class begins

- that students should know and feel comfortable with each other and with the teacher. As Carl Rogers and others keep reminding us, learning is facilitated perhaps most of all by the quality of personal relationships

- that those relationships are enhanced by a climate of trust, support, acceptance, and respect: even 'wrong' answers are legitimate

- that a student's self-image is always affected by his or her participation in discussion: feedback, therefore, is crucial for self-esteem

- that different kinds of texts, purposes, and faculty teaching styles suggest using different kinds of discussion schemes

- that even though we cannot – and should not – greatly change our personalities and teaching styles, we can, however, change the methods we use and the environments we teach in to minimise the presence of our particular style. The soft, gentle, nurturing, non-directive (and often boring) teacher can devise ways in which students provide energy and excitement; the tough, dominating, energetic, directive (and often intimidating) teacher can structure class to diminish the force of that presence.

The suggestions that follow for starting a discussion are based upon these principles. They also assume that the primary goal in any discussion is to enhance the understanding of some common text, or topic. I am using 'text' in a broad sense: essay, chapter, case study, short novel, film, speech, art object, poem, piece of music, scientific experiment, or social scientific model. Other goals of developing expressive skills, or instilling self-esteem or love of disciplinary field in students, while important, are secondary to the main purpose of achieving greater knowledge and understanding. I make no claim for these suggestions other than that they have worked, both for me and for others. Occasionally I will offer what seems to be utterly obvious, but I hope not insulting, advice. The reason for this is that I firmly believe that one of our most serious lapses in conducting discussions – and what students often need most in order to start telling each other what they are thinking – is attention to the obvious. Like, for example, insisting that students bring their book to class and reading passages out loud. Or like using student's names as often as possible. Or like clearly articulating, first to ourselves and then to our students, 'what I'd like to have happen today is...' My hope and expectation is that other teachers will adapt these suggestions and devise schemes for their own texts, purposes, and teaching styles.

## Goals and Values Testing

The students are asked to pair off and decide together what they think is the primary value of the particular text for the day, and how their consideration of it meshes with course goals. 'Why are we reading this?' 'Why now?' After five minutes or so, invite reactions. It is not necessary to hear from each pair, but hearing from a few provides a public reality test for the teacher's course goals ('is this text serving the purpose I had hoped it would?'), as well as providing a mutual basis for further probing into the text. An alternative initial question for the pairs is to ask for a list of relationships (comparisons and contrasts) between this test and another, usually the most recent one. Make the instructions explicit: 'Identify three themes common to both texts'; 'Suggest the two most obvious differences between the two texts'; 'Which did you like best and why?' 'Make a list of as many comparisons (or contrasts) as you can in ten minutes.' In this case, in order to benefit from the richness of diversity of perspective, as well as to confirm similar insights, it is probably best to check in with each pair.

## Concrete Images

It is obvious, of course, that discussions go better when specific references are made. Yet I think we often need help remembering the content of our text. A few minutes at the beginning can guarantee that the sophisticated analysis we seek will be based on specific facts. Go around the table and ask each student to state one concrete image/scene/event/moment from the next that stands out. No analysis is necessary – just recollections and brief description. As each student reports, the collective images are listed on the board, this providing a visual record of selected content from the text as a backdrop to the following discussion. Usually the recall of concrete scenes prompts further recollections, and a flood of images flows from the students.

A follow-up question is to invite the class to study the items on the board and ask: 'What themes seem to emerge from these items?' 'What connects these images?' 'Is there a pattern to our recollected events?' 'What is missing?' This is, obviously, an inductive approach to the text. Facts precede analysis. But also, every one gets to say something early in class and every contribution gets written down to aid our collective memory and work.

We have our own important questions to ask about a text. And we should ask them. But students also have their questions and they can learn to formulate better ones. Being able to ask the right questions about a particular text may be the first way of coming to terms with is. There are many ways of generating questions:

1 Ask students ahead of time (Wednesday for Friday's class) to prepare one or two questions about their reading. One can vary the assignment by specifying different kinds of questions: open-ended, factual, clarifying, connective and relational, involving value conflicts, etc.

2 As students walk into the classroom ask them to write down (probably anonymously early in the terms) one or two discussable questions about the text. 'What questions/issues/problems do you want this group to explore in the next hour about this reading?' Hand all questions to one student (a shy one, perhaps) who, at random, selects questions for class attention. Do not expect to get through all of them, but the discussion of two or three questions usually will deal with or touch on almost every other one. Students, like all of us, ask questions they really want to answer themselves, and they will make sure their point is made somehow.

3 Same as 2, except the teacher (or a student) takes a minute or two to categorise the questions and deals with them more systematically.

4 Ask each student to write down one or two questions (either ahead of time or at the start of class), but in this case the student owns his/her question and is in charge of leading the discussion until he/she feels there has been a satisfactory exploration of issues. Start anywhere and go around the table. This obviously works best in smaller groups with longer periods than fifty minutes.

5 Divide the class into pairs of small groups and charge each group to decide upon *one* salient question to put to the rest of the class.

## Finding Illustrative Quotations

We do not often enough go to the text and read passages out loud together. Students, we are told, do not know how to read any more. If so, they need practice in and to see modelled good old-fashioned *explication de texte*. Ask each student, either ahead of time or at the start of class, to find one or two quotations from the assigned text that he/she found particularly significant. There are many ways in which the instruction may be put: 'Find one quotation you especially liked and one you especially disliked.' Or, 'Find a quotation which you think best illustrates the major thesis of the piece.' Or, 'Select a quote you found difficult to understand.' Or, 'Find a quotation which suggests, to you, the key symbol of the larger text.' After a few minutes of browsing (perhaps in small groups of three or four), the students will be ready to turn to specific passages, read out loud, and discuss. Be sure to pause long enough for everyone to find the right spot in their book: 'Starting with the middle paragraph on page sixty-one – are you all with us?' Lively and illuminating discussion is guaranteed because not all students will find the same quotations to illustrate various instructions, nor, probably, will they all interpret the same passages the same way. It is during this exercise that I have had the most new insights into texts I have read many times previously. And there may be no more exciting (or modelling) experience than for students to witness their teacher discovering a new insight and going through the process of refining a previously held interpretation. 'Great class today! I taught Doc Frederick something he didn't know.'

## Breaking into Smaller Groups

No matter the size of a class, sixty or six or one hundred and sixty, it can always be broken down into smaller groups of four, five, eight, fifteen, or whatever. The purpose, quite simply, is to enable more people to say something and to generate more ideas about a text or topic. Also, groups lend themselves usually to a lively, competitive spirit, whether asked to or not. We are interested not only in the few people we are grouped with but also in 'what they're doing over there.' Furthermore, reticent students often feel more confident in expressing themselves in a larger group after they have practised the point with a safer, smaller audience. There are three crucial things to consider in helping small groups to work well. First, the instructions should be utterly clear, simple, and task-orientated. Examples: 'Decide together which of the brothers is the major character in the novel.' 'Which person in the *Iliad* best represents the qualities of a Greek hero? Which person, the same or different, best represents a hero by your standards?' 'Why did the experiment fail? What would you suggest changing?' 'Identify the three main themes of this text.' 'What is Picasso's painting saying?' 'Identify three positive and three negative qualities of King David's character.' 'What do you think is the crucial turning point in Malcolm's life?' 'If you were the company treasurer (lawyer), what decision would you make?' 'Generate as big a list as you can of examples of sex role stereotyping in these first two chapters.' 'If you were Lincoln, what would you do?' In giving these instructions be sure to give the groups a sense of how much time they have to do their work. Second, I believe in varying the ways in which groups are formed in order to create different sized groups with different constituencies. Pair off ('with someone you don't know') one day; count off by fives around the room another; form groups of 'about eight' around clumps of students sitting near one another on a third day. And third, vary the ways in which groups report out when reassembled. Variations include:

- an oral report from each group, with the teacher recording results (if appropriate) on the board

- each group is given a piece of newsprint and felt pen upon which to record its decision, which is then posted around the room

- space is provided for each group, when ready, to write their results on the blackboard

- each group keeps notes on a ditto master, which the teacher runs off and distributes to everyone for continuing discussion the next meeting

- no reporting out is necessary, or, reactions are invited from several groups, but not necessarily from all of them.

Further possibilities for small groups are described in the suggestions that follow.

## Generating Truth Statements

This particular exercise develops critical skills and generates a good deal of friendly rivalry among groups. The instructions to each group are to decide upon three statements known to be true about some particular issue. 'It is true about slavery that ...' 'We have agreed that it is true about the welfare sytem that ...' 'It is true about international politics in the 1950s that ...' 'We know it to be true about the theory of relativity that ...' And so on. I have found this strategy useful in introducing a new topic – slavery, for example – where students may think they already know a great deal but the veracity of their assumptions demands examination. The complexity and ambiguity of knowledge is clearly revealed as students present their truth statements and other students raise questions about or refute them. The result of the exercise is to develop some true statements, perhaps, but mostly to generate a list of questions and of issues demanding further study. This provides an agenda for the unit. Sending students to the library is the usual next step, and they are quite charged up for research after the process of trying to generate truth statements.

## Forced Debate

Although neither one of two polar sides of an issue obviously contains the whole truth, it is often desirable to force students to select one or the other of two opposite sides and to defend their choice. 'Burke or Paine?' 'Booker T. Washington or W.E.B. Du Bois?' 'Are you for or against achieving racial balance in the schools?' 'Should Nora have left or stayed?' 'Who had the better argument: Creon or Antigone?' 'Capitalism or Socialism for developing nations?' And so on. Once students have made their choice, which may be required prior to entering the room for class that day, I ask them to sit on one side of the table or room or the other to represent their decision. Physical movement is important and sides need to face each other. Once the students have actually, as it were, put their bodies on the line, they are more receptive to answering the question: 'Why have you chosen to sit where you are? Inevitably, there may be some few students who absolutely refuse (quite rightly) to choose one side or the other. If they persist, with reasons, create a space for a middle position. This adds a dimension to the debate and, as in the case of deciding between Burke and Paine on whether or not to support the French Revolution, those in the middle find out what it is like to attempt to remain neutral or undecided in heated, revolutionary times. I also invite students to feel free to change their place during a debate if they are so persuaded, which adds still another real (and sometimes chaotic) aspect to the experience.

## Role Playing

This is a powerful learning strategy, guaranteed to motivate and animate most students and to confuse and make nervous many. Role playing is tricky. It can be as simple (deceptively so) as asking two members of the class to volunteer to adopt the roles of two characters from a novel at a crucial point in their relationship discussing how they feel about it, or what they should do next. Or, two students can act out the President and an advisor debating some decision, or two slaves in the quarters at night discussing whether or not to attempt to run away, or a male and female (perhaps with reversed roles) discussing affirmative action or birth control. Issues involving value conflicts, moral choices, and timeless human dilemmas related to the students' world usually work best, but role playing need not necessarily be so personal. A colleague of mine in biology creates a student panel of foundation grant evaluators, before whom other students present papers and make research proposals. Or, as students walk into the class and sit down they have a card in front of them which indicates the name of a character from a novel, or an historical personage, or even a concept. For the discussion that follows they are to *be* the role indicated on their card. Knowing this might happen is not a bad motivator to make sure students get their reading done.

Any situation involving multiple group conflicts is appropriate for role playing. There are many simulation games for contemporary issues in the social sciences. But for history, I like to create my own somewhat less elaborate 'games', putting students into the many roles represented in some historical event or period. One of my favourites is a New England town meeting in 1779, in which a variety of groups (landed elite, yeoman farmers, Tory sympathizers, soldiers and riff-raff, artisans, lawyers and ministers, etc.) are charged with drafting instructions for delegates to a state constitutional convention. Another is to challenge several groups in 1866 – defeated Confederates, southern Unionists, nothern Radical Republicans, northern moderates, and Black freedmen – to develop lists of goals and strategies for accomplishing them. I play an active role, as moderator of the town meeting or as President Johnson, organising and monitoring the interactions that follow group caucuses. Our imagination can create many appropriate examples for role playing. You have, I am sure, your own.

But because role playing can be traumatic for some students and because a poorly-planned or poorly-monitored role play can get out of control, I want to make a few cautionary suggestions that I have found helpful, if not crucial.

First, except for finding the cards at the beginning of class which compel playing a role, in most playing activities students should have some choice in how much to participate, either by deciding whether or not to volunteer or by being part of a group large enough to reduce the pressures on any one individual. Teachers should monitor carefully the unspoken signals of students who may find their role uncomfortable, and intervene, often by skilfully pursuing their own role, to extricate or reduce the pressures on an actor. Generally, however, I have found role playing to be an effective way for the normally shy student, who has said little or nothing in class, to unblock in the new role and participate more readily in conventional discussions afterwards.

Second, give students some time (how much depends upon the nature of the particular role play) to prepare themselves for their role. This might mean two days or more in order to do some research, or fifteen minutes in groups to pool information, or five minutes to refresh one's memory about a character in a novel, or a couple of minutes simply to get in touch with the feelings of a character and situation.

Third, in giving instructions the definiton of roles to be played should be concrete and clear enough for students to get a handle on who they are playing, yet open enough for the expression of their own personality and interpretation. If the roles are prescribed too clearly, students merely imitate the character described (although sometimes this *is* the requirement) and have difficulty going beyond it with anything of themselves. If the roles are described too loosely, without a clear context, students will stray too far from the actual situation to be experienced and learned. And finally – and most important – in any role play experience as much (if not more) time should be devoted to debriefing afterwards as for the exercise itself. This is when the substantive lessons of the experience are discovered, explored and confirmed. This is when those students who may have served as observers will offer their insights and analysis of what happened. Above all, this is when the actors will need an opportunity to talk about how they felt in their roles and what they learned, both about themselves and about the substantive issues involved.

## Non-structured Scene-setting

Most of the ways of starting a discussion described thus far involve a great deal of structure and direction. But inevitably, when teachers suspect that they have been dominating too much ('I blew it again – talked most of the hour!'), it is clearly time to give students an opportunity to take a discussion in *their* directions, and to do most, if not all, of the talking. The teacher, however, has a responsibility for setting the scene and getting class started. There are a variety of ways to do this, some more directive than others. Put some slides on a carousel and, without a word, show them at the beginning of class. Or, as the students walk into the classroom, the teacher plays a piece of music or a speech on a tape recorder. Or, on the board before class the teacher writes a quotation or two, or two or three questions, or a list of words or phrases or names, or even an agenda of issues to be explored. The only necessary verbal instructions are to make it clear to the students that until defined time (perhaps the last five minutes) you, the teacher, intend to stay out of the discussion entirely. Even having said that, I have still found that I am capable of breaking my own contract and intervening or more likely, affecting the class by non-verbal signals. I tell my students that I find it extremely difficult to stay uninvolved, and that I need their help in making sure I stay out of the discussion. They are usually happy to oblige. If possible, adopt an utterly non-evaluative observer role and take descriptive notes on the course of the discussion. To read your notes back to the students may be the most helpful feedback you can give them.

## A Tenth Way to Start

As the term progresses students will have experienced many different exciting ways to start a discussion, most of which, we hope, enhances their understanding of a text or issue. Once the experience of variety has been established, there is even a legitimate place for the following strategy: stroll into class with your book, sit on the edge of the table, hold the book up, and ask: 'How'd you like it?'

Although it has not been my primary purpose in this article to extol the many values of discussion, I assume that my bias has been implicitly clear. The key to effective retention of learning, I believe, is in owning the discovery. Emerson wrote in his journals that a wise person 'must feel and teach that the best wisdom cannot be communicated (but) must be acquired by every soul for itself.' My primary strategy as a teacher is to structure situations in which students have as many opportunities as possible to acquire wisdom for themselves; that is, to own the discovery of the new learning insight or connection and to express that discovery to others. In this way their substantive learning is increased and their self-esteem is enhanced. How we plan the start of class is crucial in achieving this goal. 'Hey, roomie, I now know what Emerson meant by self-reliance. What I said in class about it today was that ...' Which translated means: 'Hey, I'm OK, I understand this stuff. I said something today others found helpful.' Which translated means: 'Class was good today: he let me talk.'

# 30

# Hill's Learning Thru' Discussion (LTD)

*Donald A. Bligh*

According to Fawcett Hill (1977) group discussions often fail because of a lack of direction or because the topics discussed follow the interests of the most dominant member. Hill has therefore devised what he calls a Group Cognitive Map which is a procedural tool outlining an orderly sequence for the discussion. If the tutor is to use this sequence, he must first sell the idea to his group.

Hill assumes that there should be preparatory reading for the discussion and his Group Cognitive Map is therefore most appropriate to the seminar method which in this volume is defined as group discussion introduced by a presentation. (See page 4.) The reading material need not be published material, it could be a fellow student's essay circulated before the seminar. (The practice of reading an essay aloud in student seminars wastes time, and, with the invention of the photocopier, is now outmoded.)

The Group Cognitive Map has eight steps:

> Step One – Definition of terms and concepts
> Step Two – General statement of author's message
> Step Three – Identification of major themes or subtopics
> Step Four – Allocation of time
> Step Five – Discussion of major themes and subtopics
> Step Six – Integration of material with other knowledge
> Step Seven – Application of the material
> Step Eight – Evaluation of author's presentation
> Step Nine – Evaluation of group and individual performance

Hill lists several techniques he thinks are useful to assist the direction of discussion. These may be used by the teacher, the students or both. During preparation before the dicussion:

> a Start with a copy of the Group Cognitive Map with the steps well spaced on the page.
> b As you read, jot down ideas wherever you think they best fit under the nine steps.

c Look up and learn to say the meanings of new words and concepts.
d When you have finished reading, go back through the nine steps of the
   Cognitive Map and write down reminders of what you might say during
   each step in the discussion.
e Write down questions about the material which you could introduce into
   the discussion.

## Step One – Definition of Terms and Concepts

The importance of defining terms is obvious, but I do not think, as Hill does,
that the beginning of a seminar is always the right time to define them. In
some subjects the resolution of controversial topics depends upon how you
define your terms and consequently definitions should only be formulated
when the controversies have been well considered. Nonetheless I accept as a
generalization that terms and concepts should be defined as soon as
reasonably possible. Hill suggests the following activities for either the teacher
or his students during the first stage of the discussion:

a List the words or concepts with which you had some difficulty and ask
   others to add to your list.
b Try to define or explain one of the words on your list.
c Ask the group members if you have defined it as they understand it.
d Encourage others to practise explaining what it means to them.
e Restate what someone else has said to make sure you understand it.
f Give an example to clarify the meaning.
g Ask someone else in the group to give an example.
h Ask the group members if everyone understands the new words or
   concepts.

## Step Two – Summarize the Preparatory Reading

Hill suggests the following activities. They promote a common understanding.

a State in your own words what you think the assignment was all about.
b Frame a question that will encourage someone else to state what the
   assignment was about.
c Encourage other group members to practise explaining it.
d Add to what someone else has said.
e State the ways in which your understanding or interpetation differs from
   that stated by another member.
f Ask for clarification on points you don't understand.
g Restate what someone else has said if you need to, to be sure you
   understand it.
h If you think two other members are misunderstanding each other, try to
   lessen the confusion.

# Step Three – Identification of Major Themes and Issues

Hill emphasizes the need to restate themes and subtopics in the student's own words to check that he sees which ideas are important and centrally related to all the others. In both Step Two and Step Three Hill places great emphasis upon clarifying what authors have had to say, rather than upon the opinions of students. This may be appropriate in science and engineering subjects, but it is less appropriate in the arts and social sciences.

a Note the organization of the author's material in terms of headings and subheadings used.
b Consider what makes for a logical sequence of subtopics.
c Write on the blackboard or an overhead projector, so that all can see the suggested subtopics. This speeds the process and reduces confusion regarding what subtopics are proposed.

## Step Four – The Allocation of Time

Again, because Hill thinks many discussions flounder when they are insufficiently structured, he places great emphasis upon the need for groups to plan their use of time in advance. This could defeat the purpose of a discussion when its objective is to explore the interests and opinions of group members. Nonetheless a group commitment to how it uses its time enhances group motivation and is likely to avoid the feeling that time is wasted. The budgeting of time may be particularly appropriate for tutorless groups. Hill suggests the following activities.

a Consider which topics are the most and least difficult to understand.
b For each subtopic, write down a question that would start a profitable discussion.
c Display the allocation of time on the blackboard or overhead projector so that all may see to what they are committed.
d Hill suggests the appointment of a time keeper who will tell the group when they have two minutes left for the discussion on a theme or subtopic.

## Step Five – Discussion of Major Themes and Subtopics

Get the group to state the essential elements of each theme and subtopic. These may include hypotheses, methods, techniques, arguments and sources of information.

Again emphasis is upon stating the elements of what the authorities in a field say because Hill thinks discussions will remain superficial if they move to consider participants' personal opinions too soon. This he believes should be delayed until Step Eight. He believes this delay requires maturity on the part of the group and needs to taught by practice.

# Step Six – Relating the Themes and Subtopics to other Knowledge

It is not obvious why this step should occur before Step Seven on the application of ideas presented. To consider the integration of knowledge before its application will keep the discussion on an intellectual rather than on a practical plane that is not always desirable. Hill recommends the following activities.

a State the meaning or usefulness of the new material in understanding other ideas or concepts.
b Phrase questions to put to the group members which will stimulate them to see how the new material fits into what they have studied previously.
c Ask or state how the new material contradicts, substantiates, or amplifies some previously developed point.
d Summarize into compact statements points others have made.
e Listen carefully for, and try to state puzzling aspects of the material that are giving the group trouble.
f Ask for, or give help in stating the material more concisely.
g Ask another member to restate what he has said if you think you may have misunderstood.
h Call the group's attention to and reinforce a comment that seems particularly helpful.

## Step Seven – Application of the Material

a Ask or state why and how the new material can be useful to members.
b Give examples of how you might apply it or how the knowledge of it may be useful to you.
c Compare with your own experience the author's reasons for thinking it worthwhile.
d Test the usefulness of the new material by constructing a situation for which it should be useful.
e Give examples which the new materials helps to explain or helps you to understand.

## Step Eight – Evaluation of Presented Material

Hill reserves all critical evaluation and expression of personal opinion to this stage. If powers of criticism and judgement are important educational objectives and if they take a long time to learn, considerable time should be allocated to this step. Hill suggests four activities.

a State questions to help the group evaluate the new material, the method of arriving at the conclusions, etc.
b State points supporting or questioning the validity of the arguments or the reasoning of the author.
c State why and how you think the new material is or is not useful.

d Frame questions which will help the group to test the usefulness of specific points.

# Step Nine – Evaluation of Groups and Individual Performance

Using the ideas of Benne and Sheats (1948) Hill suggests the use of a questionnaire at the end of this Learning Thru' Discussion (LTD) process (see Figure 1).

---

## MEMBER ROLES INVENTORY

Instructions: Please check which of the following roles you played some of the time today by making check marks in the A column opposite the roles you played.
      Please check which of the following roles you felt were exercised adequately by the group today by making check marks in the B column opposite those roles which were played.

### *Positive Roles*

| A | B | | A | B | |
|---|---|---|---|---|---|
| — | — | Initiating | — | — | Gave examples |
| — | — | Gave information | — | — | Asked for examples |
| — | — | Asked for information | — | — | Gave clarification, synthesis or summary |
| — | — | Gave positive reaction or opinions | — | — | Gave comments on group's movement or lack of it |
| — | — | Asked for positive reactions or opinions | — | — | Asked for comment on group's movement or lack of it |
| — | — | Gave confrontation or reality tested | — | — | Sponsored, encouraged, helped, or rewarded others |
| — | — | Gave restatement of others' contributions | — | — | Physical movement of objects |
| — | — | Asked for restatement of others' contributions | — | — | Relieved group tensions |

### *Negative Roles*

| A | B | | A | B | |
|---|---|---|---|---|---|
| — | — | Acted with aggressiveness and hostility | — | — | Sought sympathy |
| — | — | Made self-confession | — | — | Pleaded for a pet idea |
| — | — | Acted with defensiveness | — | — | Horsed around |
| — | — | Was competitive | — | — | Was dominating |
| — | — | Withdrew | — | — | Did some status seeking |

---

**Figure 1**

# 31

## The Conduct of Seminars

*Maurice Broady*

It is curious that the lecture has received so much more attention than the seminar: curious precisely because the seminar, as a method of teaching, is so much more important. The lecture requires the student to listen and annotate; in the process he may also be amused or stimulated. But he remains, intellectually, a recipient. The seminar, on the other hand, if properly conducted, involves the student more actively in argument both in speech and in writing; and learning is more effective when it entails an active rather than a comparatively passive relationship to a subject-matter. In the seminar, the student has the opportunity of coming into direct contact with his teacher and thus, one may hope, of sharing in and then catching his excitement, interest and disciplined approach to his subject. Free inquiry is caught rather than simply learned. Moreover, more time and effort are often devoted to seminars than to lectures. In the first-year social administration course at Swansea, for example, seven man-hours are invested in seminars compared with a bare one hour in lecture, and in the 'core courses' leading to the final degree, the ratio is about four to one.

These facts alone would justify our paying a good deal of attention to the conduct of seminars. But there is the further reason, that the seminar is a more difficult art-form than the lecture since it is much less static. It therefore makes greater demands upon the tutor's ability to adjust spontaneously to his students, both intellectually and psychologically. This means that he must have a far greater command both of his talents as a teacher and of his understanding of his subject-matter than is the case when he stands, with notes before him, facing a mainly passive audience, on the podium of the lecture-theatre.

It is curious, again, that this is hardly acknowledged in our teaching practice. The young assistant is assumed to be equally capable of lecturing and holding seminars without any recognition of how different are the demands which these tasks place upon him. It seems to be supposed that, since the teacher has attended both lectures and seminars, he is automatically capable of giving them competently himself. It is taken for granted that experience alone is the best teacher. But experience contributes best to

Reproduced by permission from Broady 1970.

practice only when it has been reflected upon and incorporated into the teacher's outlook: and this, given that academics tend to undervalue teaching, is neither frequently nor systematically carried out. University teachers therefore tend to teach as they were taught themselves which results in an unreflective conservatism in academic teaching which has only recently been called in question.

## The Average Seminar

How, then, does the average seminar run? There seem to be two main types. In the first, the seminar is related directly to the course of lectures. It is conceived as a way of giving students the opportunity of discussing problems that they have confronted in lectures. The tutor meets the class. 'Have you any questions?' he asks. Silence. The tutor says to himself, 'These are *dim* students', while the students sit embarrassed and, becoming steadily more and more anxious, are less and less ready to join in any discussion. But in this case it is the tutor who is at fault, since to have a question at all already pre-supposes a degree of interest and intellectual awareness which cannot be taken for granted and which it is the purpose of the seminar to foster. In any case, to have defined a question is already half-way to its solution. The tutor may then try another tack: 'Did you understand what Professor X said about alienation?'. But students often do not know what they do not understand; and even if they do, the atmosphere of the seminars is often not conducive to their admitting that they do not know. Hence more silence, embarrassment and anxiety.

So, the tutor is now 'on the spot'. He therefore starts to talk, frequently feeling obliged to fill the gap of silence by giving what is sometimes called a 'mini-lecture'. But this defeats the purpose of the seminar, which is to engage the students in active discussion. Sometimes, if the tutor recognises that he ought not to be lecturing, he may fill in the time with rather desultory chit-chat, for which the students get very little value and which only succeeds in undervaluing the seminar and intellectual activity in general.

Perhaps as many as half the seminars in the humanities and social science faculties of our universities are run like this. The waste of time and resources that this entails is obvious and urgently needs to be overcome. For waste in academic institutions is to be found not only in rooms and equipment not being used to capacity but also, and perhaps more critically, in the under-involvement of students and motivation is the most important mark of the good teacher.

In an academic context where research almost invariably counts for more than teaching, it is understandable that so little systematic attention is paid to pedagogy. For research, unlike teaching, issues in publications and is open to impartial, independent, that is to say 'objective' assessment. Objective scholarly judgment is central to the ethos of a university. But teaching is not easily assessed by objective methods. Indeed, the doctrine of *Lehrfreiheit*, of the privilege of the lecture-room in which the teacher is free to express his ideas as he wishes, also inhibits the supervision of teaching and thus prevents its being publicly assessed like research. Certainly, reputations for good or bad teaching are made on a campus, but academics are apt to be sceptical, especially of favourable judgments, since they frequently rest merely upon here-say and they suspect that they may have been won cheaply, by pandering to students' whims at the expense of those overriding virtues of rigour and discipline. The suspicion of 'the easy option' underpins many an academic prejudice. In any case, the criteria by which such judgments are made are ambiguous since the student may only perceive the full value of *some* teaching long after he has left the university. Furthermore, a reputation for good teaching is a currency which has only a low market-value on any other campus.

## Improving Seminar Teaching

What then can be done to improve the teaching seminars. A rather naïve colleague once suggested that I might put out a list of hints or 'tips' about the conduct of seminars. I asked him whether he would be satisfied to train research students on tips. Obviously not. But why should a method be proposed for teaching which is no less complex an activity than research? For though useful tips can be given, they are only likely to be effectively understood and intelligently practised if they are incorporated into a more general pattern of thinking about teaching: in a theory, in short, of what teaching is all about. This is where our teaching is weak; for without some concept of what the point of the seminar is and some idea about what factors make for success, any attempt to improve seminar teaching will be useless. Such a theory would have to begin with the proposition that the teacher's stance to his students is different from that of the research-worker to his thesis. For the teacher interprets his theory in practice: he is the agent of his own applied understanding. To apply theory to the practice of teaching involves much more than simply fitting theory to data in some impersonal and objective manner. On the contrary, it requires the teacher to interpret the significance of his theory in the dynamic context presented by the intellectual development of his students. Teaching then, inevitably involves the person *qua* person as well as the intellect, and it necessarily requires a high degree of personal commitment.

Such commitment cannot be legislated for; and many academics undoubtedly feel inhibited about expressing sentiments of any kind in the belief that too great a personal involvement prejudices the objectivity of scholarship and must be avoided. In any theory of teaching, however, the relation between intellect and personality certainly needs to be clarified, for the successful conduct of seminars depends upon very personal factors such as the tutor's imagination and his ability to communicate a sense of active interest in his discipline. The imagination, for example, which helps a tutor to understand sympathetically why a student finds it difficult to grasp a particular aspect of a subject or to find the apt example which will communicate to the student across a chasm of incomprehension: this cannot be planned for since it is part of the intuitive adjustment that each tutor must make to each of his students. But imagination and intellectual excitement, important as they are, are no substitute for the effective grasp of a discipline or clear thinking about the point and practice of the seminar.

In analysing the conduct of seminars, three factors need to be taken into account. First of all, there is the intellectual structure of the discipline which is the basic link between tutor and student. Then there is the student's pattern of intellectual development. And third, there is the social and psychological structure of the seminar. I shall comment on each of these.

## The Social-Psychological Structure of the Seminar

To consider the last point first. Conventional thinking has given most attention to the optimum size for a 'good' seminar, probably because this is an 'objective' property of the seminar which attracts the social-scientific mind. But in practice, even when the seminar is quite small, colleagues often find difficulty in knowing how to stimulate discussion. A more important question, therefore, is what processes characterise the good seminar and how can these be promoted and used by the tutor? How can the tutor influence the way the seminar runs so as to encourage the free but disciplined discussion which is the hallmark of the good seminar.

By 'processes' I refer to the many different procedures that can be adopted for conducting the seminar. One process, for example, entails the following pattern. The student reads a paper: the tutor asks the student questions: the tutor criticises the paper: the criticism finishes: the tutor then wonders why he cannot get a discussion going. An alternative process might be: student A reads a paper: the tutor asks student B to state succinctly what has been said: B does so: the tutor invites C to comment on the quality of B's resumé: C comments favourably: the tutor invites other opinions: the tutor then expresses his view, taking account of the comments made by the students: the tutor then asks D to assess the validity of A's paper: and so on.

Quite as important are such apparently trivial questions as whether students should be addressed by their christian names or their surnames. This is significant because, if tutor and students consider it appropriate, the use of christian names – reciprocally if it works out like that – can often serve to reduce the tension of the seminar and to promote easier and less formal relationships among the students themselves.

The heavier the intellectual demands which a tutor expects to make of his students, the more desirable such informality becomes.

These practices flow out of a set of assumptions of which the following are among the most important:

a The student will inevitably experience strain if the seminar is really active and demanding.

b Higher education cannot proceed without strain. 'It's no bloody good unless it hurts.'

c This involves the danger that the student can very easily take the tutor's intellectual criticism as a criticism of himself, even when this is not intended.

d If that were so, the student would feel an anxiety that could easily prejudice his academic progress, which would be counter-productive. A demanding but sympathetic tone and a corresponding teaching practice must therefore be devised so that intellectual assessment shall not be mistaken for personal criticism.

That will serve to indicate what I mean by 'the social and psychological structure of the seminar': it has to do with setting up effective conditions for free and disciplined discussion and with devising a set of procedures to that end.

# The Intellectual Structure of a Discipline

I now turn to the intellectual structure of a discipline. the most important thing that academic teachers communicate is an intellectual discipline. A discipline entails: (a) a body of concepts that are given coherence by a theory or framework of generalisations; and (b) a set of methods for establishing the validity of those general propositions. An academic discipline can be conceived either as a subject or as an argument. To regard it as a subject is to focus attention primarily upon the given body of knowledge which constitutes the subject-matter of the discipline and only secondarily upon the use which is made of that subject-matter. It is something that the student has to assimilate, passively. But to regard a discipline as an argument (which surely corresponds much more with what an academic actually does) is to see more clearly that the discipline is something which academics practise: and that raises in question how it is practised.

To practise in a discipline involves discriminating between its content and its form, between the empirical material of which the discipline makes use, and its theoretical framework or characteristic mode of argument. Without this framework, the content has little meaning; and the theory is equally devoid of meaning if it is not actively related to the factual material which theory helps one to grasp more cogently and which, in turn, serves as a check upon theory. Students often come to the university with only a weak sense of the meaning of what they are doing intellectually; and if the significance of the intellectual activity, which is their 'bread and butter' so to speak, is not made apparent, they are likely to lose heart and to give only half-hearted attention to their studies. The student's willingness to make an effort is closely related to whether or not his work is meaningful to him. The subject-matter of a discipline, therefore, together with its theory, must be so structured that the discipline can be presented meaningfully to the undergraduate. Meaning, simply put, is related to coherence. It depends upon placing each particular element of the discipline within some pattern and showing the student clearly what the pattern or form is, which gives the detailed subject-matter its significance.

Now, the academic tutor is presumed to understand the intellectual coherence of his discipline. But it is clear that he very often fails to demonstrate that coherence convincingly to his students, even in the seminar. This is partly due to the way the seminar is shaped. One common method of conducting seminar-courses is to list a set of topics *seriatim* for weekly discussion. In a typical course of seminars in sociology such topics might be: (1) Discuss Marx's theory of the state; (2) Consider the view that the functions of the family are changing under the impact of industrialism; (3) Are political élites necessarily élitist? That there is some coherence in these topics may be evident to the tutor; but how does the student see it? For him their coherence derives simply from the fact that his sociology tutor may have set them and that they go consecutively from number 1 to number 3, one week after the next. But apart from that, there is no clear intellectual coherence in these seminar topics and so they are likely to appear to the student as discrete gobbets of discussion which are somehow, but only vaguely related to some general context of 'sociology'.

An alternative method is to try to list the topics for discussion in such a way that the student can grasp the logical coherence of the subject. That means thinking out how the discipline can be presented so that the discussions are coherent from one week to the next, the topics reinforce one another and the complexity of discussion proceeds apace with the growth of the student's understanding.

## The Intellectual Structure of the Seminar

What this means in practice can only be demonstrated by reference to a specific pattern of seminars. A second-year sociology seminar which I ran in Southampton several years ago will illustrate what I mean. The aim of the this seminar was to help students how to understand, to appraise and to make use of social theories. A general theme was chosen: theoretical arguments about social change in industrial societies. In the first term, two stages were covered. First of all we studied Neil Smelser's *Social Change in the Industrial Revolution* which presents an explanation of social change in terms of a 'structural theory' of society: step 1. Then we studied an alternative type of theory based upon 'culture-personality theory' in Everitt Hagen's *On the Theory of Social Change*: step 2. this was deliberately contrasted with Smelser's work, and the reasons for each approach were clarified by studying them antithetically. The second term began with a close analysis of Emile Durkheim's study *Suicide*: step 3, which is one of the classical starting-points of sociology of the 1890s – Durkheim's approach to sociological analysis is similar to Smelser's. This was followed in turn by Max Weber's *The Protestant Ethic and the Spirit of Capitalism* which has many methodological similarities with Hagen's work: step 4. Because the comparison between Weber and Durkheim parallels that made in the first term between Hagen and Smelser, it serves to reinforce the theoretical points made earlier while giving some historical depth to the understanding of these two theoretical approaches.

A parallel theme in the development of this seminar had to do with the methodology of sociology. In my opinion, methodology is best considered only after a substantive theory has been considered. The works studied in the first term – Smelser and Hagen – discussed methodological questions only incidentally. However, they prepared the way for the more systematic treatment which these problems were to receive in the second term, where it was possible to study in some detail the essays of both Durkheim and Weber that were specifically devoted to methodological issues, *The Rules of Sociological Method* and the *Essays on Objectivity*. This discussion was taken further in the third term (steps 5 and 6) by comparing an American and a Czech theory of the future development of industrial societies, Clark Kerr's *Industrialism and Industrial Man* and Radovan Richta's *Civilisation at the Cross-Roads*, which was the theory of 'Socialism with a human face' of the 'Czech Spring' of 1968. At this stage, we were particularly concerned with the problem of how far the differences between such theories could be accounted for by differences of an ideological kind. This final transition also differed from the work of the four earlier steps in that it introduced the problem of future change, and this was further developed in the final stage (number 7) of the course in which we studied the sociological contribution to a regional plan for the period up to the year 2000, Tayside.

The most important features of this curriculum were: that it had a coherent logic that links each section to the next; that it was built upon a contrast of theoretical styles; that it expressed a clear decision about the stages in which the material was to be presented; and that each stage reinforced the points made in earlier stages by the way in which the various topics were contrasted and developed.

These principles are obviously consistent with the educational theories of Piaget and Bruner. But they also arise from hard practical experience which demonstrates that students, like other people, find it difficult to grasp complicated points at one go. Academics often fail to realise that it is hard for their students really to understand not only what we say but what we mean by what we say. But words are a very difficult medium; and our material therefore has to be presented in such a way that the really difficult issues are approached from several difficult angles. Furthermore, if the seminar is to have a coherent meaning over a year's work, and if the student can be helped to make an effort to learn if he can grasp that meaning, then the work done in each separate seminar must clearly related to a coherent pattern of development within the discipline.

The same point applies to the place of each year's set of seminars in the course of three years' work as well as to the conduct of each separate seminar. There may well be many very different ways of conceiving the purpose of each year's work and it would be unwise to be dogmatic. In any event educational purposes can only be profitably discussed if they are related to the substantive context of a specific discipline, and purposes may vary considerably in different disciplines. But for my own part, the major purpose of a first-year sociology seminar is to get students to appreciate in practice how facts and theory interrelate, which is the core of sociological argument, while the second-year seminar should aim primarily to develop the student's ability to appraise social theory critically, and the third year to explore one major strand of crucially important theoretical argument in depth.

## Coherence and Development

It is also important that, within each seminar, a theme should develop coherently. The contributions of students and the tutor need to be very subtly balanced so that the argument is the result of their collaborative work. The tutor must guide the discussion in such a way that shape and coherence is given to the argument, without in any way inhibiting the students' contributions. In my experience, this is most likely to be achieved under the following conditions. It is vitally important that every student should have done some work for the seminar. He must not only have read something but also have written something which can be read on request. The group may be required to read either a common text or else various articles or books dealing with the topic to be discussed provided that the tutor knows how this material is likely to be relevant to the course of the discussion. They should be expected to do two kinds of writing, a précis of what is read and a critique of the material. Finally, students who have not done the required work should not normally be admitted to the seminar.

Granted, this is a pretty firm regime. But it has many virtues. First of all, it ensures that each student will have practice, week in week out, in reading, annotating, criticising and discussing: some of the basic tools of scholarship.

In addition, to allow students to come unprepared to a seminar is to give the impression that anything goes and to encourage 'talking off the cuff' rather than the considered but free discussion, which is the central virtue of the intellectual tradition into which they are being inducted.

The way in which the seminar develops is not random or haphazard; and it is important that the tutor should have an idea of the method he is going to employ in order to promote a good discussion. There are innumerable procedures of which I mention here only two. The first procedure is as follows: Student A reads his critique; B is then invited to comment on A's critique in the light of what he had himself written; B points out the degree to which their views agree or disagree and gives reasons to explain and possibly to justify any divergence. C is invited to comment on this and a general discussion encouraged. The tutor intervenes to draw the threads together and perhaps also to indicate his own conclusion. He then refers back to points previously made by A, B or C and asks D's comments; and so on. Alternatively, the tutor may invite each student in turn to state briefly the points which he has raised in his critique and which he wishes to discuss. The tutor then proposes an agenda on this basis, preferably indicating in some coherent fashion how the topics are connected. The issues are then discussed *seriatim* as under the previous procedure. In this way, the tutor can ensure that each student either has the opportunity or else is placed under an obligation to contribute and that, while the discussion grows out of their comments, it also has some overall shape and strategy. This is important because only if each separate seminar generates a discussion about a meaningful and coherent theme is it likely to live.

## The Student's Intellectual Development

I turn, finally, to consider the intellectual development of the student himself. In a discipline like sociology, which is grounded in verbal rather than quantitiative argument, I have the impression that tutors rarely consider carefully enough the intellectual procedures that a student has to master in order to command a discipline effectively. In quantitative studies we do this pretty carefully; but we are much less scrupulous in insisting upon cultivating precision and clarity where verbal argument is involved. Yet the basic tool of sociological analysis is verbal argument, and unless a tutor is aware of the kind of intellectual weaknesses that the student is likely to fall into in this sphere, he will probably miss them. A few examples can be given to illustrate what I mean.

Students frequently fail to distinguish between that I call 'procedural' and 'substantive' statement. Ask a student, for example, to review a book. He will probably say: 'The author writes about the way in which output is related to social structure. He goes on to discuss the problem of....' But this is merely a procedural statement, a kind of agenda: it is simply restating, in effect, the headings on the contents page. What is obviously required is a substantive statement, such as the following: 'Smith demonstrates that firms with a centralized structure had a low output of X but a high output of Y, while firms with decentralized structures had exactly the opposite pattern of output.' Such propositions, on the other hand, clearly have a substance, since they inform us precisely what the author had to say. However, since I frequently have to require even third-year students to translate procedural into substantive statements, either the distinction is a very difficult one to grasp or their earlier tutors have allowed them to confuse the two. I suspect both to be true. But it is clear that, if a student is not made aware of this distinction but continues to produce the easier but more superficial procedural statements when substantive ones are needed, he will simply skate over the detailed substance of a discipline and be, to that extent, less effective intellectually.

First-year students sometimes do not know how to read a text adequately for academic purposes and they need to be shown how to do so. For example, when they are asked to write a commentary on a book under the two headings: What has been found out? and What was the author driving at? many students say virtually the same thing under each heading, since they have never really considered the possibility that an author might be driving at anything. But how, without understanding that, can they grasp the point of a book.

Further, students are often at a loss to know how to criticise a book or an article. As a critique, therefore, they may produce what is in effect little more than a list of quotations or points, accompanied by a simple affirmation of agreement or disagreement. As I have sometimes heard students say, 'But what can I say? It's all been written already by someone better qualified than me.' They need to be shown in the course of the seminar itself how to go about making a reasoned appraisal. Alternatively, students are also inclined to assert points of view, without giving adequate reasons for what they say, and the tutor has to insist that even their agreement with a point, if it is to be made responsibly, must be supported by evidence and good reasoning.

These examples will serve to show the kind of things that I have in mind under this heading. A seminar curriculum, in my opinion, should incorporate quite systematically a way of throwing up and of dealing with difficulties of this kind which recur so frequently year after year. One procedure designed to help students to make their criticisms more effectively is to note briefly their first attempts at a critique on the blackboard, and then by noting the stages of the subsequent discussion, to demonstrate how one actually does fashion a more sophisticated appraisal. In this way, the tutor does not simply urge or admonish his students but actually uses the seminar to demonstrate what is intended. Admonition alone is a weak educational method.

# Training Academics

University teachers clearly require some kind of training particulary in seminar method, since it cannot be assumed that they are competent seminar teachers simply because they have taken part in seminars. To be able to conduct a seminar effectively requires not only direct experience but also a good deal of practice and thought about that practice. Improvements in seminar teaching, therefore will be promoted by encouraging the tutor to reflect more carefully on what he has been doing in teaching his particular discipline. The best method of training young teachers in seminar method would be to institute some kind of academic apprenticeship, in which they would be assigned to the seminar of a more experienced tutor, who would be responsible for explaining and discussing critically what he was doing in the seminar and why he was doing it that way. To be able to do this, however, would probably require of the tutor himself a much more sophisticated understanding of how and why he teaches so that his teaching practice could be rationally assessed. What is needed above all is material such as tape recordings of seminars which would serve as a basis for teaching tutors how to tutor. Universities therefore should consider the possibilities of instituting some kind of apprenticeship system for younger academics; setting up study-groups which would aim to study systematically the processes of university teaching; and of arranging for the collation of tapes and other teaching aids which could be used in the training of teachers.

# 32

# Introduction to Student-Centred Discussion

In all the discussion methods considered so far, the agenda has been decided by the teacher. Even in tutorless task-centred groups, the tutor usually decides the tasks. If teaching consists of presenting students with certain facts and then getting them to manipulate (think about) the facts in very specific ways, that may be all right; but a lot of teaching is not like that. Specific facts and ways of thinking may be desirable in some aspects of the physical sciences, but in many subjects there is neither one 'right' way of thinking nor one correct set of facts. What the teacher tries to do in such cases is develop perceptions, thought patterns, feelings and attitudes that the student already has. Such methods are called 'student-centred'. It is not a matter of injecting new ideas and making students practise particular skills using them, but of drawing out those individual and personal perceptions, thoughts, feelings and attitudes.

Drawing out, that is 'elicitation', is the first stage. Elicitation is only possible when the student feels confident, secure, or sufficiently supported to express his private thoughts and feelings. Hence the enormous importance of developing trust in groups, of giving support, and of giving students the opportunity to express what they think and feel, rather than imposing a task or agenda.

The trouble with trying to develop students' perceptions, thoughts, feelings or attitudes is that they are normally concealed, not explicit. Only when they have been 'elicited', to make them open and no longer concealed, can they be considered in discussion. Consideration is the second stage. Such consideration in discussion raises self-awareness and gives an opportunity for feelings and attitudes to be considered rationally.

After rational discussion the student will be better able to change his thoughts and attitudes in a controlled way and be aware of what he is doing. In other words he will have freedom to develop himself as he wishes. This third stage may take place long after discussion is over.

The discussion during the first two stages is fundamentally different from the discussions hitherto described in this volume. It is centred upon the thoughts and feelings of the students, not upon topics imposed by the tutor. The students, not the teacher, determine the content. Since that content is their own experience; it is they, not the teacher, who are most knowledgeable about it. The teacher is not the authority. The students are given freedom to explore their thoughts and feelings and to take the discussion where they will. Aspects of contributions that are irrelevant or do not interest the other students are not taken up. The students decide what is relevant and they learn, albeit slowly, to take responsibility for their own learning.

Chapters 33-36 are concerned with elicitation and the techniques to achieve it. They are concerned with preconceptions and ways of thinking. Barnett (Chapter 33) does not describe an experiment in the scientific sense, but it is a concise account of the free group discussion method first developed by Jane Abercrombie. The principles stated by Carl Rogers (Chapter 34) are a classic, and once controversial, advocacy of student-centred learning. From Mary Wheeler's book on study methods counselling I have selected the chapter particularly concerned with developing personal relationships, rather than those dealing with specific study problems (Chapter 35). A great deal has been written about T-groups (the T stands for training), sensitivity groups or encounter groups, and the three are here regarded as synonymous. I have selected the article by Peter Smith (Chapter 36) because it is concerned with students, and in discussion support and confrontation it deals with techniques where many teachers are insensitive. It also relates well to other chapters in this book.

# 33

# An Experiment with 'Free Group Discussions'

## S. A. Barnett

*Quidquod recipitur recipitur ad modum recipientis*

The core of these notes is a report on work done in a tutorial class on human biology. During one session of twenty-four meetings, the teaching method used at alternate meetings differed from the conventional ones:[1] the class had previously been given a lecture during the first hour of each meeting, but during the experimental meetings the whole of the two hours was devoted to discussion.

Every teacher who has examined his own pupils knows that much of what he teaches is lost or distorted during learning. It is always tempting to attribute this to the 'natural' defects of the students: to adopt a doctrine, not of original sin, but of original stupidity or laziness. This attitude, even if reassuring to the teacher, is certainly unscientific; and it can hardly lead to any improvement in results. Rational questions which may be asked are: (a) what is it that makes the learning of many students, young or adult, so imperfect? and (b) is it possible that some part of the deficiency could be made good by changed teaching methods?'

These questions cannot yet be fully answered, but it is already possible to suggest some improved methods of teaching for the various educational levels. The method of free group discussion (FGD) can probably be applied in sixth-forms, in ordinary university teaching and in adult education classes. It is designed to overcome the difficulty suggested in the quotation at the head: the difficulty that each person has his own individual preconceptions and modes of thinking, and that these profoundly influence his understanding of any statement made to him.

I will take an example from discussions with first-year medical students. These students had read an excerpt from an essay by J.B.S. Haldane on control experiments. At the beginning an example is taken of a hospital patient given a drug to make him sleep, and it is suggested that the fact that he does sleep does not prove that the drug was effective: perhaps, for instance, he slept because he had been told he would do so. Several students,

---

Reproduced by permission from Barnett 1958.

in different groups, stated that they disagreed with the whole of the article, on the grounds that Haldane overemphasized the importance of psychology in medicine. Haldane in fact makes no statement on this subject in this article. He uses the example quoted, as one of several, to illustrate the concept of control experiments. Certain students were however, emotionally biased in such a way that they were unable to appreciate what the article was about, let alone discuss it rationally or learn from it.

The students who displayed this bias were *eventually* corrected by *other students*, as the latter *gradually* formulated their thoughts on the subject during *uncontrolled* discussion. The words emphasized in the preceding sentence indicate some of the features of FGD which differentiate it sharply from the ordinary seminar. In FGD there is little or preferably no authoritative exposition from the tutor; there is no attempt to check irrelevancies, since these reveal the unconscious polarizations and difficulties of comprehension in the student; and as far as possible it is left to the group to correct errors and to arrive at sound conclusions. The function of the tutor is to keep the ball rolling (if necessary; it usually is not); to encourage the more silent members of the group (eg if they do say anything, to refer back to it as a useful contribution to the discussion, thus increasing self-confidence); and to intervene with interpretations of students' prejudices when they become evident and no other member of the group does so.

The procedure in the extra-mural class was to issue a duplicated sheet, with a passage from a published source discussing a topic relevant to the course; this was studied for about thirty minutes. Later, the material for discussion was issued at the previous meeting. The class then discussed the passage, sitting at a table in the tutor's room. Generally, the tutor remained almost silent until towards the end, but took notes on points which seemed to him of interest. In this way the tutor himself learnt a great deal.

The passages themselves were very varied. They included one from Charles Darwin, on 'Instinct'; material on the 'Kinsey reports'; and an elementary account of reflex action. The immediate response of the class to the last was that it offered no scope for discussion, since it was purely factual and perfectly clear. Two hours later they were still arguing, having revealed a great diversity of attitudes and understanding in relation to reflexes.

The class was probably the ideal size for such discussions – about eight. The members were of diverse background and experience, but all showed a high developed intellectual curiosity which no doubt is what had led them to extra-mural study. They approved of free group discussion on the whole, but did not consider the method should be the only one used throughout the course. They liked having a typed excerpt at the beginning of (or preferably before) each meeting, apart from the exact form taken by the discussion.

The discussions were very free and animated. They brought out clearly the way in which each student looks at a topic on the basis of his or her own experience and bias. In that on reflexes one student, an active worker in the Labour movement, found it easy to raise questions connected with working-class politics. In a discussion on Kuo's work on the learning of predatory behaviour by kittens, it was clear that different students had come away with quite different sets of ideas after reading a quite short passage; one, for instance, had interpreted it entirely in terms of the desirability of educating children to desire a peaceful world. Reading a bald summary of some of the Kinsey findings induced a slight state of shock, which was reflected in a tendency to condemn the whole thing out of hand, or to dismiss it as American and so hardly relevant to us. It was agreed at the end of the discussion that a distinction should be made between a scientific report and its usefulness on the one hand, and approval or otherwise of American behaviour on the other.

At the beginning of the first discussion one student was very aggressive – almost alarmingly so: he shouted and laid down the law, and the tutor had to interrupt him, gently, to prevent him from interrupting the others. At the end, the tutor remarked on the agressiveness, amid general laughter. At later meetings much less aggressiveness was shown by this student.

Some of the discussions led to a demand for further information: a passage on the meaning of 'normal' led to a suggestion that statistical analysis should be included in next year's course. In the same discussion one student said suddenly: '"Normal" ought not to be used. After this discussion I should hesitate to use it at all.'

As the discussion went on, students came gradually to stick more to the point, and to criticize each other more effectively. There was rather less arbitrary statement of personal prejudices, and rather more attempt at rational argument. These trends were however only just beginning to appear after twelve free dicussions.

In the opinion of the writer, it is most important for the tutor to remain as silent as possible, since his words (a) are received too much as the voice of authority, (b) have very little effect indeed. Often the tutor tried to expound some particular point briefly – sometimes by request, but it was soon obvious that what he had said had not sunk in. (This fits in with the fact that enquiry at the beginning of the session showed that very little detail of the previous year's work had been remembered.) Sometimes the tutor interjected questions, but these were commonly ignored, and the students persisted (quite rightly) with their own trains of thought. Towards the end, however, there appeared a tendency to pay some attention to the tutor's questions.

In general, it seemed that the students were gradually learning to learn, but that many more meetings of a similar kind would be needed to have a full effect. This conclusion was supported during discussions held with the same group in the following session, when continued improvement was shown.

At the last two meetings the tutor's draft report was discussed; the substance of this report is contained in the preceding paragraphs of this paper.

Two of the students said that they thought that the tutor had underestimated the amount that they learnt from lectures, but on the whole the report was considered to be an acceptable account of FGD and its effects. It became clear that the members of the class had accepted the free group discussion method as desirable and effective. A middle-aged woman (who claimed to have learnt a lot from the lectures) said that during the course, and especially recently, she had become much more articulate; originally she had hardly opened her mouth, now she talked much more; moreover, she discussed the subjects of the course at home with friends. Another student, a young man in the electrical trade who was usually very quiet, suddenly spoke up at length on the importance of realizing one's unconscious bias and preconceptions, which tend to inhibit learning: the free discussions, he considered, helped him to learn to learn.

There was some exchange of personalites. One man, who tends to take a cynical and destructive line in discussion, was attacked by the rest. (One of his replies was: 'I can get even you, Mary, annoyed, now!' – referring to the effects of the discussions on the quieter members.) Another man, who used to talk a great deal, was considered to have benefited because he now talked *less*, and more to the point. The importance of the small size and intimacy of the group was emphasized.

Proposals for novel methods of teaching always meet with resistance from some teachers (both at school and university). One form of the resistance to FGD is the notion that its supporters propose to replace all other methods with FGD. This is far from being the case. It is however suggested here that a admixture of FGD can improve the effects of other types of teaching, by clarifying the thoughts of students and enabling them to unravel confusions – many of which have an origin in unconscious preconceptions. Learning is only to a partial extent a rational process, but most methods of teaching assume tacitly that it is wholly rational.

A second form of objection may be expressed in the statement that students must be taught *facts*. The implication is perhaps that discussions, of whatever form, will be woolly and unprofitable. The answer is that of course students must learn facts: the problem is, how? FGDs can deal very well indeed (as Johnson has shown) with strictly factual questions, such as the comparison of the radiographs of two hands. The learning of facts meets with just the same difficulties as the learning of generalities. Indeed, in the extra-mural classes described above, discussions of strictly factual material were particularly valuable. The material issued before the discussion provided a concrete basis for argument.

A third comment on FGD is to the effect that it is only a seminar with a fancy name, and that university and extra-mural teachers have been doing it for centuries. It is no doubt true that some informal discussions can have effects similar to those attributed to FGDs, but as a rule seminars are opened by a set paper; they are commonly controlled by someone in authority, who may consider it essential to insist on relevance and logical exposition; and in general the discussion is expected to proceed entirely on the rational plane, without considering the individual (often irrational) difficulties of the students. However, it is certainly not suggested here that ordinary seminars are useless: we need much more information on the effects of different types of teaching, before a decision can be taken on how much and when they should be used.

There is indeed no case at all for dogmatism about teaching methods. At present FGD is being used in the ordinary university teaching of preclinical medicine, clinical medicine and German in London University (Polani 1953); and of genetics in Glasgow University. As its use grows, and as further research on its effects is published, it will become easier to assess its importance. It is hoped that this article will induce some teachers to enquire into the method further by discussing it and by giving the method a trial where suitable classes are available. The indications at present are that the use of FGD will spread, and will become a valuable aid to both pupils and teachers, but this must depend on those willing to make novel experiments.

## Note

The method used was based on the work of M.L. Johnson, to whom I am indebted for much helpful advice (Abercrombie 1960).

# 34

## Student-Centred Teaching

### *Carl Rogers*

If the creation of an atmosphere of acceptance, understanding, and respect is the most effective basis for facilitating the learning which is called therapy, then might it not be the basis for the learning which is called education? If the outcome of this approach to therapy is a person who is not only better informed in regard to himself, but who is better able to guide himself intelligently in new situations, might a similar outcome be hoped for from teaching?

## The Goal of Education

It may avoid needless misunderstanding if it is clearly stated at the outset that education which embodies the principles of client-centred therapy has relevance for only one type of educational goal. It is not education which would be relevant in an authoritarian culture, nor would it implement an authoritarian philosophy. If the aim of education is to produce well-informed technicians who will be completely amenable to carrying out all orders of constituted authority without questioning, then the method we are to describe is highly inappropriate. In general it is relevant only to the type of goal which is loosely described as democratic.

This would seem to mean that the goal of democratic education is to assist students to become individuals:

who are able to take self-initiated action and to be responsible for those actions;

who are capable of intelligent choice and self-direction;

who are critical learners, able to evaluate the contributions made by others;

who have acquired knowledge relevant to the solution of problems;

who, even more importantly, are able to adapt flexibly and intelligently to new problem situations;

who have internalised an adaptive mode of approach to problems, utilising all pertinent experience freely and creatively;

---

Extracted by permission from Rogers 1951.

TTD-L

who are able to cooperate effectively with others in these various activities;

who work, not for the approval of others, but in terms of their own socialised purposes.

The method of operation of our grammar schools, colleges, universities, and professional schools is ample evidence that the usual goal is very different – more in the direction of producing a student who can reproduce certain informational material, who has skills in performing certain prescribed intellectual operations, and who can reproduce the thinking of his teacher. The approach to education which we are about to describe is not aimed towards these latter goals, but is an attempt to find a method which will achieve the goal described here as democratic.

Whether this goal is appropriate to our current culture is a question which each reader must decide for himself. Since our culture to a very large degree is organised on an authoritarian and hierarchical basis and only partially upon a democratic basis, it may seem to some that education should reflect this ambivalence. Each must reach his own conclusion on this point.

## Some Tentative Principles and Hypotheses

As we have fumbled about in our attempts to develop a student-centred teaching which would build on the concepts of client-centred therapy, certain basis hypotheses have been crystallised which are very parallel indeed to the hypotheses of therapy. Some of these are stated below, in what may seem to be a rather technical form. Stated thus as hypotheses, there is always the risk that they will be understood as flat statements of fact. It should therefore be emphasised that they are tentative in character, and still largely unproved by research in the education field.

*We cannot teach another person directly; we can only facilitate his learning.*

This is an hypothesis with which any thoughtful teacher will agree. It is indeed only a formal restatement of the old adage that 'You can lead a horse to water but you can't make him drink.' Operationally, however, most teachers utterly ignore this basic hypothesis. Watch a faculty group concerned with the formation of a curriculum. How much shall we cover in this course? How can we avoid overlap between these courses? Isn't that a topic best taught in the third year? What percentage of our first-year course shall be given to this topic? These are samples of questions discussed – and they are all of them based on the hypothesis, which every faculty member knows is false, that what is taught is what is learned.

Here, more than at any other point, is evidenced the revolutionary nature of a student-centred approach to education. If instead of focusing all our interest on the teacher – What shall I teach? How can I prove that I have taught it? How can I 'cover' all that I should teach? – we focused our interest on the student, the questions and the issues would all be different. Suppose we asked, what are his purposes in the course, what does he wish to learn, how can we facilitate his learning and his growth? A very different type of education would ensue. An educational program whether at the elementary, college, or graduate level – which had the facilitation of learning as its clear and definite and primary operational purpose – would be a program vastly different from the ones with which we are most familiar.

*A person learns significantly only those things which he perceives as being related to his self.*

Here is an hypothesis which is basic to personality theory. Perhaps the meaning of the hypothesis can be illustrated by referring to two types of student in, let us say, a course in mathematics or statistics. The first student perceives this mathematical material as being directly relevant to his professional purpose, and thus directly involved in his long-range enhancement of self. The second student is taking the course because it is required. For the maintenance and enhancement of self he regards it as necessary that he stay in the university. Therefore it is necessary that he pass the course. Can there be any question as to the differences in learning which take place? The first student acquires a functional learning of the material. The second learns how to 'get by' in the course. Or suppose that the information which is being given is in regard to the topography of a certain region. How different will be the learnings of a group listening because this is a required course in geography, and a platoon of infantry who are going into those hills and valleys to seek out the enemy! The maintenance of self is very little involved in the first group, and very deeply in the second.

*Experience which, if assimilated, would involve a change in the organisation of self tends to be resisted through denial or distortion of symbolisation.*

*The structure and organisation of self appears to become more rigid under threat; to relax its boundaries when completely free from threat. Experience which is perceived as inconsistent with the self can only be assimilated if the current organisation of self is relaxed and expanded to include it.*

These hypotheses have to do with the fact that learning, particularly if it is significant, is often a threatening thing. There are times when the new material of education is immediately perceived as making for the enhancement of self, but in a great many other instances the new material threatens the self, or, more exactly, some value with which the self has become identified. This is very obviously true in the social sciences. To learn the objective facts about prejudice may threaten prejudices which are valued. To learn about the distribution of intelligence in the population may disturb beliefs with which the individual is identified. To perceive certain facts relating to our economic system may threaten middle-class values with which the student has identified. But the threatening character of new learning holds true of the physical and biological sciences and the humanities as well. To learn a new mathematical method may imply inferiority in the old method with which the learner is identified. To learn an appreciation of classical music or literature is likely to imply a negative judgement on appreciations already developed at a lower level. We should doubtless be considerably surprised if we knew the proportions of individuals in any student group at any given time whose basic set was a sceptical, resistant,

'Oh yeah?' attitude. The reader can to some degree measure this in himself by thinking back over the last five lectures or classes or sermons he has attended. To how much of the material did he find himself inwardly resistant?

*The educational situation which most effectively promotes significant learning is one in which (1) threat to the self of the learner is reduced to a minimum, and (2) differentiated perception of the field of experience is facilitated.*

The two parts of this hypothesis are almost synonymous, since differentiated perception is most likely when the self is not under threat. If we take this hypothesis as a description of what education should provide, it will be seen that such education would be far different from present-day programs.

It may be objected that learning goes on in spite of, or even because of, threat. Witness the platoon which is likely to be fired upon as it goes into enemy territory, and because of this threat learns rapidly and effectively about the terrain. It is true that when reality provides the threat, the learning of behaviours which will maintain the self goes on apace. If the desired training has no other goal than to maintain the self as it is, then threat to self may not impede the progress of learning. But in education this is almost never true. What is desired is growth, and this involves change in the self. Whenever such a broader goal is envisaged, then threat to the self appears to be a barrier to significant learning.

# The Application of these Principles in the Classroom

The abstract hypotheses just cited are obviously the product of experience, not the forerunner. We shall endeavour to present some of the experiences out of which they grew, and the present formulation of a teaching approach which implements them.

## The Creation of an Acceptant Climate

As in counselling, our first experimental approaches to the teaching situation relied rather heavily upon teacher technique. Gradually the realisation grew that if the teacher's attitudes were such as to create an appropriate classroom climate, the specific techniques were secondary. This relationship between basic attitude and specific method is well stated by Eiserer (1949):

If teachers accept students as they are, allow them to express their feelings and attitudes freely without condemnation or judgment, plan learning activities with them rather than *for* them, create a classroom atmosphere relatively free from emotional strains and tensions, consequences follow which are different from when these conditions do not exist. The consequence, on present evidence, seem to be in the direction of democratic objectives. It is apparent that the above conditions can be achieved in more than one way – that the climate for self-directed learning by students is not the result of only one kind of practice.

As to the effect of this climate upon the student, Shedlin (unpublished), who has achieved effective results in this type of teaching, has this to say:

> A classroom climate of permissiveness and understanding provides a situation free of threat, in which the student can work without defensiveness. The decks are kept clear for him to consider the material being discussed from his own internal frame of reference. His desire for acceptance is realised, and because of this he feels the demand upon himself to be responsible for his own interpretations and insights. He feels the full strength of another person's belief in his integrity. An interesting and important outgrowth of this self-acceptance is the observable improvement in his inter-personal relations with others. He will tend to show greater understanding and acceptance of them, and develop freer, more real relationships with them. This has great importance from the standpoint of the communication and extension of the basic classroom mood.

Although the type of climate described is essential throughout the conduct of the course, the teacher who is eager to experiment with this approach in education will wish to know how to develop such an educational climate at the beginning of the course. The answer here seems to be twofold. First, a permissive and understanding climate, which respects the selfhood and purposive individuality of each student, can be developed only in so far as the instructor holds a philosophy which is consistent with these elements. In the second place, the teacher will want to implement this point of view from the very first in his work with the class. Since this experience will run almost directly counter to all the previous educational experience of the student, careful thought should be given to the techniques used.

It is desirable that the seating arrangement be a circle, or some physical arrangement which gives the instructor the same type of place as any member of the class. It is important that the purposes of the students should be foremost. The sessions may be started with a description by students of the problems they are facing, or with a discussion of problem areas. The writer has sometimes started a course with as simple a statement as this: 'This is a course labelled Dynamics of Personality (or whatever course is being taught). I suspect each of us had some sort of purpose in enrolling, even if that purpose was only to gain another credit. If we could begin telling what our purposes were, perhaps we can, together, build the course in such a way as to meet them.' As personal purposes are stated (often hesitantly and haltingly), they are simply accepted, or the attitudes connected with them are clarified. Gradually issues arise out of these purposes, and the class is embarked upon its own curriculum construction.

However, this is not to say that things will run smoothly. In students who have, for anything from one to twenty years, experienced a class in a passive experience, such an opening of a course is at first puzzling, then downright frustrating. Negative feelings, often very strong ones, are aroused. At first they are not expressed because one does not 'talk back to' or correct the teacher; but as tension mounts, some bold soul bursts out, 'I think we're wasting our time! I think we ought to have an outline, and follow it, and that you ought to teach us. We came here to learn from you, not to discuss among ourselves!' When negative attitudes such as these are understood and accepted, students begin to recognise the climate that exists. Some may not like the procedure, may heartily disapprove, but all recognise that this is a very different situation from that existing in the ordinary classroom.

The atmosphere which prevails will depend primarily upon what the teacher does and how he does it. Frequently the teacher who is considering some experimentation along these lines believes that he cannot undertake it, 'because we must use an assigned test' or because 'my section must pass the same examination as sections taught in a conventional way,' or 'I am held responsible for seeing that my class covers such and such readings each week.' Consideration of these points will perhaps serve to illustrate the primary importance of teacher attitudes. If for example this class must meet the same examination as other sections, the teacher's attitude, as expressed to the class, would take this into account: 'I would like this course to be, in so far as possible, your course, to meet the purposes you would like to have it meet. There is one limitation which is imposed upon me as well as upon you, and that is the examination which every section of this course must take. With that limitation in mind, what purposes would you like this course to serve?'

We may summarise by saying that every group has some limitations, if only the fact that they meet for a limited, rather than an unlimited number of hours each week. It is not the fact that there are limitations, but the attitude, the permissiveness, the freedom which exists within those limitations, which is important.

The essential principle might perhaps be the following: Within the limitations which are imposed by circumstance and authority, or are imposed by the teacher as necessary for his own psychological comfort, an atmosphere of permissiveness, of acceptance, of reliance upon student responsibility, is created.

## The Changing Role of the Leader

We may state briefly our present concept of the role of the leader in an educational situation when the aim is to centre the process in the developing aims of the students.

- Initially the leader has much to do with setting the mood or climate of the group experience by his own basic philosophy of trust in the group, which is communicated in many subtle ways.
- The leader helps to elicit and clarify the purposes of the members of the class, accepting all aims.
- He relies upon the student desire to implement these purposes as the motivational force behind learning
- He endeavours to organise and make easily available all resources which the students may wish to use for their own learning
- He regards himself as a flexible resource to be utilized by the group in the ways which seem most meaningful to them, in so far as he can be comfortable operating in these ways.
- In responding to expressions from the group, he accepts both the intellectual content and the emotionalised attitudes, endeavouring to

give each aspect the approximate degree of emphasis which it has for the individual and the group.

- As the acceptant classroom climate becomes established, the leader is able to change his role and becomes a participant, a member of the group, expressing his views as those of one individual only.
- He remains alert to expressions indicative of deep feeling and when these are voiced he endeavours to understand these from the speaker's point of view, and to communicate this type of understanding.
- Likewise when group interaction becomes charged with emotion, he tends to maintain a neutral and understanding role, in order to give acceptance to the varied feelings which exist.
- He recognises that the extent to which he can behave in these differing fashions is limited by the genuineness of his own attitudes. To pretend an acceptant understanding of a viewpoint when he does not feel this acceptance, will not further, and will probably hinder, the dynamic progress of the class.

## The Process of Learning in a Student-centred Class

To one who is used to highly organised classroom presentations, discussion may seem loose, may appear to jump from topic to topic. This is certainly true, but it is probable that this fluid, exploratory, even confused type of advance is more deeply characteristic of learning as it occurs, than the dead systematisation of learning after the fact. One of the things we have learned as teachers is that if the leader is uncomfortable at leaving issues 'up in the air' and tries to achieve closure by some type of summary and conclusion at the end of the discussion, this provides some relief for the group, but effecively stops any need for further thinking about the subject. If, however, the leader can tolerate the uncertainty, the divided views, the unresolved issues which the group has brought out, and if the class hour (and indeed the course) is ended without any attempt to bring an artificial closure, then the individual members of the group carry on very vital thinking outside of the class hours. The issues have been raised, some of their former conceptions and gestalts have been unsettled, they need to find some resolution of the situation, they recognise that the teacher will not give an authoritative answer to the problem, and hence there is only one alternative – to learn and learn and learn, until they have reached at least a temporary solution for themselves. And because they have achieved it for themselves, and recognise all too clearly the imperfect steps by which it was achieved, this temporary solution can never have the fixity that it would have if it had been authoritatively pronounced by a professor. Therefore, instead of becoming a fixed point, a barrier to future learning, it is instead merely a step, a way-station on the road to further learning.

## The Problem of Evaluation

How shall we solve the problem of grades, of passing of courses and examinations, when this approach is used in the classroom situation? How is the student to be evaluated?

There seems to be only one answer to this question which is thoroughly consistent with the approach itself. If the purpose of the individual and the group are the organising core of the course; if the purposes of the individual are met if he finds significant learnings, resulting in self-enhancement, in the course; if the teacher's function is to facilitate such learnings; then there is but one person who is in a position to evaluate the degree to which the goal has been achieved, and that is the student himself. Self-evaluation appears to be the logical procedure for discovering those ways in which the experience has been a failure and those respects in which it has been meaningful and fruitful. This is, indeed, the fitting climax of an 'education for rulers'. Who is to say whether the student has put forth his best effort? What weaknesses and gaps there are in his learnings? What has been the quality of his thinking as he has wrestled with the problems which his own purposes have posed? The person most competent to perform this task would appear to be the responsible individual who has experienced the purposes, who has observed intimately his efforts to achieve them – the learner who has been in the centre of the process. Here again is evidence of the revolutionary character of this approach to education, since the very heart of all our educational programme is the rigorous (one might almost say ruthless) evaluation of the student, whether by the teacher, or by a standardised and impersonal test.

Our experience has corroborated the theoretical principle that self-evaluation is the most desirable mode of appraisal in a student-centred course. The greater the freedom to use self-evaluation in such a situation, the more obviously favourable have been the results. Students experience the task of self-appraisal as one more opportunity for growth. They experience with wonderment the fact that no one is going to utilize an external locus of evaluation. They do not need to tremble for fear they will be 'failed'; nor can they look with childish anticipation for approval. The question for each student is – What is my honest appraisal of what I have done, as it relates to my own purpose? There is not even any gain to come from inflating the self-appraisal. As one student writes, 'I started to make this pretty rosy, but who would I be kidding, and why should I kid myself?' To carry through a self-evaluation is often a most difficult task. It means that the student must formulate his criteria of evaluation, must decide on the standards that he has for himself. It means experiencing to the full the implications of discovering that, in the long run, the locus of evaluation lies in one's self. Something of the flavour of this experience will be conveyed in the next section, where quotations will be given from documents concerned with self-evaluation.

Let us now turn, however, to another phase of this problem of evaluation. Most teachers are working in institutional frameworks in which the operational philosophy is almost directly opposed to that which we have been presenting. The students must be 'motivated' to work; the only proof that he has been motivated is through examinations; external evaluation is the primary function of education; grades are the balance sheet of such evaluation; and throughout the whole process the teacher must not trust the student. Is it, then, impossible for a teacher to handle his class in a student-centred fashion in such a framework? We have not found it so, though admittedly there must be some compromises, if we are to advance by evolutionary rather than revolutionary means.

Again, the problems lose their overwhelming character if the teacher is clear in his own philosophical approach to the situation. Grades and evaluation simply become one more limitation imposed by the environment, one more problem which the students and the teacher must solve. The teacher poses his dilemma to the group. 'The university demands that I sign my name to the grades given to all the members of the class, indicating that they have performed at a certain level. How do you wish to meet that problem?' Operating in such a framework, any solution is less than perfect, but various classes have arrived at working solutions which have made for far more growth than the conventional approach. Some of these may be listed.

- In some courses students have formulated the examination by submitting questions and have participated in its evaluation.
- In one small class where the students were acquainted with each other's work, they decided to arrive at grades in an open class discussion at the end of the course. Each student stated the grade he felt he had earned, and gave his reasons. The group and teacher entered into the discussion and each grade was arrived at by a general concurrence of opinion.
- In some universities a grade of Pass or Fail can be turned in. Utilizing this, classes have accepted a P grade, permitting self-evaluation to be the real judgement on their work.
- In some courses each student has written out a self-evaluation including his judgement as to an appropriate letter grade for himself. The understanding is that the teacher will turn in this grade unless he feels that he cannot agree with it, in which case the grade will be arrived at in conference between student and teacher.

These represent a few of the many compromise approaches which have been made. Even the most faulty ones have these advantages. They emphasize that evaluation of the student by the student deserves much weight in the evaluation process. The basis for grades inevitably comes into sharp focus, and students come to realise that they are often (if not always) antithetical to growth in terms of personal purposes. The student becomes quite fully aware of the fact that a grade is a highly artificial thing, based upon very human and fallible methods, and that his own judgement of his achievement is at least as valid for him as a judgement from an external locus of evaluation.

As we have struggled with this problem of grades and academic book-keeping, and have contrasted it with those experiences in which students are free to evaluate themselves, we have reached the conclusion which to some will seem radical indeed. It is that personal growth is hindered and hampered, rather than enhanced, by external evaluation. Whether that evaluation is favourable or unfavourable, it does not seem to make for the development of more mature, responsible, or socialised self, but indeed tends to work in an opposite direction.

This is not to say that we would do away with all evaluation. If I am hiring one person from among ten applicants, I evaluate them all. If a man is going out as a physician, a psychologist, a lawyer, or an architect, then perhaps the welfare of society may demand that he be evaluated in terms of certain publicly available criteria, so that society may know whether or not he is competent for his task. But let it be recognised that such evaluations are made on behalf of the welfare of the organisation, or the welfare of society. They do not, as far as we can determine, promote the growth or welfare of the individual.

## Outcomes of Student-centred Teaching

It has been our frequent practice to ask students to turn in at the end of the course some sort of personal document – self-evaluation, or a reaction to the experience of the course. One of the impressive learnings which result from perusing these documents is the sharp realisation that each student attended a different course. That is, the experiential field of each person is so different that at times it is very difficult to believe that the papers turned in were written about what was, from an external point of view, the same objective experience, namely a certain course with a certain teacher. To read such a group of papers thoughtfully is to give up forever the notion that a course will mean to all students a certain degree of 'coverage' of topics A, B, and C. Each person's experience of the course is highly unique, and intimately related to his own past and to his current desires and purposes.

In spite of this uniqueness there are certain general trends often noticeable in such reports. The first is the feeling of puzzlement, a feeling which may range from amused perplexity to real confusion and a sense of profound frustration. The student reacts with some emotion to the experience of being put on his own. A brief statement of this reaction, which would be typical of many, may be taken from a student self-evalution.

> At first I had a feeling that we were not going anywhere. Then gradually I began to feel that we were going somewhere, but couldn't determine just where. Finally, I came to the conclusion that where we were going depended on each individual.

Another general trend is that most students tend to work harder, and at a deeper level, than in the conventional course.

Another trend to which we have become accustomed is the pervasiveness of the learning which takes place in a student-centred class. It makes a difference in the *life* of the individual, not simply in the intellectual symbols which he manipulates. This is very evident in the reactions of our students. One may say that the concepts in the course, as well as the manner of teaching, accounted for the results. However, a lecture course in client-centred therapy is quite unlikely to have the type of result described.

Not every student responds favourably to a student-centred approach. Usually all but a small minority have attitudes more favourable than unfavourable. There are often, however, some who feel the course has not been of benefit to them. Sometimes even this negative reaction appears significant of progress.

Research investigations of the outcomes of student-centred teaching are in their infancy, but the findings thus far seem to corroborate the observations of teachers and students.

## A Concluding Discussion

Much of present education appears to be operationally based on the assumption, 'You can't trust the student.' Acting on this assumption, the teacher must supply motivation, information, organisation of the material, and must use examinations – quizzes, recitations, oral exams, course examinations, standardised achievement tests – at every turn to coerce the student into the desired activities.

The approach we have been discussing is based on an assumption diametrically opposed, that 'You can trust the student.' You can trust him to desire to learn in every way which will maintain or enhance self; you can trust him to make use of resources which will serve this end; you can trust him to evaluate himself in ways which will make for self-progress; you can trust him to grow, provided the atmosphere for growth is available to him.

If the teacher accepts this assumption or is willing to adopt it as a very tentative hypothesis, then certain behaviour follows. He creates a classroom climate which respects the integrity of the student, which accepts all aims, opinions, and attitudes as being legitimate expressions of the student's internal frame of reference at that time. He accepts the feelings and emotionalised attitudes which surround any educational or group experience. He accepts himself as being a member of a learning group, rather than an authority. He makes learning resources available, confident that if they meet the needs of the group they will be used. He relies upon the capacity of the individual to sort out truth from untruth, upon the basis of continuing experience. He recognises that his course, if successful, is a beginning in learning, not the end of learning. He relies upon the capacity of the student to assess his progress in terms of the purposes which he has at this time. He has confidence in the fact that, in this atmosphere which he has helped to create, a type of learning takes place which is personally meaningful and which feeds the total self-development of the individual as well as improves his acquaintance with a given field of knowledge.

# 35

# Individual Study Counselling

*Mary Wheeler*

This chapter attempts to identify the principles of counselling in study methods in as much as I have discovered them in experience. They are not derived consciously from any one 'school' of psychology though undoubtedly the insights of several have contributed to an overall view. The understanding here outlined leads on to a definiton of the distinctive role of the Study Methods Counsellor.

The particular task of counselling in study methods presents an interesting challenge to the counsellor. He shares with all counsellors – indeed with all who enter relationships of any sort that reach beyond the purely formal – the call to honesty, to 'other-centredness' (that is, letting go all known egocentric motives) and to a sort of 'living dangerously'. Just as the mountaineer who wants to leave the well-worn pathways must make acts of faith and courage as he contemplates the rock face, so there is an openness in human relationships that does not naturally 'happen' but requires similar decisions. It is this openness that is effective in breaking through the convention, the fear and the sleepiness that operate to limit the depth of an encounter. Moreover it is for the counsellor to take the lead in shedding protections. If he is not vulnerable how can he expect the one counselled to enter the vulnerability of honesty? Most of us would agree that it is impossible to engage in any relationship at this level for any considerable length of time. Yet this aim, however fleetingly and imperfectly achieved by the counsellor, has, as a kind of over-arching imperative, given a framework of purpose to the counselling.

Meanwhile the student comes with detailed practical problems and expects to find solutions from a counsellor working to a 'study methods' label. The temptation is to be hurried along and to yield to that expectation, evading the demanding challenge of a true encounter and making do with an offer of easy advice that treats behaviour as in adherence to formulae rather than as the outcome of free, willed, intelligent decisions about means and ends, made in the context of relationships. The counsellor, whose very sense of responsibility may enhance the pressure to engineer an outcome that is obviously 'successful', may desperately want to take a short-cut instead of

Reproduced by permission from Wheeler 1983.

proceeding down what looks like an unlit road, with unknown hazards and no promise of a destination. But there is no avoiding that route if the problems that are initially presented as 'out there', objective entities are to be traced back to their source in the person. And only in this way is there hope of the problems being solved via a recovery of personal responsibility.

This aim of helping a student to make his own commitment to change, rather than relegating him to the passive role of recipient of 'Rules of Correct Study', is a crucial reason for taking time to 'meet' the person. A second reason, increasingly recognised amongst researchers in this field, is that, although it is possible to collect a store of 'received wisdom' concerning study methods and indeed to use the results of research in practical advice, yet there are so many variables in terms of personal preferences, subject differences and particular problems of environment and relationships that student and counsellor must engage in a dialogue to arrive at the point at which general advice becomes personally relevant.

M. da Costa (1979) has some apposite comments in this connection.

> Study is essentially a most personal concern. No matter what techniques are tried and researched, they will be ineffective if they do not meet and bring together the needs of the individual person and the demands of the task. Study skills are there to be tried for size, reshaped, fitted again, some bits discarded and others moulded until they become a tool to serve the learner's individual size, whims and quirks. We are not automatic learning machines which need only to be fed the right programme.

Michael Howe and Jean Godfrey, in their extensive study (1977), show that even in so precise a skill as that of making notes from lectures there is no one right formula.

> The problem is that outcomes seem difficult to predict, unless one considers a variety of factors – not only presentation, conditions and activities of subjects, but also more precise details about the particular learners and also their knowledge and ability in relation to the knowledge they are attempting to acquire – and the findings one obtains can be regarded as predictive only of a narrow range of situations in which notes are made.

A third reason for engaging in a conversation in which the counsellor's listening is equally as important as his talking, is that advice, however 'good', is useless if it is unrelated to the student's *actual* needs. The invitation is not to enter some rarefied state of Ideal Studenthood but to make the next step which is the 'just-about-attainable' goal for him. The counsellor aims to present the task in such a way as to call forth enthusiasm and curiosity while stripping away the elusive goals that are so impossibly large that they are not a realistic challenge but a disguised escape from the immediate issues. Thus the counsellor must discover the threshold of change for each student. Then, by scattering a few 'clues' and allowing the student to talk, he helps draw out what the student already knows, but as yet unclearly. The counsellor confirms and thus reinforces the student's own intuitions about what is going wrong and why (and challenges evasive dishonesties if necessary) and then in a similar way works together with the student towards a resolution. It is the student who finds his own way but the counsellor may provide a spur to courage and clear-sightedness in the student's attempts to redirect himself.

Fourthly, although the special concern of the Study Methods Counsellor is with a resolution of study problems, they rarely make sense out of a 'whole-life' context. (Just occasionally a problem may be for practical purposes self-contained: poor spelling for example or impossibly slow reading.) The counselling relationship must be one that makes possible a discussion of study problems within the widest possible context.

The student counsellors at Keele have likewise discovered:

> More perhaps than ever before young people are concerned about themselves and their relationships. Some condemn this as selfish intro-spection. It is equally possible to see it as a genuine desire to come to grips with the underlying question in all human enterprises – the meaning of life itself, what am I here for, what can I do to justify my existence.

Fifthly a kind of partnership between counsellor and student is the point of resolution of the conflict that is supposed to exist between prescriptiveness and freedom and which is much debated in the annals of counselling psychology. In the context of a conversational exchange a sort of jointly decided prescription emerges. The weight of the practical decison-making is distributed variously between counsellor and counsellee. Some students need little more than confirmation of what they already sense is right for them. Others have problems in making decisions or are vague in their aims; it may be necessary to support them in a transitional process as they learn to take more responsibility for themselves.

Finally insistence on a personal relationship as the context of decision-making and advice rests on the case that the closely linked factors of motivation and confidence are crucial to the student's progress. The student will only change if he wants to enough. A counsellor may encourage that motivation – by the warmth of personal concern as much as by finding out where the student is responsive to new hope. Again, success in studying has much to do with confidence. Fears paralyse but reasonable confidence liberates powers that the student scarcely suspects. 'Positive reinforcement' by the counsellor is an essential aspect of the support he can give.

Emerging from the foregoing considerations, the distinctive role of the Study Methods Counsellor may now be defined as the combination of two, at first sight conflicting, functions. On the one hand there is a counselling relationship that contains within its scope a breadth and depth of contact, a risk-taking openness, a genuine ignorance on both sides of 'answers' and a willingness to submit to what is recognisable truth. On the other hand there is a tutoring relationship, in the learning about the practice of new strategies and specific skills. Ideally these twin poles of the task are held by the counsellor in creative tension. Certainly the requirement that there be practical outcomes acts as a healthy validation of the counselling that otherwise may veer off into esoteric maybe self-indulgent pathways.

It may be objected that the role of the counsellor in study methods is already (and better) fulfilled by each student's personal tutor. Of course there is a close link, indeed an overlapping of interests, between the tutor and the study counsellor. The advantage however of a counselling service outside the subject department is that the counsellor is in no way connected with academic assessment and therefore the student may well feel more free to confess his failures or lack of motivation. Further, a tutor's time is divided between several activities and not every tutor will have the concentration of energy that is required for such intensive and detailed counselling as is undertaken by the specialist. The help given by the counsellor must, of course, be related as sensitively as possible to the demands – methodologies and types of learning skills – of each particular subject. This involves careful listening to identify the problem from the student's viewpoint. Certainly, too there has been frequent liaison with tutors and on those few occasions where specialist academic help has been required the student has been referred to the tutor.

There may also be a query whether there is any 'territorial dispute' with the Student Counselling and Health Services. In fact there has been a most harmonious tripartite working relationship with cross-referrals as the need has arisen.

Within the university the Study Methods Service grew as one more fruit of the general concern that individual students be not 'lost' in an institution of complex structure. Certainly a sense of depersonalization and loneliness often emerge as factors in a student's distress. The Study Methods Counsellor is in effect a member of a team. Hall wardens, tutors, doctors, student counsellors and the Study Methods Counsellor each have their specialised 'sphere of interest' within an overall common concern for the well-being of students.

# 36

# Varying One's Group Training

*P. B. Smith*

The behaviour of the trainer in sensitivity training is one of the most systematically under-examined topics in the whole field. Over the years, this author's views have fluctuated wildly, from believing that the detailed content of what the trainer does in the group does not materially affect the long-term consequences to believing that trainer behaviour is crucial to the outcome of the group. This paper will not be an attempt to explore the rather sparse research literature relevant to this point but to describe the author's somewhat halting attempts to become more self-conscious about *choosing* a style of trianing to fit a particular setting. Such choice was not an urgent priority so long as the bulk of training was conducted with heterogeneous groups of initial strangers: such settings are relatively well understood and the trainer behaviour required within them is agreed between a wide range of trainers. The central requirements of such groups are probably trainers who focus attention on the group, encourage expressions of feelings and reactions, and give the group sufficient autonomy from the outside world and from the trainer himself.

Sensitivity training is now applied in an enormous range of settings in which the above prescription would be quite inappropriate. This diversification creates a situation where it becomes less useful to think of sensitivity training as a technique which under specified conditions will reliably produce a particular end-result and more useful to think of it as a craft skill which needs continuous adaptation to varying circumstances. The essence of craftmanship is that one has a clear understanding of the principles underlying one's success in a particular task, and hence can adapt one's behaviour in response to external demands.

A number of components of the culture of sensitivity training make it difficult to see it as a craft skill. One problem is the existence of a number of relatively autonomous schools of thought within the field, each of whom has considerable investment in believing that their style of training is far more effective than is that of other schools of thought. Although there is certainly a good deal in common between the approaches of all those involved in sensitivity training, much more energy goes into emphasising the differences

Reproduced by permission from Smith 1972

rather than seeking to delineate the common craft elements. The dynamics of this process are all too readily apparent in planning meetings of any large sensitivity training programme. A second difficulty is the preference of many trainers for planning their behaviour in a highly intuitive manner. One includes a particular exercise in a training design because it 'feels right'. If another trainer with different preconceptions finds that something else 'feels right' to him, then planning becomes a process of bargaining and interpersonal accommodation. Because of the lack of an explicit craft-based rationale for the training, the issue is decided on the basis of preserving amity between the trainers rather than on training needs. The belief that only when trainers' own needs are met will those of their trainees be met frequently appears implicit in planning procedures. However, it is the kind of belief which power figures have maintained in relation to their subordinates for centuries, and is no more likely to be true in sensitivity training than elsewhere.

There are a number of explicit training models available for trainers seeking to be systematic in designing their activities. Consider for instance the Rogerian model (1951). Although it refers to psychotherapy, the three therapist prerequisites of congruence, empathy and unconditional positive regard can be readily treated as prerequisites for a trainer also. Personally, I have never found this particular model too helpful, as I have never been able to see how I can both be congruent and show unconditional positive regard towards someone I dislike. To be sure, it is possible if one happens to be very close to someone, but in situations where one has some ambivalence or hostility there is a definite choice as to whether or not to express those feelings. If one does, one is being genuine but hardly showing unconditonal positive regard; if not, one is not being genuine, however much unconditonal positive regard one expresses.

As it happens, this particular dilemma, whether or not to express hostile feelings in a group at a particular time, is one on which I have frequently felt the need for some explicit guiding model. In a stronger group, I would normally feel that to express myself genuinely was the higher priority. But when working with an intact organisational group, I would be much less likely to express hostile feelings towards the boss of the group, if none of the other members dared to do so.

One model which I have found to be of considerable value in this respect is the Harrison and Lubin (1965) confrontation-support model. This maintains that learning occurs in a group where both support and confrontation are present. In other words, if a member finds that someone both likes him and dislikes some aspect of him, this experience generates change. Harrison and Lubin (1965) write about the presence of support and confrontation in the group, but I prefer to look at it in more individual terms. If an individual experiences support from one member of his group and confrontation from another, this will not lead to learning. It will more likely lead him to like the person who supports him and dismiss the person who confronts him. Only where both support and confrontation come from the same source will he need to face up to the confronting material.

I regard the support half of the Harrison and Lubin (1965) model as the easy part. Given time, autonomy, and the encouragment of the trainer, a group can be relied upon to create a warm, supportive climate. Some groups find it more difficult than others, but these, I shall argue, are those in which some kind of confrontation is stucturally inherent. At least within stranger groups, support is easy. Confrontation, on the other hand, varies considerably. Confrontation in the group may derive from the trainer or from the group. In Table 1, four possible group settings are diffferentiated, with examples in each cell which I shall be discussing. It should be noted that Table 1 makes no reference to the presence or absence of support in the group. This is a consequence of my view that support as a component of the T-group culture is the easy part to obtain. As a trainer I would not feel it right to take on a commitment to train a group to whom I was unable to offer support. I have occasionally found myself with groups whose own capacity for support was rather low, but I shall not be considering such settings here.

| | Trainer is confronting | Trainer is not confronting |
|---|---|---|
| Group is confronting | Groups of under-graduates whom I also teach | Intact organisational work groups/ Groups of work colleagues |
| Group is not confronting | Student personal growth workshops | Heterogeneous stranger groups |

**Table 1**
Varying settings in which I engage in sensitivity training.

In assigning types of groups to cells in Table 1, account is taken not so much of the personal predispositions of groups or trainers, but rather of pre-existing and continuing role relationships with one another. At the interpersonal level, I assume that most people have the capacity to confront one another if they so wish. The entries in the cells obviously reflect my own situation as a university lecturer. Had I been in some other occupation, the examples in the left-hand column would not be drawn from university settings. I shall now discuss some examples from each of the four cells drawn from recent training experiences. In each setting, my goal is firstly to think through the nature of the setting and then clarify how, I, as trainer, should behave if I am to optimise the possibility of group members' experiencing support and confrontation from the same source.

# Both Trainer and Group are Confronting

For a number of years past, I have organised a three-day residential sensitivity training laboratory for undergraduate students majoring in social psychology. The University of Sussex has twenty such students per year. The programme is scheduled towards the end of the students' second year at the university, at a stage when they also spend time doing course work concerning studies in experimental social psychology.

I am a confronting figure to the students because among others I am involved in assessing their final degree results a year later, and more generally because I am in touch with other faculty members at the university. The group situation is inherently confronting to them in so far as it resembles group teaching situations which predominate at Sussex, such as tutorials, seminars, and practicals. In each of these, there is some element of peer evaluation implicit in the setting.

The confronting preconditons for these groups mean that I see my main task in them as that of creating support. This involves both my giving support and also encouraging the emergence of support systems within the groups. It is difficult for me to establish the authenticity of my support. For instance, the groups have always been clearly labelled as voluntary rather than as a course requirement. Voluntariness should signal both that the groups are not related to the assessment system and that, unlike other parts of the degree programme, the groups are based on individuals taking responsibility for their own behaviour. The voluntariness of the groups is, however, sometimes interpreted in "other ways by students, who may state that they do not feel really free not to come. In practice, about two-thirds of the students have come in recent years. The groups tend to be very centred on the trainer. His trustworthiness as a person is a matter for extended examination, and the groups often seem unable to explore other issues until some resolution of this issue is achieved. My response to this in terms of programme design is to maximise the amount of time spent in T-groups and not to propose other types of sessions. A sparing use is made of non-verbal exercises within the T-group when they fit in with issues salient in the group. The exercises used are often those which highlight issues of trust or support, such as 'trust falls', 'cradling', 'eye gazing' and the like.

The groups do not feel as exhilarating or 'freeing' as some other kinds, but their effects are often marked in terms of their beneficial effect on later tutorials and seminars. A second effect is often some kind of reorientation of the gulf which many students find between their own experience and the research literature on experimental social psychology.

## The Trainer is Confronting but the Group is Not

A number of faculty at Sussex recently initiated a programme of personal growth workshops. In their first terms, these workshops were attended by more than 100 of the 3,000 undergraduates at the university. The format of the workshops varied, some being residential, others being marathons or week-end groups, while yet others met on a once-weekly basis. The groups were open to all undergraduates in the university, while most of the trainers were teaching staff. The confronting nature of the group leaders does not arise in these groups from specific assessment relationships; it arises rather from the experiences of these students with faculty in general. Student/faculty relations at Sussex are informal compared to those at some other universities. Nonetheless, there exists a considerable distance, which no doubt arises out of the different life-styles of students and faculty. Initially, students in the groups were typically strangers to one another, felt somewhat isolated, and shared a wish to achieve some kind of personal growth or new experience from the group.

The principal difficulty found in these groups was that of developing a sense of shared responsibility for what occurred. Members' orientation tended to carry over from campus culture as a whole, and could perhaps be expressed as,

'It's the leader's job to make this a worthwhile experience for me; if he's not up to it, I'll drop out and try something else.' The problem was one of building a supportive climate in which this 'consumer' orientation was superseded. This was much more effectively achieved in the intensive groups than in the weekly groups. Somehow the leader needs to steer a course between excessive confrontation, which will eliminate from his group those who are not strongly committed to it, and the kind of support which will build very high cohesion but very little carry over from the group into other settings. I personally feel much more at ease in settings where I am not, myself, a main source of confrontation, and will now turn to some of these.

## The Trainer is Not Confronting but the Group is

This situation arises when one works with intact-work-groups in an organisation other than one's own. This discussion draws on recent experiences with a mental health clinic and with a drug addiction unit run on therapeutic community lines. In the mental health clinic, a number of professional groups – doctors, nurses, social workers and occupational therapists – worked together. They encountered frequent difficulties in building a climate of shared trust. Each professional group felt strong loyalties not only to the clinic but also to their professional training. When one group threatened another, it was easy to fall back on one's professional reference group for protection. In the drug centre, confrontation derived more from the inherent difficulty of the unit's task, the constant suggestions of failure and the all-too-rare indications of success.

In these groups, the trainer's required role is relatively clear to me. The groups are burdened with difficulties and confrontations they dare not face up to. The trainer's task is to generate enough support in the group to make it possible to confront these problems. In order to do this, he does not need a central position in the group; indeed, he is inevitably no more than a transient visitor to it. What he does need is an ability to devise supportive procedures for the group. These may be task-centred procedures or they may have a stronger emotional focus, depending on the culture of the group one is working with. For example, with the mental health clinic group a sequence of activities was used in which they sought to diagnose what problems they were faced with, what possible solutions might be entertained, and what procedures they might use to decide between them. In the drug unit, on the other hand, a sequence of non-verbal exercises focusing on 'helping' and 'empathy' were used. Both interventions were supportive but they were at a level congruent with the group's existing procedures.

In existing groups, one of the trainer's main difficulties is that key events occur before he arrives and after he leaves. These events colour the quality of the intervention, and yet the trainer has very little control over them; indeed, he may not even be told that they have occurred. In the mental health clinic, the director made a proposal for a radical reorganisation of the clinic, just a few weeks before the group met. In the drug unit, the most important issues were 'who should or should not be present at the groups', since this effectively determined which issues would be worked on during the group. Thus, the trainer can make an effective contribution to an existing group only if that group establishes an open communication link with him ahead of time. The establishment of such a link is a first test of the trainer's ability to contribute to the client group the support they are seeking.

Another existing organisational group with which I have worked is the postraduate degree programme in social work at Sussex University. This is a highly cohesive two-year programme admitting around eighteen students per year. Although this programme is within my own institution, I do not see my role in it as a confronting one. Assessment plays a minor role in the programme and the students on the programme identify as strongly with their future profession as they do with the university. They have an opportunity to attend a three-day residental sensitivity training programme in their first year. In the second year, I run a course for them entitled 'Social group work'. This is designed as an intervention in the social system of the course. The basic procedure involves the use of a one-way observation mirror. The course meets for a half-day per week for about ten weeks. The course splits into two groups. For half the time, group A observes group B, while group B works on their own concerns. These concerns may be interpersonal ones or they may be problems concerning the practice of social group work. After half-time, the groups reverse roles. Each group is charged with making constructive interventions in the other.

The most likely event is that A and B become two groups in 'win-lose' conflict, with each supporting themselves and confronting the others. Since the course group has considerable salience for its members, such a breakdown in it could become quite painful. The situation, therefore, requires that each group develop skills in *confronting* the other group *supportively*. Early on they often comment on how much easier it is to analyse the failings of the other group, while feeling paralysed in developing one's own group. From this point, the groups work towards support and confrontation in combination rather than in opposition.

## Neither the Group nor the Trainer is Confronting

I have left until last the situation which represents the 'classic' T-group, the heterogeneous stranger group. If confrontation occurs in such groups, it occurs because of the behaviour of the members, not because it is structured into the group. Compared to the other types of group discussed, the attraction of a stranger group is its sheer freedom to develop in a self-determining way. The culture of such a group is to emphasise the common elements in human experience and to cherish the sharing of those elements. The danger of such a group climate is that it fosters a denial that there are any divisive or confronting issues in society. My view of the trainer's task in a stranger group is consequently that his task is to confront the members. He will want to do this in a supportive setting and in such a manner as preserves the individual's freedom to be confronted or not confronted, but within this framework he will generate opportunities for members to grow through confrontation. This frequently involves both verbal feedback and non-verbal activities. The non-verbal activities will include a broader range of both supportive and confronting activities.

I have now reviewed instances of groups falling within each of the four cells of my table. Through the use of the support-confrontation model, I have tried to explain how I have started to think about planning my interventions. Thinking about intervention and design suggests a degree of self-conscious-ness which seems to conflict to some extent with other values of the sensitivity training movement, which I also esteem, such as spontaneity and genuineness. It is my belief that disciplining one's trainer activities within broad frameworks such as support or confrontation, need in no way detract from spontaneity or genuineness. At no point does the model propose that as a trainer one should behave in any way other than how one feels; it does, however, suggest that one should select from among one's feelings some rather than others. The manner in which one chooses to express them is always a matter for spontaneity.

Choosing between one's feelings does imply that one has a range of available feelings in a particular situation to choose between. Consequently, one might argue that the implicit values of this model are that the human condition is one of ambivalence. I find that this fits my own position, but others may feel more at ease with Rogerian unconditional positive regard or Sartrean despair.

# 37

# Introduction to the Evaluation of
# Teaching by Discussion

There are, of course, many ways to evaluate teaching. Not every method is applicable to teaching by discussion, but a good many are and it would be impossible to deal with them all. The essence of teaching by discussion and thinking together is interaction.

In this book we are therefore confined to evaluation of interaction in groups. Interaction is a difficult feature of groups to evaluate. So Part V is divided into evaluations teachers can do for themselves and those requiring assistance from audio-visual staff or professional evaluators.

Chapter 38 lists methods teachers can use for themselves and describes factors influencing interaction in groups which they might consider. Chapter 39 deals with methods requiring professional assistance, with a particular emphasis upon two methods of interaction analysis.

Why this emphasis? I see evaluation as a process of inquiry and for this reason, so far as possible, evaluators should use research techniques. But the researcher's techniques may seem a little forbidding even to some professional evaluators. I have therefore attempted to simplify the methods of two influential researchers in the field of interaction analysis in the hope that some readers will be tempted to try the methods for themselves, particularly now that so much more public attention is being paid to the accountability and evaluation of teachers. I found the methods rewarding once I got used to them, not only for the delight that comes to any researcher, but because the knowledge acquired continues to be useful in my teaching.

The Flanders Interaction Analysis is based upon the premise that the initiation and response of a teacher or student is the salient characteristic of interaction. It is particularly useful in evaluating teaching using the methods described in Chapters 28-31 in this book. Bales' Interaction Process Analysis is most useful for methods described in Chapters 32-36, particularly when there is a task, problem or series of tasks requiring a decision-making process by the group, or when the major objectives are concerned with students' feelings.

# 38

# Evaluation by Teachers

## *Donald A. Bligh and David Jaques*

## Methods of Evaluation

Evaluation usually involves gathering information upon which a value judgement can be made. There are practical problems for us as teachers when we try to evaluate our own teaching: 'How can the information be gathered?' and 'What information should we gather?' These practical questions are tackled here. The more philosophical question, 'How can we justify our value judgement?' is not considered.

How can teachers gather information about their teaching by discussion? There are three broad ways. They can ask themselves some questions. They can seek information from the students. Or they can derive information from side effects of the teaching such as examination marks or library records.

### *Teachers' Checklist*

If they are going to ask themselves questions, the danger is that teachers will avoid the kinds of awkward or embarrassing questions they would rather not face. The possession of a checklist prepared on a previous occasion, or by someone else, avoids this evasion. The content of the checklist should depend upon the purpose of the evaluation and some suggestions with reference to interation in groups are made later in this chapter.

### *Diaries*

When a group has a number of meetings over a period of time and with the particular aim of students' personal development, students can benefit from keeping diaries in which they record:

– what ideas, concepts, principles and information they have learned

Adapted by permission from Jaques 1985.

- what they have learned about themselves; and
- what their perceptions are of the processes at work in the group.

The use of diaries in this way is normally a teaching method, not a method of evaluation, for a diary is normally confidential to its author. But teachers may contract, or otherwise seek permission, to see them. When they do so, diaries may give valuable feedback on the effectiveness of a course, provided teachers and students have a certain amount of mutal trust. Without trust diaries become dishonest and a worthless chore. As evaluators, teachers must be vigilant for signs of low trust and insincerity in students' writing.

## Rating Scale Questionnaires

Perhaps student questionnaires are used more than any other method of evaluating teaching. They are useful in that teachers can rapidly gather a lot of information on specific issues from every student. Students can remain anonymous. The data can be treated quantititively if rating scales are used so that responses for different questions or groups of students can be compared. Cahn's rating scale designed to assess trust in a teaching group is shown in Chapter 5 in this volume.

However, the limitations of questionnaires should be recognized. Although students' responses are usually very consistent, their perceptions may not be accurate. That is to say, their responses are highly reliable but of doubtful validity. In spite of the comment in the last paragraph, quantitative treatment requires cautious interpretation – most discussion groups are too small for most statistical tests and, though numerical, the data is really subjective and impressionistic. It can also be argued that, when using rating scales, teachers will naturally select criteria they think are important; but if they think the criteria important, they are likely to have paid particular attention to them already. The factors teachers neglect will be neglected on the questionnaire too. Students may have different ideas.

## Free Response Questionnaires

One answer to the last point is to seek criteria from the students. This could be done in a two-stage process: first seeking the criteria and then presenting a traditional questionnaire based upon the students' consensus.
However it is much easier to use free response questionnaires on which students are asked to write under fairly general headings. For example:

- Give your opinion on the discussion as a whole.
- How far did you achieve what you wanted from the discussion?
- Describe three things you liked about the discussion.
- In what way do you think the teaching could be improved?

There are reasons for using each of these questions. It helps avoid distortions if we get a general evaluation before making students focus on specifics. Work with rating scales shows that general evaluations are often more favourable than any specific item. The second question above focuses on crucial objectives. The next two not only focus on specifics, but allow students to let their feelings go. They tell the teacher what was 'good' and what was 'bad' as far as the students were concerned. These two questions could be used as hints for the next discussion, but it is the last question that is specifically looking to the future.

One advantage of free response questionnaires is that they allow each individual to express a personal, and possibly idiosyncratic, opinion. This is particularly important when teaching by discussion, because group harmony depends upon every member. In lecturing, by contrast, the feelings of one student are less likely to be crucial to teaching effectiveness.

Free response questionnaires can also be a diagnostic tool for a teacher who feels a discussion did not go well but doesn't know why.

A mixture of free response and rating scales can be used if a space is left for comment after each item in a traditional questionnaire, or at the end.

## Participant Observation Description

This method may be spoken or written. In so far as it asks participants for descriptions of what happened during the discussion, rather than free expressions of feelings and opinions, it aims to be more dispassionate and objective. In practice different group members have different perceptions and interpretations of what takes place and this method helps all members of a group, including the teacher, to see each other's point of view, thereby developing tolerance and harmony.

Jaques (1985) makes this point for all evaluation by discussion. Evaluation is likely to improve training

1 If it enhances the experience of teaching by creating a climate of openness and honesty where there might otherwise be a sense of secretiveness and mistrust
2 If it is organized as a co-operative act in which both teacher and students articulate their experiences and both learn from it
3 When there is no question of its being used for promotion or other public purposes, except where this option has been clearly chosen
4 Where it is organized at stages in the life of a group rather than at its conclusion and all concerned have the opportunity to develop and change for mutual benefit.

Participant observation requires some maturity from group members; on the other hand it also develops it.

There are several criteria for the usefulness of feedback. It should be descriptive rather than evaluative. Let the receiver make his own judgement. It is better to be specific than to make generalizations. Generalizations tend to be abstract. It should satisfy the personal needs of both the receiver and the contributor. Feedback is better sought than imposed. Its acceptability often depends upon its timing and whether it is confirmed by the rest of the group.

## Critical Incident Analysis

The difficulty with the methods considered so far is that they are dependent upon perceptions that could be very subjective. The difficulty with the more objective techniques is that they are often so specific that they do not tell the teacher very much. Thus when choosing methods of evaluation there is often a conflict between global but subjective methods and objective but over specific observations.

Specific observations therefore have to be interpreted with caution. For example, records of when students hand in work, of when the teacher returns it, and of books referred to in essays or borrowed from the library might be used as an indication (but only as an indication) of attitudes in the group.

Having gathered such data there is a sequence of questions that the teacher can usefully ask. Does interpretation of the data suggest there is any kind of problem? If so, what are the signs or symptoms of the problem? What are the conditions that created the problem? What are its most likely causes? Which cause(s) seems to be most critical? How could the situation have been avoided or overcome? (In other words, what are the possible solutions to the problem?) Select the best solution. If the situation is likely to recur, prepare a strategy to implement the preferred solution when the time comes.

# Factors Affecting Interaction in Groups

If teachers want to evaluate how their students have behaved in discussion they will need to understand why their students interact in the way they do. This understanding will influence the content of checklists and questionnaires, and interpretation of feedback and critical incidents. The remainder of this chapter describes factors influencing students' behaviour in groups, and suggests not precise questions but general questions teachers will need to refine for their own purpose. Much of this section is from Group Teaching (Jaques 1985) in *International Encyclopaedia of Education*.

## Aims and Motives

Aims are implicit in most, if not all, groups, though they are all too rarely considered and even less often discussed. These aims may be intrinsic to the group process: 'to enjoy each other's company', 'to discuss environmental pollution', or they may be extrinsic and concerned with the group's product: 'to make decisions about the course' or 'to prepare for an examination'.

Aims also have social and task dimensions. Social aims include 'to develop supportiveness within the group and a sense of belonging', while task aims refer to qualities like judging ideas and checking students' progress. They are complementary. If the social dimension is not given attention, students may feel cool about the group and have no sense of commitment. If the task dimension is missing they may become dissatisfied and feel frustrated at not achieving anything worthwhile. The social dimension has an additional educational scope. It includes qualities like self-awareness and the ability to work independently yet co-operatively in a team – all-important aspects of the students' personal development.

Members of any group are likely to have their own personal, and sometimes hidden, aims and these may have little to do with the aims of the group as a whole. Sometimes such personal aims (for example, impressing the tutor, scoring off another student, wanting approval of the group or capitalizing on other students' ideas) may undermine the intended aims of the tutor. It is the tutor's job to accommodate or mobilize students' personal aims within the overall aims of the group. There is usually no better way to do this than by discussion, as open as possible, of all the aims arising from the group.

Issues about aims to be considered for evaluation include:

- What were the aims of teaching by discussion?
- Were they clear to the students?
- Were they acceptable to the students?
- To what extent did everyone inside (and outside) the group share the aims?
- What aims were not shared by all?
- Was the method/technique/interaction appropriate to achieve the aims? What was the evidence?
- What unintended outcomes were there?
- Did the group evaluate its progress during or at the end of the meeting/series of meetings?

## Tasks

A task is what must be done in order to achieve an aim. Not enough attention or imagination is usually given to the design specification of tasks in group teaching. Too often teachers assume that the task is simply to discuss a topic. To design stimulating tasks particular attention should be paid to their key verbs, for example: identify, contrast, predict, select, differentiate, organize, judge, criticize, and so on. If the aim for a group is to develop awareness of different strategies for solving problems, suitable tasks might be:

- to try to solve a given problem;
- to monitor the strategies used;
- to share the findings and compare with research evidence;
- to draw up a set of guidelines on problem-solving strategies.

Tasks will vary in the skills they practise, the abilities they demand, the amount of work they require, their ease or difficulty for members in a particular group, the time they take to complete, and their optimum size of group. It is part of the tutor's job to select tasks accordingly.

Issues to be considered for evaluation might include:

- What prior tasks, for example, writing, reading, consulting, and so on, were required?

- Were the tasks acceptable to the group?
- How thoroughly were they carried out?
- What tasks were set at the meeting? Were they clear and attainable within the time allowed?
- Did the tasks take into account the students' developmental needs? Did they encourage imaginative and deep thinking?
- What tasks were agreed or specified for the next meeting?

## Group Climate

Though it may be difficult to define, the social climate in which group discussion takes place is of enormous importance, and is usually fairly easy to sense. Forecasting the details of the weather is more difficult. The tutor has an important role to play in creating a climate in which warmth, spontaneity, support, tolerance, realism, openness, and informality exist. A mutually supportive climate can release more energy and imagination in a group, and affect the way students feel about belonging to it.

Questions to ask about climate include:

- Was the group harmonious or dissonant, warm or cool, relaxed or tense, free or constrained?
- Was there a sense of competition – how did it arise?
- Did students seem willing to take risks – for example, express uncertainty and half-formed ideas, reject the tutor's ideas, or express their feelings?

## Members' Past Experience

Members of a new group bring with them sets of expectations arising out of what they know of the origins, history or composition of the group – which significant people are to be in it? They build up expectations from any statements they have heard about the group's purpose and task. Members may also bring with them attitudes to other members born out of prior relationships outside the group, and the group itself may carry a reputation for a particular style, climate, or level of achievement. In education, students will probably have picked up comments about how well or badly the group went in the previous year. The formation of a group requires that someone made decisions about place, resources, and the size and composition of the group. Whoever undertakes this task, for example the tutor, will have considerable influence in the success of the group, at least in its initial stages.

In an established group, members may carry with them feelings derived from previous meetings; they may look forward to the resumption of an exciting interchange or may dread the re-enactment of conflicts and time-wasting tactics. They may have to do preparatory work, such as a paper or a report, and their anticipation of what will happen may cause them to approach or engage with the group in a predetermined way. New members may need careful briefing on the group's norms and procedures.

Questions about the previous experience of group members include:

– What do students need to know beforehand – place, time, aims, membership, roles, prior tasks?
– What expectations are they likely to have – from previous studies, from other students?
– What prior experience of group discussion are they likely to have had?

## *Physical Environment*

Several critical factors in group dynamics – the flow of communication, the perception of status and the emergence of leadership, for example – are affected by factors such as the physical position of group members, their distance apart, and their body orientations. These in turn are strongly influenced by the shape and size of the room in which a group meets, and the spatial arrangement of charts and tables. A long, narrow room will probably limit eye contact along its length and impel members to talk to others across the room, but not along it. Anyone who sits at the end of a long table or behind the only desk in the room is more likely to be regarded as a leader. Dominant members will tend to choose the more central seats in any group situation, and reticent ones may even try to sit outside the group. The further apart members are, the less talkative and more formal is the interaction likely to be. Tables create a physical barrier which may be reassuring in groups where formality is of the essence, or where there is a wish to maintain personal distance or space. They may also encourage members to lean forward and closer to each other or be invaluable as a writing surface. A lack of tables may be threatening to some but it usually encourages openness and informality.

Personal space, the area around a person which he or she regards as private, will of course vary from one person to another, but it is clear that people of higher status often prefer, or are accorded, greater distance between them and others. (The seats on either side of a tutor in an otherwise undifferentiated circle of chairs are often the last to be filled by students.)

The location of a group meeting has its effect too. The tutor's room is his or her territory and underlines the authority role. The student union bar on the other hand is a more egalitarian venue but can be invaded by others, and its use may be limited by licensing limitations. Just as groups may assume territorial rights over physical space and objects, so may members act territorially about positions in a room. (see Sommer 1969).

Evaluations may need to consider:

– What association does the room have in the minds of the students?
– Is it the tutor's room, a formal classroom, or some neutral area?
– Is the room to be a regular venue?
– Might discussion be vulnerable to noise or interruption?
– Can everyone be equally spaced?
– Is anyone (especialy the tutor) likely to have a special position, eg behind a desk or at the head of a table?
– What can be done by moving furniture, to improve communication in a group?

- Can everyone make eye contact with each other?
- How possible it is to rearrange the grouping of chairs and tables?

## Group Size

There are two opposite tendencies with regard to the number of people in a group. The larger the group, the greater is the pool of talent and experience available for solving problems or sharing the effort: on the other hand, as the size increases fewer members have the chance to participate, and indeed the differences in relative participation increase to the point where one or two members begin to dominate. It thus becomes more likely that reticent members will fail to contribute, though they may well enjoy the relative anonymity a large group affords them.

The smaller the group, the greater is the likelihood of close relationships, full participation, and consonance of aims. Whereas in a small group or team leadership and other roles are likely to be shared or rotated, in a large group the formation of sub-groups and the increasing differentiation of roles will ensure the emergence of a leader. Where there is an agreed leader (eg the teacher) the need to counteract these tendencies places special demands on his or her awareness of the problems and skills in coping with them.

When does a group become 'large' and does it still have any merits? Most theorists or researchers and practitioners agree that five to seven members is the optimum for leaderless groups. In the case of led groups, as for academic discussion, the maximum for member satisfaction according to students (NUS 1969) is ten to twelve. Larger groups are an advantage when it requires the combining of individual efforts as in brainstorming (see Chapter 16). They are of less value when everyone must accomplish the task, which is the general situation in most discussion groups. If the group is small (ie two or three in number), the tutor is likely to be dominant from the start. With a large group (eight or more) the divergence of aims and the need for role differentiation may push the tutor into a dominant position. However, the use of sub-groups can overcome some of the difficulties of large group discussions.

If the tutor has any choice in the matter the tutor might ask:

- What size of group is appropriate to the aims?
- How many people can be fitted into the room and still have good eye contact?
- Will the tutor take a leadership role or will students take responsibility for the process?
- Does the tutor intend to split the group into sub-groups?
- Is the group large enough to avoid total dominance by the tutor?
- Will the group still be large enough if one or two memberes are absent?

## Group Composition

Whether a homogeneous or a heterogeneous mix of students in each group provides the best chemistry for interaction and achievement depends upon the task. For example, where the task requires creativity, diverse experience is an advantage. When the task requires comprehension of subject matter, a wide spread of intelligence may be frustrating for group members. Such qualitities as age, sex, nationality, and personality may also need to be taken into account, though it is always difficult to be sure what mixture will lead to good participation. Students will contribute differently according to their perceptions of other group members. There is what is known as an 'assembly effect' in which the presence of other people makes students feel more keyed up; but this factor is difficult to predict. Indeed the tutor may contribute to it, for example when a group of dependent students are led by an assertive tutor.

Yet often the most powerful influences are the personal likes and dislikes of fellow members. People tend to agree with individuals they like and disagree with those they dislike even though both may express the same opinion. By and large, groups composed of compatible people learn well when they want to. The opposite may often be the case with a disaffected group.

When evaluating the effects of group composition, the tutor may want to ask questions like:

- What are the main differences between students? What kinds of task are suitable?
- Which students seem to identify with and support each other?
- Which students continually disagree with each other?
- What cliques do there seem to be?
- How well do the personalities enmesh or trigger each other in a positive way?

## Communication

It is through communication that members of a group learn to understand one another and to influence, or be influenced by each other. Yet communication is not just a matter of expressing ideas clearly. It is often suffused with unintended effects, fears and dislikes, and unconscious motives. Often the non-verbal part of communication is the most eloquent. A great deal is revealed about what a person is really thinking and feeling by their facial expression, posture, and gestures.

The content of communication is important too. In every subject area there is a specialized vocabulary which a newcomer may find off-putting. A clique within the group may sustain a private joke which intentionally excludes the rest.

For any communication to take place, speaking must be complemented by listening. Students may often, through preoccupation with their own thoughts or scorn for another's opinions, fail to hear what is being said. Ground rules in which each speaker in turn has to summarize what the previous one said can encourage more purposeful listening.

Questions about communication to be considered are:

- Were members expressing their ideas clearly?
- Were they evidently listening to each other?
- Did they make connections to or build on each others contributions?

- Did they check for understanding or ask for clarification when they were not sure of what somebody else meant?
- Was there good eye contact round the group?
- Were feelings as well as thoughts communicated?

## Participation

The degree of participation in a group is dependent to a large extent on its size and the physical environment. The pattern of interaction may also vary. For instance, it may take the form of a one-way 'mini' lecture by the leader or tutor, or be a two-way question-and-answer format, again directed by the tutor. In some cases, comments may be channelled through a member, not officially the leader, because of his or her dominant role outside the group, and in others a small clique may set up as an interaction to the exclusion of the rest of the members. As a general rule communication is directed upwards in the status hierarchy and the upward communication tends to be more positive than that directed downwards. Consequently, the tutor may receive more rosy information than is appropriate: an important fact to remember in conducting an evaluation of the group or the tutor.

Patterns of interaction in a group may be consistent over time or may vary. They can certainly be changed through the structuring of discussion with sub-groups or by introducing helpful ground rules. The more widespread the participation in discussion, the better will be the interest and involvement.

Questions the tutor may wish to ask are:

- Did everyone appear involved, either verbally or non-verbally?
- Were quieter students encouraged to participate? How?
- To whom were questions usually addressed: the whole group, the tutor, particular members?
- For what proportion of time did the tutor talk?
- If a grid is constructed showing the number of times each group member responds to every other, what pattern emerges?

## Cohesiveness

Cohesiveness is a measure of the attraction of the group to its memberes (and the resistance to leaving it), the sense of team spirit, and the willingness of its members to co-ordinate their efforts. Compared with members of a low-cohesive group, those in a high-cohesive group will be keen to attend meetings, be satisfied with the group, use 'we' rather than 'I' in discussions, be co-operative and friendly with each other, and be more effective in achieving the aims they set for each other themselves. A low-cohesiveness group will show greater absenteeism, the growth of cliques and factions, and a sense of frustration at the lack of attainment.

Questions for the tutor to ask on group cohesiveness are:

- How satisfied are members with the group and their part in it?
- Did members seem glad to see each other again?

- Did there seem to be a sense of shared purpose or was everyone 'doing their own thing'?
- Did any sub-group or private conversations develop?
- Was the quality and quantity of communication high or low?
- Did members turn up on time and stay to the end without looking distracted?
- What evidence was there of interest or lack of interest among members in what was happening or where the group was going?
- Did members talk inclusively about the group – 'our group', 'we', and 'each one of us' rather than 'the group', 'I', or 'you'?

## Unspoken Norms

Every group has a set of norms: a code of conduct about what is acceptable behaviour. It may apply to everyone in the group or only to certain members. Some norms will be strictly adhered to while others permit a wide range of behaviour. The group usually has sanctions (eg disapproval) which it may apply in the case of 'deviation'. Common norms in groups include: discouragement of open expression of feelings, avoidance of taboo subjects, reluctance to interrupt or challenge the tutor, hesitation in volunteering one's services, avoiding conflict, and restraining long and frequent contributions. All of these are usually hidden or implicit and new members may find it difficult to adjust. Over the first few meetings of a group there may be confusion about what the norms are, with consequent frustration, discomfort and lost momentum. It may be helpful to invite a group to break into sub-groups to discuss its norms and perhaps to discard some of these which seem counter-productive.

Questions about norms for a teacher to consider include:

- Are there any taboo subjects?
- How do norms appear to be enforced? Who does it?
- Does anyone consistently break the norms? How does the group respond?
- Are the norms well understood by everyone?
- Do the norms seem to help or hinder progress?

## Explicit Procedures

Procedures are really metarules or conventions for ensuring that what a group wants to happen, does in fact happen. They are the means of handling problematic events like making decisons, conflict, distribution of tasks, assessment and evaluation: and they may be invoked by, or applied to, any member of the whole group. Procedures may also be seen as devices for ensuring the smooth running of the group and the achievement of agreed aims. They may be formal and strictly codified, as in many committees, or informal and loose as for teams and working groups. The main virtue of a procedure is that it is usually set up before the event and thus detaches discussions of how the group should handle problems in general from the problem-solving process itself. Examples of rules and procedures for groups include:

– All decisions should be made by consensus.
– Anyone may call time-out at any stage in order to review progress.
– The time and duration of the meeting.
– The group starts and finishes on time.
– The first five minutes of every meeting are spent milling around the room talking.
– The group follows an agenda like that proposed by Hill (1969), see Chapter 30.
– Members take on functional roles like time-keeper, summarizer, and so on (again see Hill 1969).
– Each member has a maximum time limit for contributions.

A very sophisticated group might also agree a metaprocedure which determines how any of the above rules of procedures might be changed.
Rules and procedures may be invented in response to questions like these:

– How will the group decide on aims, tasks, and agendas?
– How is the group to make decisions?
– What regular process problems are likely to arise?
– How can it make best use of the resources of its members?
– How is it going to ensure full involvement in discussion?
– How will it monitor and evaluate its progress?
– How will it co-ordinate the various activities outside the group or in sub-groups?

## Structure

When a group comes together for the first time and begins to interact, various differences between the members begin to appear: differences in status, influence, role, ability and so on. The pattern of relationships that is thus established is known as the group structure. The pattern will, of course, change according to the nature of the task or the stage of discussion and the most influential person for one purpose may not be so for another. Where there is no appointed leader, as in tutorless groups, the leadership may, therefore, move round different members of the group. A structure that emerges in these ways is known as the invisible structure.

A visible structure exists when the group agrees a division of labour, roles and responsibilities, in order to get essential tasks performed. Hill (1969, see Chapter 30) proposes a set of roles to be distributed in the group: initiating, giving and asking for information, giving and asking for reactions, restating and giving examples, confronting and reality testing, clarifying, synthesizing and summarizing, gatekeeping and expediting, timekeeping, evaluating and diagnosing, standard setting, sponsoring and encouraging, and group tension relieving. Such a method, though it is valued by some students, is found by others to be too socially demanding. Northedge (1975) describes another kind of structure to encourage participation: a sequence of stages involving individual work, followed by discussion in pairs, then in fours, and a final session with the whole group or class.

Questions to ask about structure include:

- What kind of pecking order(s) emerged among the students?
- What kind of group roles or functions (see Hill above) were missing, and what effect did this have?
- What role did the tutor adopt – instructor, facilitator, chairperson, resource, consultant? Was it clear?
- Did students have any specified roles?
- Was the assessment role of the tutor clear to the students?
- How did the invisible structure match any visible one?
- How was the invisible structure manifest? Who influences whom? Who volunteers, defers to others, etc.?
- Was the group structure, visible or invisible, appropriate to the task?

## Groups in Context

Wherever group teaching occurs – in the seminar, the laboratory, or the project, there are two further factors which the alert tutor will want to consider: the social and educational context in which the group meets and how to evaluate the work of the group. The problems in teaching by discussion may not lie inside the classroom at all. Students can be profoundly affected by aspects of institutional life outside the formal curriculum: departmental norms, the structure of the buildings, and the accessibility of various people to each other (see Parlett and Simons 1976). The value of chance encounters and space for ad hoc groups to meet should not be underrated. In the educational sense, group teaching has to form an integral part of a sometimes complex and, to the student, bewildering curriculum.

Tutors need to ask themselves:

- How does this group link to the lectures/laboratory work/field trips?
- How can some group work be included in lectures?
- How do the norms and requirements of groups marry with those of other tutors?

# Conclusion

This chapter has been concerned with methods the teacher can use to evaluate his teaching by discussion. It is primarily concerned with evaluating the defining characteristic of groups – the interaction of their members. The chapter first briefly describes a number of methods the teacher himself can use to evaluate his teaching by discussion; and then considers influencing interaction to which he may wish to pay attention.

# 39

# Professional Assistance in Evaluating Teaching by Discussion

*Donald A. Bligh*

## Stages in Professional Evaluation

*Initial approach.* I am sometimes asked by teachers to 'evaluate their teaching', to which I must reply 'I can't – not all of it!' The point is that teaching is so complex that it would be impossible to evaluate everything, and if I tried, I would interfere with what I was observing in such an all-pervading way, that any evaluation would be invalid. Like assessment of students, any evaluation necessitates a sampling procedure. This is particularly true in the evaluation of discussion and small group teaching. There is so much going on, even in the shortest extract from a discussion, that no one could ever observe all of it.

So after an initial approach by a teacher (or 'requester') the second task is to decide what is to be evaluated. This involves a *consultation* with the teacher to clarify the objectives of the evaluation and to consider methods by which they can be achieved.

After the consultation, I, as the consultant, usually go away to prepare a *draft proposal* on how I might help the teacher.

After this I return with my draft for a *second consultation* so that it may be modified. It is essential that the teacher agrees with what I am going to do. Sometimes it is necessary to get the agreement of other people, such as the students and the head of department.

At the end of this consultation, when there is agreement on what we should do, there is, in effect, a *contract* between the teacher and me (and possibly others). This may not be a formally written contract, but I like to firm up the agreement with a letter or memorandum outlining what each of us will do. In the case of questionnaire methods, and other methods using special pieces of paper, I send a copy of the document with the contract.

The next stage, which might occur before the contract and sometimes does not happen at all, is to collect some data as a pilot study or *feasibility study*.

Thereafter there is a major period of *observation and data collection*; by which I do not necessarily mean quantitative data.

Adapted by permission from Bligh 1972a.

The data is *processed and interpreted*. I write a *draft report*.

The draft report is then *checked* for factual inaccuracies. I don't normally find that teachers want to change other things.

This is an interesting point because it is normally part of the contract that I will let anyone who has taken part in the evaluation have a copy of the final report. Since reports are of no value if they are not honest, they could contain statements the teacher would not like others to see; but I have never found this a difficulty.

I will then produce the *final report*, which is sent to all who took part, and this commonly includes the students. Nonetheless I regard the report as confidential until 'released' by the teacher. Others receiving a copy must also treat it as confidential until that time. It is not professional to put teachers under pressure to release their evaluations and most never do so.

Finally I like to have a *follow-up discussion* with the students or whoever else is involved, to consider recommendations – not only my own, but any they might suggest.

## Practical Principles in Helpful Evaluation

There are certain practical principles involved when evaluating the teaching of others.

By 'practical' I mean to exclude all those theoretical and rather philosophical principles about whether we should only evaluate the achievement of objectives, whether evaluators should know what the objectives are, whether evaluation is a kind of aesthetic judgement, how far empirical evidence is necessary, whether the evaluator should make a value judgement or leave it to the teacher, and what generalizations in teaching can justifiably be made on which to base a judgement.

These are issues an evaluator may ponder in his armchair. His opinions will influence his general approach and he may write learned articles expounding them. But they need not be issues in the forefront of an evaluator's mind when doing the practical job of helping a teacher. They are issues about the realism of his evaluation, but they are not concerned with his own compassion and openness; and these two factors are equally important. For the teacher, evaluation is a sensitive issue, not a theoretical one.

First the evaluator should *actively look for conflicts in teaching*. Teaching situations are nearly always conflict situations. This is particularly true of discussion and group teaching. The very authority that makes a teacher a brilliant lecturer may inhibit student participation in his tutorials and seminars. The willingness of a tutor to consider the personal needs of individual students in his group may lead him to neglect the needs of the majority, or the other way round. A high regard for the organized clarity of his subject matter may prevent a tutor from exploring the interests of his students.... The conflicts are endless. In a sense the teacher can never win.

In recognizing this, the evaluator should give support to teachers, showing how in every teaching situation there are gains and losses, pros and cons. Recognition that the teacher is in a situation of conflict makes empathy easier and makes it less likely that the evaluator will make dogmatic judgements about what the teacher ought to have done. However, the skills to look for and recognize the conflicts, are not easily acquired.

Empathy and low dogmatism, recognition that there are no right answers to the conflicts of which teaching consists, should lead the evaluator to a third principle. There is no one correct way of teaching: therefore *encourage variety in teaching*, not a stereotyped model.

From the variety principle it is a short step to recognizing another principle: not only that different teachers are good at different things and that their different skills, styles and approaches are to be encouraged, but that *evaluation for staff development involves cultivating a teacher's strengths*. Eradicating his weaknesses is often less important. (It depends on the weakness, of course.)

Two more principles emerge from this recognition: *actively look for a teacher's talents and think how they could be developed and used in new ways*. In particular, think how they can be used to compensate for, or avoid, activities in which the teacher is less skilled. For example, if a teacher is particularly good at organizing his subject matter with great clarity in lectures but is insensitive and impatient in tutorials discussions, there is little immediate chance of changing his tutorial personality. He might do better to plan a careful sequence of questions or tasks for buzz groups in tutorials. This would remove his presence from the discussions while using his talent for organizing subject matter.

Notice, looking for talents reverses a natural tendency. Most of us look for things to criticize and then think how to soften the criticism with praise.

If we develop institutions in which different teachers are each doing what they are good at, they will soon have different perceptions of their roles as teachers. The open-mindedness of the evaluator will then be extended from 'there is a variety of acceptable ways of teaching the same thing' (the third principle), to 'it is acceptable that teachers should be trying to do totally different things'. These things could conflict, possibly reflecting different choices in one of the conflicts mentioned earlier. (See the first principle.) But a variety of possibly conflicting roles and teaching styles could be confusing for the students. Though not if a teacher can take students into his confidence, explaining his perception of his role and his particular abilities.

A seventh practical principle follows: *maximize openness*. Complete openness is never possible, but it should be possible to find out from teachers what they think their role and their talents are, check their self-acceptance of their own self-appraisal and check how far openness has been, and could, be achieved. Hence this discussion with a teacher is normally part of a professional evaluator's method when staff development is involved.

## Methods to Assist Evaluation of Interaction

Three common methods are direct observation, electrical recordings and post discussion interviews.

The seven principles described in the last section are all particularly pertinent to *direct observation* by an outsider, the professional evaluator.

Two difficulties dominate this method: the observer effect and the multiplicity of things that could be observed. The observer effect can be reduced, but never overcome. The observer can be introduced and his purpose explained either at the beginning or at a previous meeting. He can try to be unobtrusive and hope that his presence is forgotten after ten minutes; or abandoning that hope and the pretence that he is not there, he can openly join the group and attempt to evaluate as an insider. The range of things to be observed can be reduced by preparation of a checklist after discussion with the teacher. (See for example the checklist by Powell on page 29 and the one by Hill on page 152.)

The observer's hope that his presence will not be noticed after ten minutes is often unsuccessful because human beings are very sensitive to the presence of other people, particularly if they make small movements or sounds. Microphones and video cameras are more easily forgotten. Thus the observer effect appears not to be so great when recordings are made. *Recordings* have the obvious advantage that, by repeated play, many observations and complex anlyses can be made. Provided he can face himself, the teacher can obtain his information for himself rather than through interpretation by another. A very valuable approach is to invite the students to view the recording with the teacher. If done fairly soon, this can give lively feedback as students recall their thoughts and feelings. The students benefit from a second run through the subject matter; and experience shows that the openness of this approach results in lasting improvements in teacher-student relationships because the teacher has opened himself to face-to-face student criticism.

The use of *post discussion interviews* is one way to remove the observer effect. By this method the evaluator does not himself experience the richness of interaction. Non-verbal behaviour, for example, is unlikely to be elicited by interview. Consequently, though interviews can be well used in other areas of educational evaluation, in evaluation of teaching by discussion the questions must be very carefully planned and limited to specific issues. Interviews can be useful for eliciting covert feelings, but this requires considerable interviewing skills on the part of the evalutor.

## The Flanders Interaction Analysis

The Flanders Interaction Analysis is performed either by an experienced observer in the classroom or by subsequent playback of a tape-recorder. In either case the teacher should take his students into his confidence, explain that he wishes to study his own style of teaching, and make evaluations on a number of different occasions. If the teacher always records his lessons, the tape-recorder will more easily become part of the usual environment and students are more likely to ignore it. If this is not done he may need to wait until the class or group feeling is well established. The time when it is being established is the most difficult for this kind of innovation, although, from the point of view of the teacher, it is then that the interaction is at its most interesting and important.

The analysis is made by categorizing, at intervals as regular as possible, the last completed communication as one of 1–10 in Table 1. The table needs to be learned so that the recorder thinks easily in terms of the numbers. Four to six hours' practice is desirable before live observation using the interaction analysis is attempted. The trained observer will categorize what is being said every three seconds and write the appropriate numbers in a sequence as they occur. For example, if a teacher asks short questions which are briefly answered by his students a pattern 4 7 4 7 may be recorded. Although such a pattern may occur in school teaching, it is less common in higher education. It suggests the teacher is quizzing the students, probably with an emphasis on knowledge of factual information rather than thought, and a teacher-directed rather than a student-centred approach. Both questions and answers in higher education are more expansive, so that 4 4 7 7 7 4 4 7 7 is more likely. This pattern still implies that the teacher directs the lesson. If it is the students who ask the questions and the teacher who answers, 8 3 5 will be recorded. In lectures there are sustained periods when nothing but 5 is recorded, while small group teaching may show little but 9 if the teacher is successful in obtaining fluent student participation. If the Flanders Interaction Analysis reveals sustained periods of 5 in a small group, the situation is probably not being used to develop student powers of thought and expression, which is frequently claimed to be one of the objectives of small group teaching.

| | | | |
|---|---|---|---|
| TEACHER<br>TALK | Response | 1 | Accepts feeling. Accepts and clarifies an attitude or the feeling tone of a student in a non-threatening manner. Feelings may be positive or negative. Predicting and recalling feelings are included. |
| | | 2 | Praises or encourages. Praises or encourages a student action or behaviour. Jokes release tension, but not at the expense of another individual: nodding head, or saying 'Um hum?' or 'go on' are included. |
| | | 3 | Accepts or uses ideas of students. Clarifying, building or developing ideas suggested by a student. Teacher extensions of student ideas are included, but as the teacher brings more of his own ideas into play, shift to category 5. Answer questions. |
| | Questions | 4 | Asks questions. Asking a question about content or procedure, based on teacher ideas, with the intent that a student will answer. |
| | Initiation | 5 | Giving facts or opinions about content or procedures, lecturing, expression his own ideas, giving his own explanation, or citing an authority other than a student. |
| | | 6 | Giving directions. Directions, commands or orders to which a student is expected to comply. |
| STUDENT<br>TALK | Response | 7 | Student talk – response. Talk by pupils in response to teacher. Teacher initiates the contact or solicits student statement or structures the situation. Freedom to express own ideas is limited. |

| Questions | 8 | Student questions. Questions concerning content or procedure that are directed to the teacher. |
| Initiation | 9 | Student talk – initiation. Talk by students which they initiate. Expressing own ideas; initiating a new topic, freedom to develop opinions and a line of thought going beyond the existing structure. |
| SILENCE | 10 | Silence or confusion. Pauses, short periods of silence and periods of confusion in which communication cannot be understood by observer. |

**Table 1**
The Flanders Interaction Analysis (modified).
The Flanders categories have been modified to include 'student questions' (8) and omit teacher 'criticizing and justifying authority' (7). Flanders' category (8) is therefore written as (7) here.

## First Steps in Interpretation

The value of this technique lies in comparison. Statistics showing that the teacher talked for 60 per cent of the time do not mean much on their own. Comparisons between two or more lessons, teachers, parts of the same lesson, or with some kind of norm, are more instructive. (There are so far no general norms, since objectives, subject matter, student level, size of class, etc. are very variable.)

The first stage is to check the total number of recorded tallies against the time spent in coding. If tallies were made at 3-second intervals there would be 1,200 per hour. A total of less than 400 is not very reliable for comparative purposes.

The second stage is to find the percentage of time for each category and for totals of teacher talk (TT) and student talk (ST). (A slide rule permits quick working.)

In the third stage the teacher's tendency to react to the ideas and feelings of his students, called the Teacher Response Ratio (TRR), is found from categories:[1]

$$\frac{1 + 2 + 3}{TT} \times 100$$

The TRR may give an indication of the teacher's sensitivity to his class which is particularly important in small group teaching. If 4 is included in the numerator

$$\frac{1 + 2 + 3 + 4}{TT} \times 100$$

[1] The categories referred to here correspond to those in Table 1, which are modified from the original.

the resulting ratio (sometimes known as the 'Indirect-Direct' teacher influence ratio) may provide useful comparisons on how far a teacher's approach is student-centred. In contrast the proportion of time spent in categories 5 and 6 may be an indication of authoritarianism, but obviously relevantly similar situations must be compared if any valid inference of this kind can be made. All the previously mentioned variables are relevant to the need of a teacher-centred, or student-centred approach.

The formula

$$\frac{4 + 5}{TT} \times 100$$

may give an indication of how far a teacher is concerned with subject matter. The contrast is sometimes made between those who teach a subject and those who teach students although it will be noticed that 4 is here included in both, and 6 in neither.

An indication of student freedom to express their own opinions may be obtained by finding the proportion of student contributions that are in category 9 by the following formula:

$$\frac{9}{7 + 8 + 9} \times 100$$

This is known as the Student Initiation Radio (SIR). Caution must be exercised in the interpretation of these statistics, but we should expect a higher SIR in a free group discussion and situations requiring student creativity and decision-making than in a seminar where the tutor may offer comments and criticisms of an essay, or a group tutorial where he may be required to answer questions.

A similar index of student questions may be obtained (Student Question Radio – SQR) by the formula:

$$\frac{8}{7 + 8 + 9} \times 100$$

At the end of a fairly formal lecture students may only be expected to ask questions for the purpose of clarification, rather than participate in lively discussion. This would present a pattern with a long period of 5 followed by a period with a high SQR.

Let us suppose that the following sequence has been recorded in which the sign / has been used to separate one group member's contribution from another to give a quick impression of the length of individual contributions. Silence or confusion is recorded as 0 rather than 10 for the sake of speed and to save any confusion with 1 in a row of figures.

0 5 5 5 5 4 4 / 0 / 7 / 2 3 3 5 5 / 9 8 / 1 3 3 4 / 7 7 9 9 9 / 0

This sequence represents the beginning of a group tutorial in which, after initial silence (0), the tutor states a few facts or opinions (5 5 5 5) and asks a question (4 4). After a momentary pause (0) the student gives a brief response (7) which the tutor rewards by saying 'Yes' encouragingly (2), and accepts (3) and uses to develop his opinion (3 5 5) which is challenged by another student, first by expressing a contrary view (9) and then, more cautiously, by asking a question (8). The tutor is pleased at the student's critical attitude (1), accepts his point (3 3), but asks if he has considered a further point (4), to which the student replies (7 7) developing his own views (9 9 9). The tutor then waits for further student reaction (0).

This example has been telescoped (with a three-second interval it represents only one and a quarter minutes). Such a small sample would be quite unreliable for any significant comparisons. Neverthless the reader is invited to calculate the following for practice.

| Ratios | Per cent |
| --- | --- |
| Total of Teacher Talk (TT) | |
| Total of Student Talk (ST) | |
| Teacher Reaction Ratio (TRR) | |
| Indirect-Direct Influence | |
| 'Authoritarianism' | |
| Subject matter | |
| Student Initiation Ratio (SIR) | |
| Student Question Radio (SQR) | |

So far the suggested interpretations have only used totals for each of the ten categories. These ignore the sequence in which the events occurred. If, as suggested, the order has been recorded, there is much more information available. For example, totals take no account of the difference between 4 7 4 7 4 7 and 4 4 4 7 7 7 although we have seen that there is an important contrast in the pattern of interaction, while the class atmosphere and level of thinking may also be very different. Totals, in fact, do not measure *interaction* at all. This may be done by recording each communication in relation to the previous one, to which it is a 'reaction' on the matrix shown in Figure 1. Each cell corresponds to a 'pair of communications' such that the first number of any pair designates the row, and the second number designates the column. If a lesson has distinct periods it is useful to record these on separate matrices.

The sequence already described may be represented as shown in Figure 1 such that the letters (used here for explanatory purposes) represent 'pairs of communications' and correspond to those given in the matrix.

Although the TRR gave us some idea of the teacher's reaction to his students, his Instantaneous Teacher Response Ratio (TRR 789) may now be studied by looking at the 18 cells (7+8+9) (1+2+3+4+5+6) at the bottom left quadrant of the matrix. The tallies here will give the teacher's spontaneous reaction to student contributions. These may be more revealing of the teacher's attitude and be particularly relevant to the climate of the class. *If* one could judge from the example given, although the teacher's TRR was 40 per cent, his TRR 789 shows him to be a teacher very sensitive to student feelings. TRR 789 is defined as 'the tendency of the teacher to praise or integrate student ideas and feelings into the class discussion at the moment the student stops talking'. It is calculated from the formula

$$\frac{(7+8+9) \ (1+2+3)}{(7+8+9) \ (1+2+3+4+5+6)} \times 100$$

Similar ratios may be calculated to find out the proportion of student questions that are immediately answered by the teacher. This is found by the proportion of tallies in (row 8) (columns 1 to 6) that are in cell (8) (5). Some experienced teachers interlace questions with factual information, thus producing a 5 4 5 5 4 mixture. This mollifies a quizzing style. It may be calculated by comparing the number in (4) (5) and (5) (4) cells with the number in (4) (7).

| | | TEACHER TALK | | | | | | STUDENT TALK | | | | TOTAL |
|---|---|---|---|---|---|---|---|---|---|---|---|---|
| | | 1 | 2 | 3 | 4 | 5 | 6 | 7 | 8 | 9 | 10 | |
| TEACHER TALK | 1 | | | $q_1$ | | | | | | | | 1 |
| | 2 | | | $j_1$ | | | | | | | | 1 |
| | 3 | | | $kr_2$ | $s_1$ | $l_1$ | | | | | | 3 |
| | 4 | | | | $f_1$ | | | $t_1$ | | | $g_1$ | 3 |
| | 5 | | | | $e_1$ | $bcdm_4$ | | | $n_1$ | | | 6 |
| | 6 | | | | | | | | | | | - |
| STUDENT TALK | 7 | | $i_1$ | | | | | $u_1$ | | $v_1$ | | 3 |
| | 8 | $p_1$ | | | | | | | | | | 1 |
| | 9 | | | | | | | | $o_1$ | $wx_2$ | $y_1$ | 4 |
| SILENCE CONFUSION | 10 | | | | | $a_1$ | | $h_1$ | | | | 2 |
| TOTALS | | 1 | 1 | 4 | 3 | 6 | - | 3 | 1 | 4 | 2 | 25 |
| % | | 4 | 4 | 16 | 12 | 24 | - | 12 | 4 | 16 | 8 | 100 |

**Figure 1**

The Flanders Interaction Matrix.

Normally a tally mark is used (instead of a letter) and the total (here in subscript) is circled.

Although Flanders admits that Categories 3, 6, 7, 8 and 9 may represent remarks about the subject matter, he believes that a high proportion of all tallies in rows and columns 4 and 5 (The Content Cross Radio or CCR) indicates the main focus of class discussion was on subject matter, the teacher took an active role and attention to student feelings and motivation was minimal.

The Steady State Ratio (SSR) reflects the tendency for contributions to last over three seconds in the same category and may be calculated as the percentage of all tallies lying on the (1) (1) to (10) (10) diagonal. It will be noticed that in the short sample given these are the only cells with more than one tally and they constitute 40 per cent of all tallies. The SSR can be used to gain a quick impression of the length of individual contributions. Teachers are usually able to extend their talk longer in the same category than students, consequently the Students' Steady State Ratio (SSSR) is a particularly sensitive measure of student confidence, and sense of freedom to express themselves.

The proportion of all tallies in cell (9) (9) gives an indication of student ability to develop and argue their own ideas. The limitations of this ability may be determined either by the teacher or themselves. A good free group discussion could have such a high proportion of contributions in this cell that an alternative system of analysis is advisable (see Bales' Analysis on page 215). Sustained talk between students will be indicated by the bottom right quadrant (7+8+9) (7+8+9).

The speed of teacher-student interchange is indicated by the proportion of all tallies in the bottom left and top right quadrants. With many short contributions these quadrants would be full. As the TRR 789 shows, examination of particular cells in these quadrants may also indicate the most common conversation pattern when there is interchange. For example, what proportion of students' first remarks are answers to questions ((4) (7))? What proportion of their remarks finish with questions ((8) (1+2+3+4+5+6))?

If a record is made of who made each contribution, interesting comparisons may be made between students. Is there one who asks questions but never ventures an opinion? Is there one who ventures opinions but never in response to a previous contribution? Is there one who responds to the teacher but never to his fellow students, or vice versa? What are the proportions of student and teacher talk in two halves in the same lesson and are there some students who never talk in the first half of a group tutorial? All these questions can be answered fairly objectively without much difficulty with the Flanders technique.

## Design your own Categories

It may be that the kind of information supplied by the Flanders (modified) categories are not what the reader wants. It may be, for example, that the interaction between teacher and student in clinical medicine, or visiting a student teacher on 'school practice', require additional or different categories. Possibly the analysis is to be done with a specific kind of evaluation, with specific objectives in mind. The answer here is 'invent your own categories'! This is quite possible if a few simple rules are observed:

1 Make the categories logically complete.
2 Make the categories as exclusive as possible.
3 Make sure the choice of categories will give the information required.
4 Make sure the major divisions of categories are the most easily discriminated.

The first rule is to make sure that all communications can be allocated to a category. The second is to try to make sure that they cannot be allocated to more than one category. In practice this second ideal can never be perfectly achieved. For example, any statement of fact can be said in an emotional way so that it conveys both feelings and information and it is doubtful whether a satisfactory system of categories could be devised that did not distinguish these two. Consequently there is nearly always difficulty in classifying emotionally expressed statements giving information. The third rule requires that the purpose of the evaluation is made clear. The fourth may be illustrated by the Flanders categories themselves. It is easy to tell whether it is the teacher or student talking, or whether there is silence, and this is the major division of categories (see Table 1). It is less easy to tell whether what they say is a response, a question, or an 'initiation'; and this is the second order set of categories. The third order is even harder to discriminate.

## Conclusion

The Flanders type of analysis has several advantages. Although the choice of categories and the allocation of particular contributions to them may be subjective, the high correlation between different observers suggests that it is fairly objective. (Perception of group processes is always a subjective process.)

The methods of interpretation provide more information than most alternative methods of analysis.

The use of modern portable cassette tape-recorders permits its use in practical classes (including some clinical contexts) and without the intrusion of external observers.

Its speed permits fairly rapid feedback for the teacher before he completely forgets the lesson.

The possibility of designing tailor-made categories within the interpretative framework creates a very flexible system for assessing one's own teaching.

## Bales' Interaction Process Analysis

The Flanders Analysis is primarily concerned with the interaction between teacher and student. Hence a large proportion of the categories are allocated to the teacher. This is not very satisfactory where the teacher plays a small overt role, or where the emotive aspects of student contributions (which Flanders neglects) are important.

The analysis by R.F. Bales (1970) in Table 2 is more satisfactory in these contexts. This means it is more likely to be useful for evaluating free group discussion, individual tutorials, T-groups, counselling and some role-play situations. (However the emotive nature of some teaching by these methods may preclude the wisdom of using a tape-recorder for their evaluation. This must inevitably be left to the teacher's judgment.) Most of Bales' work has been with problem-solving groups so that it may be used in individual buzz groups, brainstorming, synectics, syndicates, problem-centred groups and some forms of case study discussion.

The techniques of recording are not very different from Flanders' except that each communication is categorized irrespective of length (ie recordings are not at regular three-second intervals); it is necessary to note who speaks at each point; and non-verbal communication may be included.

In considering his findings it must be remembered that Bales' groups were leaderless, mostly consisting of Harvard students who had not met before and who were to reach an agreed solution to a human relations problem. Since it is unlikely that teachers will normally find themselves in such

| Social-emotional area POSITIVE | A | 1 | Shows solidarity: raises others' status, gives help, reward. | |
| | | 2 | Shows tension release: jokes, laughs, shows satisfaction. | |
| | | 3 | Shows agreement, passive acceptance: understands, concurs, complies. | |
| Task area NEUTRAL | B | 4 | Gives suggestion: direction, implying autonomy for other. | |
| | | 5 | Gives opinion: evaluation, analysis, expresses feeling, wish. | |
| | | 6 | Gives information: orientation, repeats, clarifies, confirms | |
| | C | 7 | Asks for information: orientation, repetition, confirmation. | |
| | | 8 | Asks for opinion: evaluation, analysis, expression of feeling. | |
| | | 9 | Asks for suggestion: direction, possible ways of action. | |
| Social-emotional area NEGATIVE | D | 10 | Shows disagreement: passive rejection, formality, withholds help. | |
| | | 11 | Shows tension: asks for help, withdraws 'out of field'. | |
| | | 12 | Shows antagonism: deflates other's status; defends or asserts self. | |

a b c d e f

| A Positive reactions | a Problems of communication |
| B Attempted answers | b Problems of evaluation |
| C Questions | c Problems of control |
| D Negative reactions | d Problems of decision |
| | e Problems of tension-reduction |
| | f Problems of re-integration |

**Table 2**

circumstances it is suggested, as with the Flanders technique, that they use the Bales categories in a comparative manner with situations known to them. Bales has carried out many thorough and detailed studies. The findings reported here are given in order to suggest possible points of interest which the teacher may wish to study, not as norms against which he should judge himself.

Like Flanders, Bales suggests a number of ratios as indices of the nature of the discussion. For example

$$\frac{8}{8+5}$$

gives some indication of range of opinions in the group and this in turn will affect the speed of agreement to a problem's solution. He too has been concerned with the differences between participants' first reactions to a previous speaker and their subsequent contributions (see Figure 2).

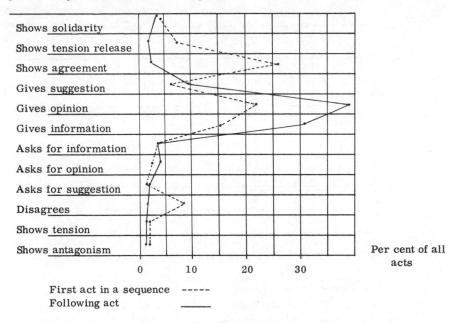

First act in a sequence  -----
Following act            _____

**Figure 2**
A comparison of a person's first and following acts in a conversation sequence (Bales 1950).

Much of his interest has been on differences in group size and the changes in pattern of contributions in time. Figure 3 shows change in certain kinds of contribution during three phases of discussion. It has been interpreted as showing that during the first phase the group is gathering information; during the second, evaluating it, and during the third giving some suggestions for a solution which arouse both positive and negative socio-emotional reactions to their maxima. Bales suggests that in a decision-making group there is a steady movement from categories 'a' to 'f' (see Table 2, especially upwards towards the lower numbers).

In another study he found that tension release (2), giving suggestion (4) and showing solidarity (1) shows increases with the size of the groups. Showing tension (11), agreement (3) and asking opinion (8) show a decrease. If groups with only two members are excluded, giving information increases, and giving opinions or evaluations (5) decrease. He thinks variations are the result of having more relationships to maintain and less time to do so.

In groups of two, categories (11), (8), (7), (6) and (4) are high; and (10), (12), and (5) are low. Bales thought this reflected the need to 'save face' for the other person and concluded that the dominant person needs to 'avoid the implication of superiority and to persuade the other by gentle self-effacing means'. If such findings are applicable to teaching it may be necessary to revise traditional opinions of the intimacy of the individual tutorial in which the

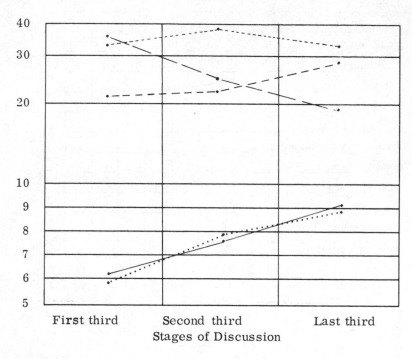

Rate per
100 acts

First third    Second third    Last third

Stages of Discussion

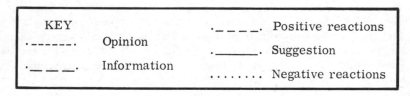

KEY

.------. Opinion

.— — —. Information

.— — —. Positive reactions

._____. Suggestion

........ Negative reactions

**Figure 3**
Changes in the pattern of contribution through a discussion (Bales).

student *feels* free to express his personal lines of thought. They reinforce the need for training counsellors.

A profile of the kind of contributions made by each individual can be contrasted. This is useful for insights into the behaviour of students, particularly when combined with studies of 'who responds to whom' in a group tutorial. Is there, for example, a pecking order amongst students such that contributions by one are criticized by none of the others, while at the other end the ideas of another may be questioned by all? Such studies of one's students are fascinating. If sensitively used, teaching may replace 'preaching'.

The interpretations must not be reached too hastily. For example Bales has shown that each individual's behaviour shows greater variability as the size of the group increases and one explanation of this is a more frequent change in roles because of the larger number of people to whom each role (eg leader, joker, butt) may be allocated. In particular, categories (2) and (4) increased with increasing group size, while (3), (10) and (11) decreased.

Figure 4 shows that the distribution of participation in groups of different sizes forms a J-shaped pattern. The most vocal member is not normally the most liked after the first meeting. The most liked person at the first meeting usually scores highly in the 'task area', but in later meetings preference shifts to one who shows 'positive' feelings, or who expresses the group's 'negative ' feelings towards the vocal 'task specialist'.

Bales' analysis is useful for evaluating a group climate. And as it is assumed here that it is part of a teacher's job to foster group harmony towards a working atmosphere, the analysis is recommended for its value when assessing a teacher's effect in this respect. It is suggested that changes in a group's climate and the roles of individuals are worth observation while the effects of group size must also be borne in mind.

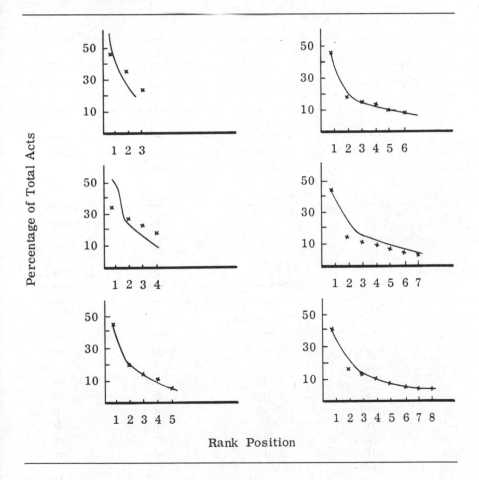

**Figure 4**
The distribution of participation in groups of different sizes (Bales 1950).

# Bibliography

Annotated by

## Janette M. Baker and Donald A. Bligh

Abercrombie, M.L.J. (1960) *The Anatomy of Judgment* London: Hutchinson
A classic. Read the 'Argument' at the end first. (DAB)
Abercrombie, M.L.J. (1966) Small groups. In Foss, B.M. (Ed.) *New Horizons in Psychology* Penguin.
Abercrombie, M.L.J. and Terry, P.M. (1978) *Talking to Learn: Improving Teaching and Learning in Small Groups* Guildford: SRHE
    The first section of this book for teachers and students interested in learning about their own behaviour in teaching/learning situations, discusses lessons that can be learned from analysing videotapes of their tutorial sessions. The second part discusses the nature and nurture of group discussion – discussion in new and in mature groups, assessment of students, control of participation, student/teacher relationships, etc. (JMB)
Abercrombie, M.L.J. (1-4 editions: 1970, 1971, 1974, 1979) *Aims and Techniques of Small Group Teaching* Guildford: SRHE
    Abercrombie reviews developments which have contributed to the growth of the small group method of teaching, then discusses the uses and outcomes of group work. She offers a number of general principles for running small groups and includes suggestions for further reading. She concludes by considering the traditional aims of a university education. (JMB)
    Probably the best introduction so far. Brief, with a broad coverage. Quotes empirical evidence. Useful bibliography. (DAB)
Argyle, M. (1967) *The Psychology of Interpersonal Behaviour* Pelican original.
    Ch. 6 on 'Eye contact and the direction gaze' is particularly fascinating in the context of discussion methods. (DAB)
Argyris, C. (1964) T-groups for organisational effectiveness *Harvard Business Review* March/April
Argyris, C. (1967) We must make work worthwhile *Life* 5th May
Armstrong, M. and Boud, D. (1983) Assessing participation in discussion: an exploration of the issues *Studies in Higher Education* 8 (1) pp33-44
    Discusses some issues involved in assessing student participation in discussion, the reasons for its use, limitations, and ways to increase its effectiveness. (JMB)

Asch, S.E. (1960) Effects of group pressure upon the modifications and distortion of judgments. In Cartwright, D. and Zander A. *Group Dynamics* 2nd Edition. London: Tavistock

Bales, R.F. (1950) *Interaction Process Analysis: A method for the study of small groups.* Cambridge, Mass.: Addison-Wesley

Bales, R. F. (1953) The equilibrium problem in small groups. In *Working Papers in the Theory of Action* 2, 199-231. New York: The Free Press of Glencoe

Bales, R.F. (1970) *Personality and Interpersonal Behavior* Holt Rinehart Winston

Balint, E. and Balint, M. (1955) Dynamics of training in groups for psychotherapy *British Journal of Medical Psychology* 28, 135-143

Balint, M. (1964) *The Doctor and his Patient, and the Illness* London: Pitman Medical

Barnett, S.A. (1958) An experiment with 'free group discussions' *Universities Quarterly* 12(2) 175-180

   A report on the use of the free group discussion method in a tutorial class in human biology. Changes in student behaviour and objections commonly given against the use of this technique are discussed. (JMB)

   Describes the technique quite clearly, but is not really an 'experiment'. (DAB)

Bass, B.M. (1950) The leaderless group discussion technique *Personal Psychology* 3, pp.17-32

Beard, R.M. (1970) *Teaching and Learning in Higher Education* Penguin

   Techniques of teaching small groups are well related to various kinds of objectives. (DAB)

Beard, R. M. (Ed.) *Varieties of Group Discussion in University Teaching* University of London Institute of Education

Beard, R.M. and Bligh, D.A. (1978) *Research into Teaching Methods in Higher Education* 4th edition. Guildford: SRHE

   A concise review of empirical findings for the experienced teacher. (DAB)

Benne, Kenneth D. and Sheats, P. (1948) Functional roles of group members *Journal of Social Issues* 4(2)41-49

Bennis, W.G. (1959) Leadership theory and administrative behaviour: the problem of authority *Administrative Science Quarterly* 4(3)

Bennis, W.G. (1964) Patterns and vicissitudes in T-Group development. In Bradford, L.P., Gibb, J.R. and Benne, K.D. *T-Group Theory and Laboratory Method; Innovation in our Education* New York: Wiley

Berger, P.L. and Luckman, T. (1967) *The Social Construction of Reality* Allen Lane the Penguin Press

Bion, W.R. (1961) *Experiences in Groups* London: Tavistock

Black, P.J., Dyson, N.A. and O'Connor, D.A. (1968) Group Studies *Physics Education* 3, pp.289-293

Black, Paul J. (1972) Group discussion in the planning and reporting of group projects. In Beard, R.M. (Ed.) *Varieties of Group Discussion in University Teaching* University of London Institute of Education

Blaine, G.B. and McArthur, C.C. (1971) *Emotional Problems of the Student* London: Butterworths

Bligh, Donald A. (1972a) Evaluation of teaching in groups by interaction analysis. In Beard R.M. (Ed.) *Varieties of Group Discussion in University*

*Teaching* University of London Institute of Education.

Bligh, Donald (1972b) Small group teaching methods – A classification. In Beard, R.M. (Ed.) *Varieties of Group Discussion in University Teaching* University of London Institute of Education

Bligh, Donald (1972c) Some suggestions on the use of terms. In Beard, R.M. (Ed.) *Varieties of Group Discussion in University Teaching* University of London Institute of Education

Bligh, Donald (1973) Developing skills for small group work. In Bligh, D.A. (Ed.) *Introductory Course for Lecturers. Volume 11 Background Papers* UTMU, University of London Institute of Education

Bligh, Donald A. (1978a) *What's the Use of Lectures?* D.A. and B. Bligh, Briar House, Clyst Honiton, Exeter.

Bligh, Donald (1978b) The buzz group technique. In *What's the Use of Lectures?* D.A. and B. Bligh, Briar House, Clyst Honiton, Exeter

Bligh, Donald (1978c) Problem centred groups. In *What's the Use of Lectures?* D. A. and B. Bligh, Briar House, Clyst Honiton, Exeter

Blumer, H. (1967) Society as symbolic interaction. In Manis, J.G. and Meltzer B. W. (Eds) *Symbolic Interaction* Boston: Allyn and Bacon

de Bono, Edward (1977) Brainstorming. In *Lateral Thinking – A Textbook of Creativity* Pelican Books, Penguin

Bradford, L.P., Gibb, J.R. and Benne, K.D. (Eds) (1964) *T-Group Theory and Laboratory Method* New York: John Wiley and Sons

Broady, Maurice (1970) The conduct of seminars *Universities Quarterly* 24, pp. 273-284

Burns, T. (1969) On the plurality of social systems. In Burns. T.(Ed.) *Industrial Man* Penguin

Burns T. and Stalker, G. M. (1961) *The Management of Innovation* Tavistock

Cahn, Meyer M. (1975) *The Development of Trust in Learning Groups* Mimeo, San Francisco State College

Caldin, E.F. (1968) The tutorial. In Layton, David (Ed.) *University Teaching in Transition* Edinburgh: Oliver and Reed, pp.58-62

A tutorial should be 'a discussion of written work based on special readings,' according to Caldin. Ways to conduct tutorials, functions and the organization of them are discussed in this brief chapter. (JMB)

Canter, Francis and Gallatin, Judith (1974) Lecture versus discussion as related to students: personality factors *Improving College and University Teaching* 22 (2) pp.111-112, 116

Reports on a study which related student preferences for lecture or discussion to personality factors. The subjects were students in an introductory psychology class. The researchers concluded that personality factors are less important than the specific situation which is encountered. No support was found for the idea that authoritarian personalities will prefer lectures to discussions; nor that discussions will be preferred to lectures when a choice is offered with class size and subject matter equated. (JMB)

Capes, M. (Ed.) (1960) *Communication or Conflict: conferences, their nature, dynamics and planning* London: Tavistock

Cartwright, D. and Zander, A. (1968) *Group Dynamics* 3rd edition. London: Tavistock

Clement, D.E. (1971) Learning and retention in student-led discussion groups *Journal of Social Psychology* 84, pp.279-281

Cockburn, Barbara and Ross, Alec (1977) *Working Together* Teaching in Higher Education Series 3. Lancaster: University of Lancaster, School of Education.

 The authors describe the nature of the small group and the role of the tutor. They note the importance of understanding and utilizing communication patterns, knowledge about how students learn, and the importance of each student's contribution to the group. The role conflict of the tutor (group member and authority figure) is pointed out. (JMB)

Cockburn, Barbara and Ross, Alec (1977) *Patterns and Procedures* Teaching in Higher Education Series 6. Lancaster: University of Lancaster, School of Education

 Patterns of small group instruction including the seminar, syndicates, associative discussion groups and tutorless groups, are examined. The authors also include examples of how small groups can be organized. (JMB)

Cockburn, Barbara and Ross, Alec (1980) *A Kind of Learning* Teaching in Higher Education Series 5. Lancaster: University of Lancaster, School of Education

 Points out that small group work is active learning that is deeper and more enduring than passive learning. The research suggests that this method is a superior one for the transmission of thought. The authors distinguish between process-centred and task-centred groups and discuss, with illustrations, both types. (JMB)

Collier, K.G. (1962) Examinations in higher education *Unicorn Review* 1 (3) Autumn

Collier, K.G. (1966) An experiment in university teaching *Universities Quarterly* 20 (3) pp.336-348

Collier, K.G. (1968) *New Dimensions in Higher Education* Longman, Chapters 1, 3 and 4

Collier, K.G. (1969) Syndicate methods: further evidence and comment. *Universities Quarterly* 23 (4)431-436

 Useful for a quick understanding of the method. (DAB)

Collier, K.G. (Ed.) (1983) The *Management of Peer-Group Learning: Syndicate Methods in Higher Education* Guildford: SRHE

 Describes how a teacher with a group of 20 or more students can incorporate small group teaching to the course by dividing the students into syndicates (groups of 5 to 8). Syndicates are given joint assignments. Resources are provided for private study that then becomes the basis for intensive discussions for consensus in the syndicates. (JMB)

Cooley, C.H. (1902) *Human Nature and the Social Order* New York: Scribner

Crutchfield, R.S. (1955) Conformity and character. *American Psychology* 10, pp.191-198

Curtiss, Frederic R. and Hurd, Peter D. (1980) Implementation of case study, role playing and small group discussion in a course in pharmaceutical law and ethics *American Journal of Pharmaceutical Education* 44 (1) pp.55-61

 A course in pharmaceutical law and ethics at the University of Rhode Island was redesigned to provide time for small group discussion, role playing and case studies. This format was developed as a means to elevate learning activities above the recall level and to incorporate activities into the areas of personal and professional ethics. Information about learning levels and course material are included with the article. (JMB)

Da Costa, M. (1979) Profiles of a Study Skills Workshop. In Hills, P. (Ed.) *Study Courses and Counselling*, Guildford: SRHE

Davis, Robert T. (1955) *Some Suggestions for Writing a Business Case* Boston: Harvard Business School

Davis, S.A. (1967) An organic problem-solving method of organisational change *Journal of Applied Behavioural Science* 3 (1)

Deutsch, M. (1949) The effects of co-operation and competition upon group processes. In Cartwright, D. and Zander, A. *Group Dynamics*. 2nd edition. London: Tavistock

Denzin, W.K. (1969) Symbolic interactionism and ethnomethodology: a proposed synthesis *American Sociological Review* December

Dyer, F.C. (1962) *Executive's Guide to Effective Speaking and Writing*
   Describes features of various kinds of group conference and ways of handling each type of conference. (DAB)

Eiserer, Paul (1949) The implications of non-directive counselling for class-room teaching *Growing Points in Education Research* Washington: American Education Research Association.

Emkey, William L. (1979) The small group approach to introductory physics *American Journal of Physics* 47 (8) pp.695-697
   A description of an alternative to the lecture-recitation approach for teaching introductory physics to science and engineering majors. The class is divided into small groups that work on their assignments during the class. The students interact both with their peers and the instructor during this time. (JMB)

Festinger, L. and Aronson, E. (1960) The arousal and reduction of dissonance in social contexts. In Cartwright, D. and Zander, A. (Eds) *Group Dynamics* London: Tavistock

Flanders, N.A. (1970) *Analyzing Teaching Behaviour*. Cambridge, Mass.: Addison-Wesley.

Flood Page, Colin (1972) Problems in group work and how to handle them. In Beard, R. M. (Ed.) *Varieties of Group Discussion in University Teaching* University of London Institute of Education.

Foster, P.J. (1981) Clinical discussion groups: verbal participation and outcomes *Journal of Medical Education* pp.831-838
   Transcripts of more than 75 hours of discussion drawn from 62 groups comprising of 119 third-year medical students and 22 faculty were analysed. Lectures by teachers occupied 45.6 per cent of the time, student reporting 23.6 per cent, and teacher/student interaction 28.2 per cent. Two thirds of the teachers' questions were at the knowledge level, 7.7 per cent at the application level and 3.3 per cent at higher cognitive levels. Three-quarters of the student talk was at the knowledge level, 18.8 per cent at the comprehension level and 2.0 per cent at higher cognitive levels. (JMB)

Foulkes, S.H. and Anthony, E.J. (1965) *Group Psychotherapy* Harmondsworth, Middlesex: Penguin

Frederick, Peter (1981) The dreaded discussion: ten ways to start *Improving College and University Teaching* 29 (3) pp.109-114
   Ways to initiate good discussion include: examining goals and values, noting concrete images in the text, generating questions about goals and

values, finding illustrative quotations, generating truth statements, holding forced debates, role playing, non-structured scene setting, and eliciting opinions about the textbook. (See chapter 00) (JMB)

Fremont-Smith, F. (1961) The interdisciplinary conference *AIBS Bulletin* 11, 17-20

Friedrich, C.J. (1964) Authority. In Gould J. and Kolb, W.L. (Eds) *A Dictionary of the Social Sciences* Tavistock

Garrett, R.M. and Roberts, I.F.L. (1982) Demonstration versus small group practical work in science education: A critical review of studies since 1900 *Studies in Science Education* 9, pp.109-146
   Reviews research on demonstration versus small group instruction in four phases (up to 1926, 1926-1946, 1946-1960, and 1960-1982). (JMB)

Gibb, C.A. (1969) *Leadership* Penguin Modern Psychology
   A collection of 25 articles with 'personality factors' and 'interaction with the group' being relatively well considered; but since understanding leadership assumes some understanding of groups, preliminary reading of introductory texts, such as Sprott's 'Human Groups', is advised. (DAB)

Gibb, J. (1964) Climate for trust formation. In Bradford, L.P., Gibb, J. R. and Benne, K. D. *T-Group Theory and Laboratory Method; Innovation in our Education* New York: Wiley

Goffman, E. (1959) *The Presentation of Self in Everyday Life* New York: Doubleday

Goffman, E. (1961) *Encounters* Indianapolis: Bobbs-Merrill

Gordon, W.J.J. (1961) *Synectics* NYC: Harper & Row

Gordon, William J. J. (1971) *Synectics: The Development of Creative Capacity* Collier McMillan, p.180

Gordon, W.J.J. and Poze, T. (1968) *Making it Strange. Books 1, 2, 3, 4 and Teacher's guide* NYC: Harper and Row

Gordon, W.J.J. and Poze, T. (1972) *Teaching is Listening* Cambridge: Porpoise Books

Gordon, W.J.J. and Poze, T. (1974) *From the Inside* Cambridge: Porpoise Books

Gordon, W.J.J. and Poze T. (1975) *Strange and Familiar. Books I, III, and VI* Cambridge: Porpoise Books

Gordon, W.J.J. and Poze, T. (1979) *The Metaphorical Way* (New edn.) Cambridge: Porpoise Books

Gordon, W.J.J. and Poze, T. (1980a) *The New Art of the Possible* Cambridge: Porpoise Books

Gordon, W.J.J. and Poze, T. (1980b) SES synectics and gifted education today *Gifted Child Quarterly* 24 (4) Fall

Gore, A.E. (1962) *Individualised Instruction through Team Learning in a College Course in General Psychology* Doctoral dissertation, Boston University. Reprinted in Dissertation Abstracts, no. 23/04/1273

Gorman, A.H. (1969) *Teachers and Learners: The Interactive Process* Boston: Allyn and Bacon Inc.
   Although partly with reference to school teachers, the sections on 'interaction exercises' and 'evaluation instruments' are useful. (DAB)

Greene, R. (1964) *A Sentence Completion Procedure for Measuring Self-Disclosure* Unpublished MA Thesis, Ohio State University, Columbus.

Hale Report (1964) *Report of the Committee on University Teaching Methods* HMSO, para 30

Hare, A.P., Borgatta, E.F. and Bales, R.F. (1965) *Small Groups* New York: Alfred A. Knopf
    Sixty-five papers covering a wide field including historical and theoretical background, the individual in group situations, factors affecting interaction within groups such as group size, composition and leadership. (DAB)
Harrison, R. and Lubin, B. (1965) Personal style, group composition and learning *Journal of Applied Behavioural Science* 1,pp.286-301
Henderson, Norman K. (1969) *University Teaching* Hong Kong University Press
    Patchy in quality. Good on 'Student Debates' and evaluation of discussion. Clear style. Other chapters are worth attention, especially Ch. 5, 'Practical Sessions'. (DAB)
Hendrix, Jon R. et al. (1983) Facilitating effective small group discussions of controversial issues *Journal of College Science Teaching* 13 (1) pp.21-25
    Describes four components (instructional guidelines for the group leader, information about alphafetoprotein (AFP), specific discussion questions, student evaluation forms) in a package of materials designed for small group discussions on AFP screening for neural tube defects. Copies of the materials discussed are included. (JMB)
Herbst, P.G. (1962) *Autonomous Group Functioning* Tavistock
Hill, W.F. (1969) *Learning Thru' Discussion: A Guide for Discussion Group Leaders and Members* London:Sage
Hill, William Fawcett (1977) *Learning Thru' Discussion: A Guide for Leaders and Members of Discussion Groups* Beverly Hills, CA: Sage Publications
    Discusses a method of student-led discussion groups. The technique encourages students to do their assigned readings and analyse the content. (JMB)
Homans, G.C. (1951) *The Human Group* London: Routledge, Kegan Paul
Howe, M. and Godfrey, J. (1977) *Note-taking as an Aid to Learning* Exeter University Teaching Services
Huczynski, A. (1983) *Encylopaedia of Management Development Methods* Gower
Jaques, D. (1984) *Learning in Groups* London: Croom Helm
Jaques, D. (1985) Evaluation by teachers. In *International Encyclopaedia of Education*. Oxford: Pergamon Press
Jersild, A. (1955) *When Teachers Face Themselves* New York: Teachers College, Columbia University
Jersild, A. and Lazar, E.A. (ND) *The Meaning of Psychotherapy in the Teacher's Life and Work* New York: Teachers College, Columbia University, p.115
Jourard, S.J. (1964) *The Transparent Self* Princeton: Van Nostrand
Journet, Alan R.P. and Journet, Debra (1979) Structured discussion in introductory biology *Improving College and University Teaching* 27 (4) pp.167-170
    Describes a series of highly structured, criterion-referenced, small group discussion tutorials which are designed for use in a large introductory biology class. The design of these groups and their role in achieving course objectives are discussed. (JMB)
Keegan, Warren J. (1977) A note on case preparation for students. In Levin, James K. (Ed.) *Learning via the Case Method* World Trade Institute of the Port of Authority of New York and New Jersey

Kirk, M. (1968) The seminar. In Layton, David (Ed.) *University Teaching in Transition*. Edinburgh: Oliver and Reed, pp.63-70.

This article is concerned with the seminar as a teaching method for undergraduate instruction. The author briefly discusses techniques and objectives, then touches on problems related to the quality of students, the quality of teachers, and the library and ancillary services. (JMB)

Klein, J. (1956) *The Study of Groups* Routledge Paperback

Proceed from the whole to the particular by reading the 'contents' and chapter summaries carefully before going on to the detailed argument. (DAB)

Klein, J. (1961) *Working with Groups* Hutchinson

An excellent book. the summaries at the beginning of each chapter give a quick impression but relation to one's own situation is essential for full value. (DAB)

Knickerbocker, I. (1969) Leadership: a conception and some implications, In Gibb, C.A. (Ed.) *Leadership* Penguin

Knowles, Lyle (1976) Tutorial mode: practising humanistic principles with inner city adult graduate students *Education* 96 (4) pp.374-378

Within a framework of a tutorial approach, the applications of humanistic principles in a graduate programme are discussed. Student-centred techniques, while requiring more time on the part of the instructor, are successful with students who are full-time employed, inner city adults. (JMB)

Lancaster, Otis Ewing (1974) The discussion method. In *Effective Teaching and Learning*. New York: Gordon and Breach, pp.125-141.

Opens with definitions of the terms: discussion method, lecture method, and recitation method. Reasons for using the discussion method are given, then experimental evidence for its use cited. The instructors' and students' responsibilities in the group are listed. A brief discussion on class size is also included. (JMB)

Lawrence, Gordon (1970) Social Processes in task oriented discussions *Spode House Review* 6 (71) pp.3-11

Layton, D. (Ed.) (1968) *University Teaching in Transition* Oliver and Boyd

Lewis, Harry (1979) The anatomy of small groups *Studies in Higher Education* 4 (2) pp.269-277

Discusses five studies on the advantages and disadvantages of small groups in higher education. These include the works by M.L.J. Abercrombie; B. Cockburn and A. Ross; M.L.J. Abercrombie and P.M. Terry; and J. Ruddock. (JMB)

Mann R.D. (1967) *Interpersonal Styles and Group Development* New York: John Wiley and Sons

Maslow, A.H. (1968) *Toward a Psychology of Being* 2nd edition. Princeton: Van Nostrand.

McGrath, J.E. and Altman, I. (1966) *Small Group Research* New York: Holt, Rinehart and Winston.

McKeachie, Wilbert J. (1965) The discussion group. In *Memo to the Faculty* 14. Center for Research on Learning and Teaching, University of Michigan.

McKeachie cites research pertaining to the discussion versus the lecture method and develops his ideas on the instructor's role. He suggests that a discussion leader should be skilled in starting discussion, asking questions and appraising progress. He elaborates on how to ask a question, handle arguments and stimulate discussion. He concludes with the predictions that 'small discussion groups are likely to become more common, and the selection, supervision and training of teaching fellows is likely to become even more important. (JMB)

Merry, Robert W. (1954) Preparation to teach a case. In McNair, Malcolm P.(Ed.) *The Case Method at the Harvard Business School: Papers by Present and Past Members of the Faculty and Staff* New York: McGraw-Hill

Mill, C.R. and Ritvo, Miriam (1969) Nonverbal techniques: some precautions. In Mill, Cyril, R. (Ed.) *Selections from Human Relations Training News.* Washington DC: NTL Institute for Applied Behavioural Science

Mills, H. R. (1967) *Teaching and Training* London: MacMillan

Mill, T. M. (1967) *The Sociology of Small Groups* New Jersey:Prentice-Hall

Mixson, Imogene M.(1983) Making group-work work in the writing classroom *Teaching English in the Two-Year College* 10 (1) pp.57-61
    Describes serveral techniques for making discussion groups work effectively in composition courses. (JMB)

Morris, B. (1965) How does a group learn to work together? In Niblett, N.R.(Ed.) *How and Why do we Learn?* London: Faber and Faber.

Morris, William E. (1975) Having a graduate seminar 'with' rather than 'from' *Improving College and University Teaching* 23, pp.221-226
    Morris believes that a seminar can be a 'lively, mutually profitable adventure in scholarship'. He tells how he planned a graduate seminar about the world of John Donne, how it proceeded and whether it was successful. (JMB)

Myers, M. S.(1968) Every employee a manager *California Management Review*

Newcomb, T.M. (1960) Varieties of interpersonal attraction. In Cartwright, D. and Zander A. *Group Dynamics* 2nd edition. London: Tavistock

Newcomb, T. (1961) *The Acquaintance Process* New York: Holt, Rinehart and Winston

Northedge, A. (1975) Learning through discussion in the Open University *Teaching at a Distance* No. 2 Milton Keynes: Open University

Northway, M.L. (1959) *A Primer of Sociometry* University of Toronto Press

Osborn, A.F.(1953) *Applied Imagination* New York: Scribner

Ottaway, A.K.C. (1968) Teaching in small groups. In Layton, David (Ed.) *Teaching in Transition* Edinburgh: Oliver and Reed, pp. 53-57
    Ottaway is concerned with the nature of instructor/student relationships in small groups (7-15 students). The value of small groups depends on the opportunity for free discussion with all memberes participating and the development of a special type of rapport between the instructor and the students. He lists seven advantages to the student and the instructor of this method and concludes with a discussion of the non-directive group. (JMB)

Page, Warren (1979) A small group strategy for enhanced learning *American Mathematical Monthly* 86 (10) pp.856-858
    Presents a summary-review strategy for use in mathematics classes. Outlines the specific objectives that are attainable and two procedures for using this strategy.

Parlett, M.R. and King, J.G. (1971) *Concentrated Study: A Pedagogic Innovation Observed* London: SRHE

Parlett, M.R. and Simons, H. (1976) *Learning from Learners. A Study of Students' Experiences of Academic Life* London: Nuffield Foundation
Payne, J. (1969) *Research in Student Mental Health* London: SRHE
Pfeiffer, W.W. and Jones, J.E. (1969) *Structured Experiences for Human Relations Training* Vol. 1. Iowa City: University Associates Press
Polani, P.E. (1953) *Health Education Journal* 11, pp.126-133
Potts, David (1977) Paired learning: a workshop approach to humanities *Times Higher Education Supplement* October
Powdermaker, F.B. and Frank, J.D. (1953) *Group Psychotherapy* Cambridge, Mass.: Harvard University Press
Powell, J.P. (1964) Tutorials without tutors *Vestes* 7, pp.207-210
Powell, J.P. (1971) *Universities and University Education: A Select Bibliography. Volume 2: 1965-70* Slough: NFER
Powell, J.P. (1974) Small group teaching methods in higher education *Educational Research* 16 (3) pp.163-171
    Report of a research project that evaluated the small tutorial group by the amount of speech of each member and the cognitive content of the verbal interaction. Groups with and without leaders were included. There was more and a wider distribution of participation in leaderless groups than in tutored ones. Powell concluded from the data that many instructors view themselves primarily as information givers. He also reports on the advantages and disadvantages of leaderless groups and points out obstacles in evaluating teaching methods. (JMB)
Powell, J.P. and Jackson, P. (1964) A note on a simplified technique for recording group interaction. *Human Relations* 17, pp.289-291
Revans, R. (1964) Morale and effectiveness of hospitals *New Society* 21, pp.6-8
Rex, J. (1961) *Key Problems of Sociological Theory* Routledge & Kegan Paul
Rice, A.K. (1965) *Learning for Leadership* Tavistock
Richardson, E. (1967) *Group Study for Teachers* Students Library of Education. Routledge & Kegan Paul.
    A personal account which may, or may not, fit the experience of others. Not easy for the busy reader to skim. Strong emphasis on Bion's theory. (DAB)
Riddles, W. (1969) The unquiet revolution *Improving College and University Teaching* XVII (3)
Rippetoe, Joseph K. and Peters, George R. (1979) Introductory courses and the teaching assistant *Improving College and University Teaching* 27 (2) pp.20-24
    Discusses whether graduate teaching assistants influence student satisfaction with introductory sociology courses and whether students feel they derive the essence of the course from the lecture or the tutorial group. (JMB)
Rogers, Carl R. (1951) *Student-Centered Teaching in Client-Centred Therapy* Boston: Houghton Mifflin; London: Constable Publishers
Rogers, C.R. (1961) Significant learning in therapy and in education. In *On Becoming a Person* Boston: Houghton Mifflin
Rogers, C.R. and Roethlisberger, F.J. (1952) Barriers and gateways to communication *Harvard Business Review* July-August XXX
Rosenbaum, M. and Berger, M. M. (Eds) (1963) *Group Psychotherapy and Group Functions* Basic Books

Rotem, A. and Manzie, P. (1980) How to use small groups in medical education *Medical Teacher* 2 (2) pp.80-87
   Gives the advantages of small group interaction and suggests ways to facilitate its use. (JMB)
Royal College of General Practitioners (A Working Party) (1972) Teaching styles. In *The Future General Practitioner: Learning and Teaching* The Royal College of General Practitioners
Rudduck, Jean (1978) *Learning Through Small Group Discussion: A Study of Seminar Work in Higher Education* Guildford: Society for Research into Higher Education
   Rudduck sees small group work 'as essentially a formal rather than an informal activity.' She includes in this book comments from student interviews, statements from seminar leaders, and a summary of Nisbet's method. She lists some of the roles a seminar leader may adopt – instructor, participant, model, devil's advocate, chairman, consultant. (JMB)
Schacter, Steven C. (1979) Death and dying education in a medical school curriculum *Journal of Medical Education* 54 (3) pp.661-663
   This student-initiated course at Case Western Reserve University's School of Medicine features a small group format, multidisciplinary representation, and student leadership. The course objectives and content, teaching methods, course design, and student and faculty evaluations of the course are discussed. (JMB)
Schroder, H.M. and Harvey, O.J. (1963) Conceptual organisation and group structure. In Harvey, O.J. (Ed.) *Motivation and Social Interaction* New York: Ronald Press
Schutz, Alfred (1953) Common sense and scientific interpretations of human action. *Philosophy and Phenomonological Research* 19(1)
Schutz, W.C. (1958) *FIRO: A Three Dimensional Theory of Interpersonal Behaviour* New York: Rinehart
Seabourne, A.E.M. (1963) Social effects on standards in gauging tasks *Ergonomics* 6, pp.205-209
Shaw, M.E.(1971) *Group Dynamics: The Psychology of Small Group Behaviour* New York: McGraw-Hill
Shedlin, Arthur J. (ND) *A Psychological Approach to Group Leadership in Education* Unpublished
Shepherd, C.R. (1964) *Small Groups* San Francisco: Chandler
Shepard, H. A. (1965) Changing interpersonal and intergroup relationships in organisations. In March, J. G. (Ed.) *Handbook of Organisation* Chicago: Rand McNally
Slavson, S.R. (Ed.) (1956) *The Fields of Group Psychotherapy* New York: International University Press
Smith, Clyde R. (1981) Cotextualizing pattern drills: The 'German Circle Games' *Foreign Language Annals* 14 (3) pp.203-208
   Describes German 'circle games', a small group activity which turns grammatical exercises into meaningful and communicative activites. Pantomime, props and pictures are used to provide context. (JMB)
Smith, Peter B. (1968) The small group as a teaching medium. In Layton, David (Ed.) *University Teaching in Transition*. Edinburgh: Oliver and Reed, pp.47-52

Sometimes, in small groups, students adapt a passive, receptive role when the instructor's teaching method is similar to the one he uses in lectures. Smith first lists the situations which will defeat the small group teaching method, then suggests instructor behaviours that will increase the learning in small group situations. The effect of communication patterns and structural variables (eg group size, frequency of meeting, subject matter, etc.) are discussed. (JMB)

Smith, P.B. (1969) *Improving Skills in Working with People; the T-Group.* Department of Employment and Productivity Information Paper No. 4. London: HMSO

Uses a model in which behaviour is 'public', 'blind', 'hidden' or 'unconscious'. (DAB)

Smith, Peter B. (1970) *Group Processes* Penguin Modern Psychology

Twenty-two psychological papers on small groups considering definitions, models, roles, behaviour change and intergroup relations. (DAB)

Smith, Peter B. (1972) Varying one's group training style to take account of the setting *Interpersonal Development* 3, pp.159-166

Sommer, R. and Ross, H. (1958) Social interaction on a geriatrics ward *British Journal of Social Psychiatry* 4, pp.128-133

Sommer, R. (1959) Studies in personal space *Sociometry* 22, pp.247-260

Sprott, W.J.H. (1958) *Human Groups* Harmondworth, Middlesex: Penguin

Sets the subject of 'groups' in its wider context. (DAB)

Stanton, H.E. (1978) Small group teaching in the lecture situation. Improving College and University Teaching 26 (1) pp.69-70

Four stages of student participation in small groups – working individually, working in pairs, working in groups of 4 to 6, and reporting back to the whole group – are adapted to the lecture situation. The technique allows the instructor to intervene at each stage to direct progress towards the previously determined objectives. (JMB)

Stanton, Harry E. (1982) Improving the university tutorial *Improving College and University Teaching* 30 (2) pp.87-90

Suggests that student participation in a tutorial can be increased by varying the teaching method, reducing the size of the discussion group, using brainstorming and other idea development techniques, and using student leaders. (JMB)

Strauss, B.W. and Strauss, Frances (1960) *New Ways to Better Meetings* Tavistock

Although written for the American reader, the principles described are widely applicable. (DAB)

Thiagarajan, Sivasailam (1978) *Grouprograms* The Instructional Design Library, volume 8. Englewood Cliffs, NJ: Educational Technology Publications

Describes the 'groupprogram' format, which consists of four elements: information, group task, feedback, and instruction. The purpose of this technique is to help students teach and learn from each other. (JMB)

Trakman, Leon E. (1979) Law Student Teachers: An Untapped Resource *Journal of Legal Education* 30 (3) pp.331-357

Discusses the practice of using senior law students as instructors as a means to reduce the teacher-student ratio in law school. The extent to which these students have contributed to teaching, supervision and instruction is analysed. The European tutorial experience is compared with the North American one. (JMB)

Tuckman, B.W. (1965) Developmental sequence in small groups *Psychological Bulletin* 63 (6)

University of London Teaching Methods Unit (1976) Small group discussion. In *Improving Teaching in Higher Education* London: University of London Teaching Methods Unit, pp.40-61
    Discusses topics such as why learn in small groups, ways to encourage group discussion (physical environment, ways to get interaction, how to ask questions, the instructor's role), varieties of small groups tutorials, buzz groups, problem-centred groups) and the evaluation of group work. A checklist for observation of discussion is included. (JMB)

Valentine, Carol Ann (1976) Using small group methods for social education *Clearing House* 50, pp.115-117
    Small groups allow members to contribute their special knowledge, are more efficient than large, non-interacting groups, provide opportunites for purposeful oral communication, and are more likely to result in attitude changes. Valentine, after citing these advantages, discusses the effectiveness of the small group method in social education and points out some cautions that should be taken. (JMB)

de Volder, M.L. (1982) Discussion groups and their tutors: relationships between tutor characteristics and tutor functioning *Higher Education* 11 (3) pp.269-271
    At Limburg State University, medical students meet a tutor twice a week to discuss case studies on selected topics. A questionnaire-based study of 125 of these groups indicated that the effectiveness of tutors, as assessed by students, is related to tutor knowledge of subject-matter, and not to tutor age or length of tutoring experience. (JMB)

Webb, N.M. (1982) Student interaction and learning in small groups *Review of Educational Research* 52 (3) pp.421-445
    Review of the literature, focusing on the role of the students' experience in small group interaction. Examines research pertaining to the relationship between interaction and achievement, the cognitive process and social-emotional mechanisms that provide a bridge between interaction and achievement, and group and reward structures that predict interaction in small groups. (JMB)

Webb, N.J. and Grib, T.F. (1967) *Teaching Process as a Learning Experience: The Experimental Use of Student-led Discussion Groups* Final Report, Project No. 5-0923-2-10-1. Washington, DC : US Department of Health, Education and Welfare

Webster, J. (1951) *Dictionary of Synonyms* Springfield, Mass.: G. & C. Merriam

Wheeler, Mary (1983) Individual counselling. In *Counselling in Study Methods* University of Exeter Teaching Services Centre

White, R. and Lippitt, R. (1960) Leader behaviour and member reaction in three 'social climates'. In Cartwright, D. and Zander, A. *Group Dynamics* 2nd edition. London: Tavistock

Wilson, Andrew (1980) Structuring seminars: A technique to allow students to participate in the structuring of small group activities *Studies in Higher Education* 5 (1) pp.81-84

Wilson describes the ways he tried to improve his small group teaching sessions. His preferred approach uses a pattern system which enables students to participate in structuring the discussion. (JMB)

Wood, A.E. (1979) Experience with small group tutorials *Studies in Higher Education* 4 (2) pp.203-209

Summarizes the experiences of small group tutorials in biology in which the leader acts as a participant rather than as leader. For this technique to work effectively, the material used must be of the type that will stimulate discussion and at the correct level for the group. Other significant factors include the skill of the tutor, the physical surroundings and the level of preparation by the students. (JMB)

Zophy, Jonathan. (1982) On learner-centered teaching *History Teacher* 15 (2) pp.85-96

Suggests ways to encourage learning through a learner-centred approach to the teaching of history. Discusses small group discussions, tutorial sessions and learner-centred lecturing. Also looks at problems associated with these methods. (JMB)

# Index of References

# Subject Index

# The Society for Research into Higher Education

The Society for Research into Higher Education exists both to encourage and co-ordinate research and development in all aspects of higher education, including future policy, and to provide a forum for debate on issues in this field. Through its activities, it draws attention to the significance of research and development and to the needs of those engaged in this work. (It is not concerned with research generally, except, for instance, as a subject of study or in its relation to teaching.)

The Society's income is derived from subscriptions, book sales, conferences and specific grants. It is wholly independent. Its corporate members are universities, polytechnics, institutes of higher education, research institutions and professional and governmental bodies. Its individual members include teachers and researchers, administrators and students. Members are found in all parts of the world and the Society regards its international work as amongst its most important activities.

The Society discusses and comments on policy, organizes conferences and encourages research. Under the imprint SRHE & NFER-NELSON it is a specialist publisher, having some 30 titles in print. It also publishes Studies in Higher Education (three times a year), Higher Education Abstracts (three times a year), International Newsletter (twice a year), a Bulletin (six times a year), and jointly with the Committee for Research into Teacher Education (CRITE) Evaluation Newsletter (twice a year).

The Society's committees, study groups and local branches are run by members (with limited help from the small secretariat at Guildford), and aim to provide a forum for discussion. Some of the groups, at present the Teacher Education Study Group, the Staff Development Group and the Women in Higher Education Group, have their own subscriptions and organization and publications; so too do some Regional Branches. The Governing Council, elected by members, comments on current issues and discusses polices with leading figures in politics and education. The Society organizes seminars on current research for officials of DES and other ministries, and is in touch with official bodies in Britain such as the NAB, CVCP, UGC, CNAA and the Britsh Council and with sister-bodies here and overseas. Its current research projects include one on the relationship between entry qualifications and degree results, directed by Prof. W. D. Furneaux (Brunel) and one on Questions of Quality directed by Prof. G. C. Moodie (York).

The Society's annual conferences take up central themes, 'Standards and Criteria in Higher Education' (1986), 'Re-structuring' (1987). Joint conferences are held, viz. on Information Technology (1986, with the Council for Educational Technology, the Computer Board and the Universities of Glasgow and Strathclyde) and on the Freshman Year (1986, with the University of South Carolina and Newcastle Polytechnic). for some of the Society's conferences, special studies are commissioned in advance.

Members receive free of charge the Society's Abstracts, annual conference papers, the Bulletin and International Newsletter, and may buy SRHE & NFER-NELSON books at trade price. Corporate members also receive the Society's journal Studies in Higher Education free (individual members at a heavy discount). They may also obtain Evaluation Newsletter and certain other journals at a discount, including the NFER Register of Educational Research. There is a substantial discount to members, and to staff of corporate members, on annual and some other conference fees.

Further information from SRHE At the University, Guildford GU2 5XH UK. Telephone 0483 39003 Book catalogue from SRHE & NFER-Nelson, 2 Oxford Road East, Windsor SL4 1DF, UK. Telephone Windsor 858961.